EVEN THE RIVER STARTS SMALL

A COLLECTION OF STORIES FROM THE MOVEMENT TO STOP LINE 3

Self-published by the Line 3 Storytelling Anthology Team, 2023

All rights reserved. However, we acknowledge that all anonymous contributors gifted their works to us to use for this collection, and that they reserve the rights to their own art and writing. We encourage contributors to keep their stories alive by reproducing them independently.

First Edition

ISBN: 979-8-218-05789-3
LCCN: 2022923900

Printed by Smart Set, Inc. in Minneapolis, MN.
Typeset in Minion Pro & Proxima Nova

Cover artwork by ten artists from the movement to stop Line 3.

—

Three pieces in this collection were originally published elsewhere:

"On This Land Where We Belong," American Craft Council, September 2021
"The Umbilicus," Atmos Magazine, May 2022
"A Letter to The Water Protectors," Earth First! Journal, September 2021

EVEN THE RIVER STARTS SMALL

This anthology is for everyone who resisted and struggled for a better world through the movement to stop Line 3. In this book, we have collected stories and reflections from organizers, Indigenous leaders and community members, allies, land defenders, legal workers, artists, scientists, and hundreds of other people who came together in solidarity against this extractive project.

The book you hold in your hands is a collection of stories from nearly a decade of fierce resistance. Our initial team began collecting stories in the fall of 2021, when oil began flowing through the pipeline and when our movement was reflecting and grieving. At that time, a few of us — three organizers who had been involved in the movement for years — wanted to ensure that memories of the movement were not lost, even as we moved into a new phase of resistance.

We believe in the power of storytelling and collective memory making and decided to embark on this project with the hope that we could create a container to hold some stories from the movement. We began reaching out to our community and discovered that the idea of collecting stories resonated with many. We grew our team as we incorporated feedback and recognized the need for more capacity. In total, we spent over a year gathering, reviewing, and compiling these stories, photographs, poems, and works of art. This book is a selection of the many submissions that we received.

Many people had their lives transformed by this movement, though the nature of that transformation is not the same for everyone. This fight took place on Anishinaabe and Dakota land, led by Anishinaabe people. They were, and continue to be, most impacted by this violent rupture. Many people chose to come to Minnesota and join the fight, but Indigenous people from this land often didn't have a choice. Our team was comprised of people who had the privilege to choose to participate in this movement. We hope that this collection can honor the people Indigenous to this land and the movement leaders who so generously invited us to fight alongside them.

Through this collection, we tried to highlight a diversity of experiences, identities, tactics, and emotions that existed within our collective attempt to stop this pipeline. We hoped to honor a range of the experiences people had and to commemorate the years of resistance. We attempted to create space for people to show some of the many different ways they showed up for the land and water, and we are grateful for the wide range of storytellers and diverse voices who chose to share their reflections with us.

This book is not a history of the movement. It is not even close to a complete collection of the diverse personal and collective experiences this movement held. It is simply a collection of some moments, some memories, and some musings from the movement, for the movement. This book is meant as an offering that can be revisited over the years. It is not meant to be read cover to cover or in one sitting. Please flip through it, read stories here and there, and take your time with it.

All of the submissions in this collection are anonymous. We chose to publish the submissions anonymously for a few reasons. We wanted everyone to feel comfortable submitting their work with as much honesty and vulnerability as desired without fear of incriminating or implicating themselves or others. We also wanted to make sure that everyone who participated in the movement, no matter their role, knew that they were welcome to share their story. We hoped that anonymity would help people feel empowered to share, but we also acknowledge that anonymity can render readers unable to comprehend the positionality of the author. We trust that the stories included here were written and submitted with good intentions.

We intended for this collection to contain personal stories and reflections, rather than critiques of movement tactics and strategy, discussion of specific leaders, or broad political analysis. While those tactical reflections are crucial, gathering them was not a goal of this project and those on our team were not the right people to foster that dialogue. We do encourage people who want to share their analyses, lessons, and experiences of harm to disseminate them in other forums so we can all learn from the lineage of this movement and engage in rigorous dialogue and healing.

This movement held many contradictions, and so do the stories in this book. Some of these stories might not resonate with you. You may disagree with or dislike some of them. This movement was made up of many different people trying many different things to make a change in the world. We've done our best to hold those contradictions within these pages. Just because a piece appears in this anthology does not mean that our team agrees with the author or endorses their position. We ask that you give grace to the authors in this collection and remember that individuals shared their stories for a variety of reasons and that these experiences were deeply personal. We also acknowledge that this may not always be possible for you, and we want to hold space for that, too.

At several junctures in this project's history, we have responded to feedback, listened to criticisms, and adjusted course, sometimes significantly, as best we knew how. This book is the sum total of all that; imperfect but here. We know that there are voices missing from the collection, and that there are many valid reasons why people chose not to submit. We hope that this anthology is just one project among many that attempts to make meaning out of our collective experiences in the movement to Stop Line 3. In building this collection, we were reminded that there is no one way to participate in movements, no perfect shared understanding of how to build a better world, and that no one project can adequately hold and commemorate those struggles.

These stories serve as a reminder that everyone had a reason for being a part of this fight, even if everyone's reason was different. We would like to thank everyone who trusted us with your words and art. Even if we were not able to include your piece, please know that we read each submission with gratitude and care. We are honored that so many people were moved to share their reflections with this project, and we are proud of the hard work our team put in to create this final book.

We hope that in reading these stories you find moments of joy, grief, and reflection that allow you to connect with this past era of resistance as we prepare for the fights to come.

With gratitude and in solidarity,
The Line 3 Storytelling Anthology Team

Notes on Process

From the fall of 2021 through the summer of 2022, members of our team conducted extensive outreach to people across the movement to invite them to submit to this anthology. Through the outreach process we had a team that offered support on writing, including ghostwriting, conducting interviews, and editing stories that people wanted to share.

As people submitted their work, we had a team read through each piece to determine if it should be included in the final collection. This team met weekly for many months to decide democratically what submissions should be included, make a style guide to outline the types of edits that we would and wouldn't make, and eventually edit all the pieces. Our goal was to include submissions from numerous perspectives and experiences of the movement. We received hundreds of submissions and included as many as we could that both aligned with the goals of the project to create a representative collection and fit within our limited print capabilities.

As you read through the collection, you may notice that your submission has been changed. We copy-edited for spelling and grammar to achieve consistency across the collection, although at times we kept particular choices in place to preserve the voice of the author. All pieces have been edited for clarity and length. Some stories included here are excerpts of longer pieces. We chose to trim pieces depending on the length of the submission, its relevance to the goals of this particular project, and for the writing to flow as a part of a collection, rather than as a standalone piece. Our editorial team worked very hard to manage the volume of written work submitted to the project and developed a rigorous and intentional process for collaborative editing. We also had the final draft of the project professionally copy-edited.

The written pieces in this book are not organized in any particular order. They are not chronological or grouped in any thematic way. Some art and photos were submitted or commissioned to accompany a piece of writing. Other art and photos may be arranged with written pieces that fit tonally or topically but are meant to be appreciated on their own as standalone submissions.

We consulted with an attorney to review a draft of the book to mitigate any risks that might be associated with sharing and publishing these stories. We tried to ensure that there is no information in this book that is not already in the state's possession. We also took steps such as changing people's names (while leaving in place all organizational names where we could), avoiding photos with recognizable faces, and committing to anonymity for all submissions throughout the collection. Our team had lengthy discussions about the personal risks we might face for the publication of this collection and applied a security culture lens to the edits we made to the book. We know there is no way to guarantee the actions and reactions of the state to movement work, but we did our best to prioritize the safety of our team and of the people who submitted to this collection.

Additionally, Indigenous matriarch, movement leader, and writer Great-Grandmother Mary Lyons reviewed a first draft of the book and provided feedback on the written content. We are grateful for her thoughtful contributions at the early stages of this project.

We raised money to print and distribute this book through grants and nonprofit contributions. One of our primary goals for this project was for this book to be available, free of charge, to anyone involved in the movement who wanted one. We used the funds raised to print this initial run, and any money made from donations will be used to fund the printing and distribution of future copies of this book.

To those of you whose work we could not include

Thank you for trusting us with your stories, photos, and artwork. We are so grateful that so many people wanted to be involved in this project. While we were not able to include your piece in this final collection, we encourage you to continue sharing your stories and thoughts. We greatly appreciated the opportunity to read and review your work, and we promise that we read each piece with care. Thank you for your time and your resistance.

The new Line 3 is a tar sands oil pipeline built to replace and expand an existing line owned by Canadian energy company Enbridge Inc.

The pipeline crosses unceded Anishinaabe treaty land in northern Minnesota.

It also crosses more than 200 water bodies and miles of wetlands. Construction of the pipeline has harmed ecosystems across the state, and future oil spills threaten more damage. In particular, Line 3 threatens the health of manoomin (wild rice), which is a sacred cultural food for the Anishinaabe and which their people have relied upon and stewarded for centuries.

This book is not a history of the movement. However, it includes stories that span nearly a decade of resistance and reflect on dozens of different movement tactics. These stories are not arranged chronologically, so for readers who may be less familiar with the history of the Line 3 pipeline, we hope that this brief timeline can help you orient to the stories that you will find in this collection.

1968 — The original Line 3 began operating to transport Canadian oil from Alberta, Canada to Superior, Wisconsin and beyond for refining and distribution.

2014 — Enbridge Energy proposed a so-called "replacement," or expansion, of the Line 3 pipeline that would increase the volume of oil the company could transport and open up a new pipeline corridor between Clearbrook, MN and the Fond du Lac reservation.

2017 — The project's state-authored Environmental Impact Statement highlighted dozens of concerns with the project. The report identified, among other issues, the threat that inevitable oil spills pose to water and wild rice beds, the tar sands industry's contribution to catastrophic climate change, and the disregard for Indigenous sovereignty, communities, and lands inherent in pipeline construction and operation.

2018 — The Public Utilities Commission (PUC) initially granted Enbridge the foundational permits they needed to build the new Line 3 pipeline.

February 2020 — After legal appeals had overturned Enbridge's initial permits, the PUC reinstated them in a split vote. Additional federal and state regulatory agencies approved the project over the course of the year.

December 2020 — Construction of the new Line 3 pipeline began in Minnesota.

September 2021 — Enbridge completed construction and oil began to flow through the new stretch of pipeline the following month.

Over the years prior to and during construction, thousands of people fought to stop Line 3 from being built in Minnesota. To quote a story from the collection:

> *"We fought Line 3 throughout the permitting process and the construction process. We fought with petitions, rallies, marches, banners, graffiti, lockdowns, blockades, camps. We fought in the courtrooms, at the banks, on the construction sites. [But] Enbridge built the pipeline anyway."*

For the better part of a decade, Indigenous leaders, climate justice organizers, and community members built a tremendous grassroots movement that resisted this extractive project at every turn. Some stories from their years of resistance are collected here.

Although oil is now flowing through the new Line 3 pipeline, those who joined together in the resistance are carrying the lessons and relationships from this fight forward to further movements for liberation all across Turtle Island.

Content Warning

People submitted stories to this collection that reflected their own experiences, and used the opportunity to write and share as a means of processing a range of intense events. There are many stories that reflect on harm and violence. Individual stories do not have specific content warnings, but themes in the book include:

Police brutality

Incarceration

Gender-based violence, transphobia, and homophobia

Sexual assault and violence against women, including discussion of Missing and Murdered Indigenous Women and Relatives

Addiction, overdose, and death

Reflections on and experiences of white supremacy, colonialism, and racism

Graphic language and mature themes

Please take care of yourself as you read this collection, as we know that revisiting these experiences can be overwhelming and triggering for many of us.

EVEN THE RIVER STARTS SMALL

A Collection of Stories from the Movement to Stop Line 3

The car we were driving home from an action got a flat tire in the middle of a dirt road. The lug nuts wouldn't budge in the 98-degree heat. I had a few mouthfuls of water left in my water bottle. I gently poured the water into my mouth and sprayed it on the lug nuts of the sagging tire. The wrench began to turn. Saved once again by water. •

There was that time when we were asked what scientists could do to help stop the Line 3 tar sands pipeline. We didn't have a good answer, but we found so many along the way.

That time we went to the statehouse with dozens of our comrades and stood under bloody civil war murals while the governor's handlers talked to us like we were children.

That time we ran through the statehouse chanting, singing, and found the next governor in a small office.

That time the governor, Walz, his name a symbol of what he would become, lied to us, told us in soothing tones what he thought we wanted to hear. That time we knew he was lying.

That time we wheeled live macroinvertebrates in coolers across the east bank to show people the abundance of life depending on water.

That time we bird-dogged Laura Bishop, and didn't she cry? And Peggy Flanagan tried to evade us, but we ran her down.

That time we organized scientists to go back to that bloody room in the capitol. We knocked on doors, knocking on the press door, the staffer being like, "here's three chairs" and we were like, "oh no we need 50."

That time we spoke.

That time we yelled.

That time we reasoned.

That time we knew. We knew.

That time we tried to explain "the process" and we made a video, because we knew the absurdity needed to be captured. That time we showed Line 3 was a hot potato.

The times we learned from Indigenous teachers about Indigenous sovereignty, and our responsibilities as treaty people. We are still learning.

That night we sat together in someone's kitchen, writing detailed reports, trying against their avalanche of data and money. That mismatched power staring us in the face. But we had snacks.

That time we went to Clearbrook to confront Enbridge. It was Indigenous Peoples' Day, a day of mourning, a day that we realized what rural white supremacy looks like.

The time we first saw those beautiful banners. It was the same time we saw those tractors and heard those screams and saw the violence.

The times we heard a leader say, "What happens to the water happens to the women," to whole roomfuls of us, to friends and colleagues shaken to our core.

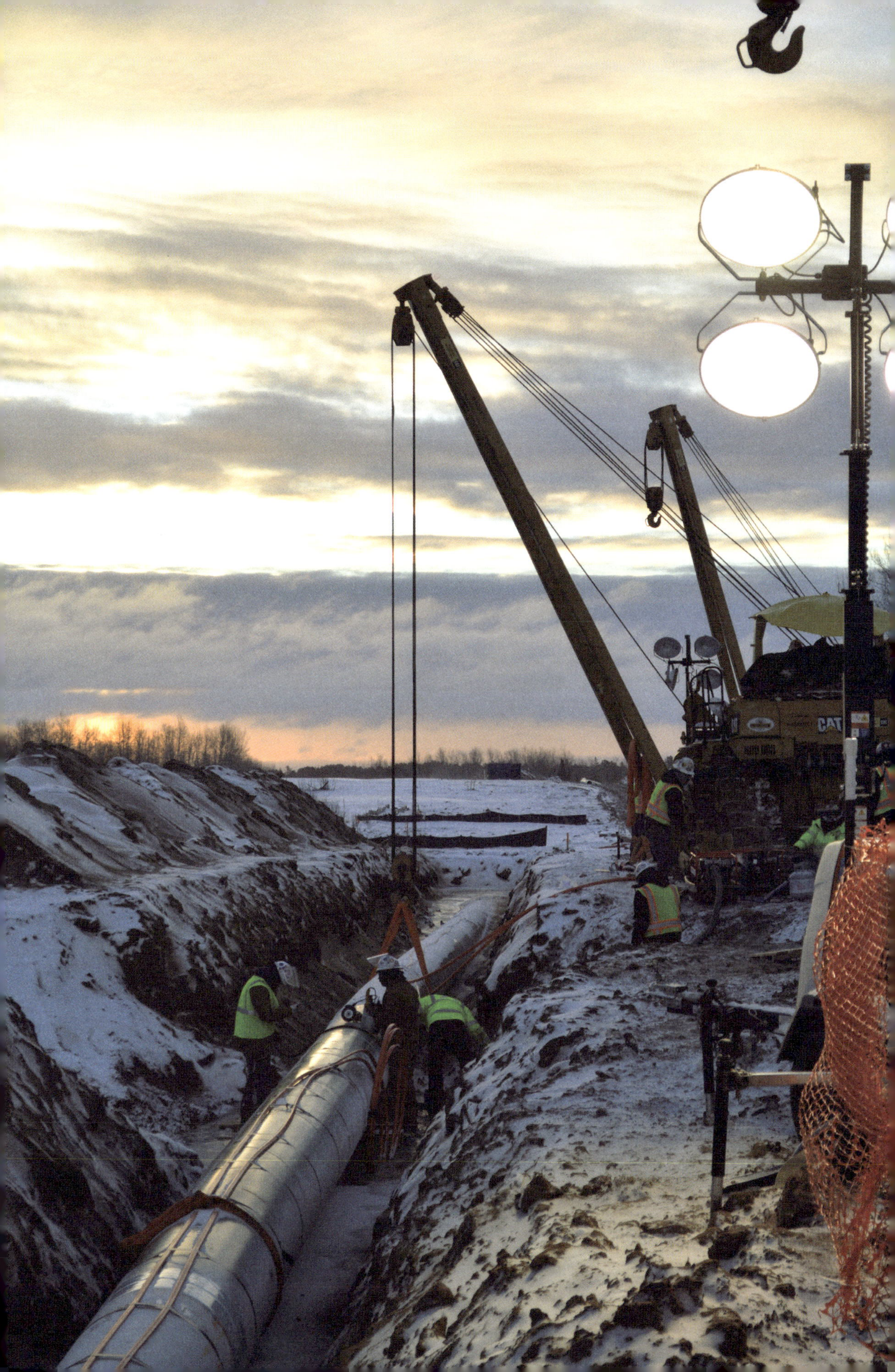
CAT

The time we met with the Pollution Control Agency about the permit and it sucked our souls out.

That other time we got up at 3:30 am to sit in the front row at the Public Utilities Commission to testify. We didn't have the matching shirts that Enbridge's paid attendees had, with their donuts and big buses. But we got up and we sat in the front row. That time we were seen.

That time we went north. The cops, or sheriffs, or armed guards followed us. Stopped us. Talked to us. Harassed us. Threatened us. That time we talked back to them, allegedly.

The times, so many times, we met. And all of that time on Signal, allegedly plotting and planning, but sometimes making jokes.

The times we tried to figure out how to write collective public comments about permits, why there should be no permits, why we should not build Line 3.

The times we made maps and diagrams, making visible the destruction across webbed networks of blue, across the green swath of floodplains.

The times we each grappled with our identities, with positionality, with "expertise," with who faces forward, with privilege, with whiteness, with solidarity, with justice.

The time we spent all summer writing legal testimony.

The time we saw the frac-out in real time at Firelight.

The times we were carried forward by the energy, the vigilance, the bravery of fellow water protectors.

The time we had to talk down the park ranger of Itasca State Park from kicking people out of the headwaters press conference.

The time we taught about the groundwater and the river waters, and their relationship.

All the times we talked to the press, so often like ramming our heads against the wall.

That time Enbridge pretended to clean up the frac-out with brooms and mops and buckets and no protective gear and it looked like a photoshopped picture. But it wasn't.

That time we got the water samples, and watched the drone footage, and knew it had happened.

The time we hung up that poster at the state fair. (We're still laughing.)

That time, all sweaty in the kitchen, when we only had two hours to go through 200 pages. Thanks Department of Natural Resources.

That time we confronted the governor for his support for tar sands and the Twin Cities Coalition 4 Justice 4 Jamar campaign confronted him first and we felt solidarity echo.

That time at Hard Times.

That time we confronted power, shouted at it, and we were told to be civil, we were told about free speech and process and we were told it would all save us. Instead, we disrupted, and we told them about direct action, and we got kicked out for handing out pamphlets. That time it all happened again.

Those other times at Hard Times.

That time we were there, in the hot and dusty fields and the sticky pavement, and the cold and lonely cells.

That time we sang.

That time we shut shit down, allegedly.

That time we stayed up all night long, stuffed in a van, under the stars, with nerves wracked, dusty, tired, to be there when we got out of jail.

That time we watched the gate, fixed it too, and got caught in a rainstorm, and then the fat chipmunks came out to run through the garbage bags.

That time we stayed up all night for our security shift, listened to the sounds of the pipeline being built, seeing the glare from the lights, hearing the stream gurgle, feeling like we had already lost.

That time the police pulled us over, for no reason, and we feared being dragged back to jail.

That time we spent trying to stop a mistake, a crime. That time we spent trying to make sure we all had a future. •

They Said It Would Happen

They said it would happen, and it did.

We were warned by the victims themselves.

Just as it has been for four hundred years.

In 2017, Indigenous women of Minnesota traveled from all directions to the State Capitol to testify against a permit to Canadian Enbridge's Line 3. With the knowledge that it wasn't just Uni Maka or Shkaakaamikwe, Mother Earth, who would be violated, but our own women, girls, and communities. That's the way it has been from the moment Colonizers stepped foot on this continent or any other, for that matter. The women came to speak their truth of historic trauma endured by themselves, their relatives, and ancestors when loved ones went missing and were murdered with no justice.

That same summer, having completed my first legislative session in the Minnesota House of Representatives, I listened one evening to a report on BBC radio reviewing Canada's initial report on their MMIW (Missing and Murdered Indigenous Women) Task Force. The data and the stories were heartrending to listen to. Truth is, comparably in the U.S., most Native women expect that they will be victims of violence within their lifetime. Approximately 80% of Native women will experience some form of physical abuse and over half will experience some type of sexual assault. Those who are victims of homicide are often killed by a non-Native or an intimate partner.

> *It wasn't just Uni Maka or Shkaakaamikwe, Mother Earth, who would be violated, but our own women, girls, and communities.*

It was at the same time that Savanna LaFontaine-Greywind, Spirit Lake Nation, went missing in Fargo, North Dakota. Savanna's body was found floating in the Red River near the North Dakota-Minnesota border by a group of kayakers. She was 22 years old and eight months pregnant when she was murdered by a neighbor, having stolen the baby from her womb.

When legislation was immediately proposed by U.S. Senator Heidi Heitkamp, combined with the action of our northern neighbors, I knew that it was time for Minnesota to step up and address the generational injustice. With those incidents in mind, I marched back to the Capitol and began working on our own MMIWG (Missing and Murdered Indigenous Women and Girls) task force with input of our Indigenous community. We passed that legislation and completed the report despite the pandemic, in just 18 months. We went on to establish the first-in-the-nation permanent MMIR (Missing and Murdered Indigenous Relatives) office within our state government and continue to work on systemic change to ensure the safety of all.

Fast forward to 2021.

They said it would happen, and it did.

When those Indigenous women of Minnesota arrived from all directions to the State Capitol to attend the Line 3 PUC (Public Utilities Commission) permit hearing, they traveled to tell the history of violence against our communities and loved ones. To speak of their fears that they knew to happen time and time again, that violence would come to their communities. Evidence and data have proven that the pandemic of missing and murdered Indigenous women is directly linked to fossil fuel production. According to Seeding Sovereignty, "there is a direct correlation between increased rates of sexual abuse, trafficking and domestic violence against women and children in regions where fossil fuel extraction companies set up 'man camps' to house workers." The link between oil extraction and violence is a fact. The high rates of sex trafficking of Native women and girls is proven.

Knowing this, the women faced an indomitable force of Enbridge employees, supporters, and hired seat holders. They dared to ask the question: whether, when, and how do the experiences of women matter? Are women's lives, particularly Indigenous women, valued?

The women testifiers warned the public and Minnesota PUC with their hearts in their voices and tears in their eyes, but were scoffed at, laughed at, and blatantly disrespected as their testimony was dismissed with the arrogance of white patriarchy. They were the voices of American Indian women who are survivors of sexual, physical, and emotional abuses. Their vulnerability was controlled by men through addiction and violence to be used, abused, and trafficked for sex.

The violence against Native communities during the Dakota Access Pipeline was fresh in their minds when the women spoke in alarm against Enbridge and Line 3. Unfortunately, as we know, the permit was allowed, Line 3 was rushed through and just as the women prophesized, communities became unsafe, and the men came…

It was ironic that on the final day of Minnesota's historical MMIW task force meeting, June 2021, we received the news of new arrests from the second sex trafficking sting operation. Booked into the Beltrami County Jail on solicitation of prostitution and commercial sex were six men who had responded to an advertisement placed on a sex ads website. At least two of the men were subcontractors of Enbridge's Line 3.

The first sex trafficking sting happened in February 2021, resulting in two of Enbridge's Line 3 employees charged in an Itasca County human trafficking bust. All along the process, Enbridge touted zero tolerance for illegal behavior — but what could be expected when rural communities are flooded with 4,000 men, flush with cash, time on their hands?

They said it would happen and it did.

Nevertheless, we're not done fighting for the safety of our communities, for justice and a safer future for the next seven generations. Our ancestors did not give up, neither will I. •

8

Across Canada and the United States, red dresses are hung as a symbol to commemorate and raise awareness about the epidemic of missing and murdered Indigenous women, girls, and relatives.

Migizi Will Fly: often delivered as a battle cry or the final thought of a poignant speech. These are words of consolation, touching enough to forever etch into a forearm. It is a vow.

Those magical, serendipitous moments when someone spotted Migizi in flight, an audience of comrades would suddenly unslouch, dust off, and gaze upwards at the Eagle coasting on an air current. I never cared much for bird watching, but in those moments I was captivated by something so free.

Even on those days when no winged spirits materialized, the essence of the Eagle was ever-present. It is his piercing glare we cast onto Enbridge. He gave his talons to slash our chains, his screech to carry our chants, it was his tenacity that fueled us.

Once, from the jumble of art and things hung over time on the fenced perimeter, we managed to untangle a length of string, tied to the very end of which was a kite: a bald eagle painted brightly with gaping mouth, protracted claws, and a dazzling rainbow tail. The chilling winds and lengthy security shift suddenly took on new possibility. We released the bird. People gathered. The usual deep stillness accompanied by a sighting left us, and on that day there was hollering and so much running. From far away, one might have mistaken us resistance camp residents for patriotic children. With laughter jumping from our cold bodies, many people tried and mostly failed to keep the flimsy, plastic frame airborne.

However, Eagles were never meant to be chained; eventually, the frail string snapped, and the kite careened to the dirt. But for a glorious second, despite so much, the promise was fulfilled, and Migizi flew. •

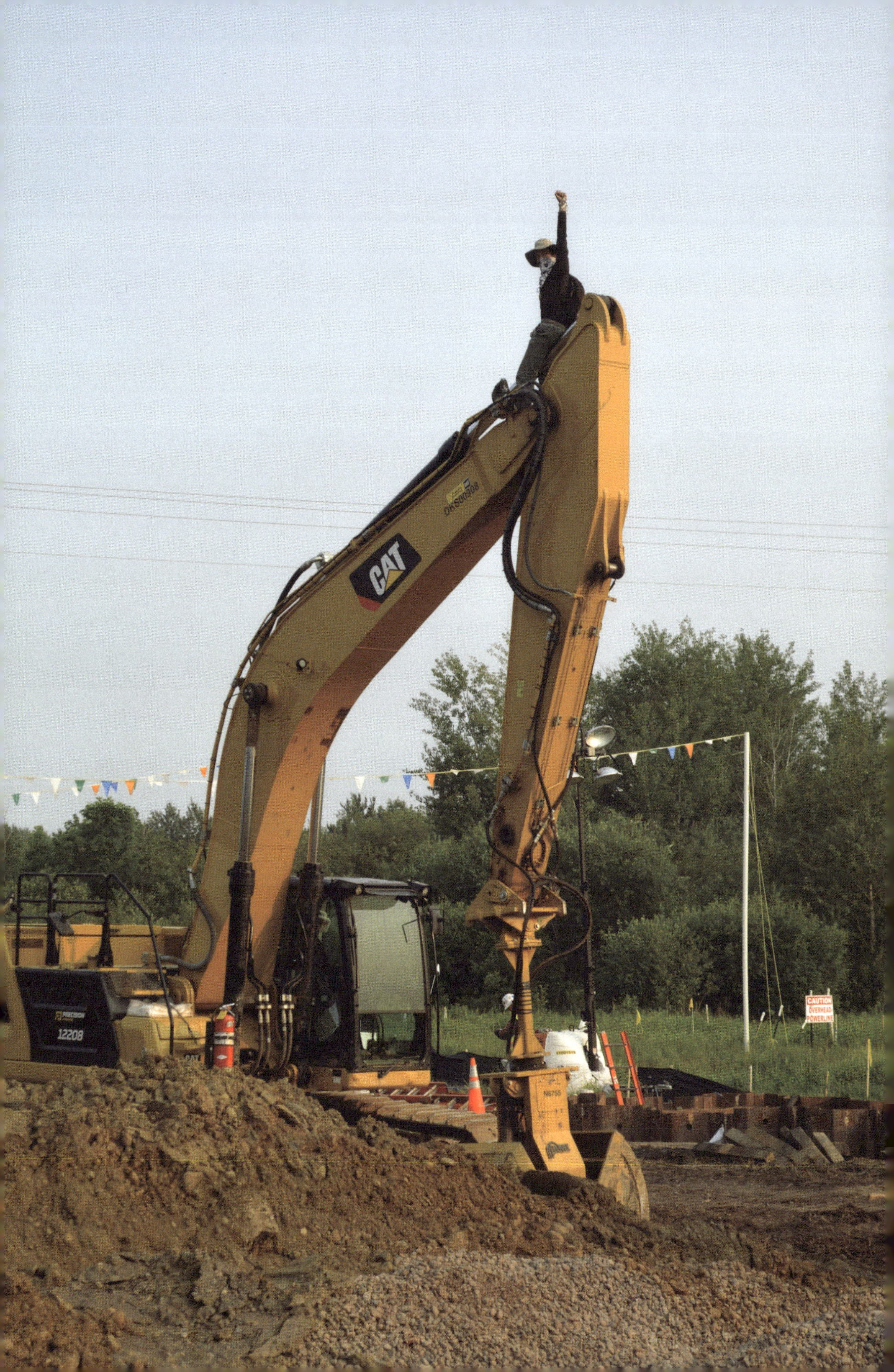
CAT
12208
CAUTION
OVERHEAD
POWERLINE

Tobacco, and the sharing of it, is sacred.

For most of my life, I only had cigarettes my sister shared with me
Eight months after her death, on my way to the frontlines,
I missed the smell of smoke and the moments we healed together

My second day at the capitol, over eggs, coffee, and a community pack of cigs,
I shared my extra narcan and the knowledge to use it

Does it feel to you like something is missing here?

Near the grass outside Walz's mansion,
between escaping being kettled in the alley and the arrests
K and I sat and smoked on the curb
A brief and beautiful gift

I could still taste tobacco
when I linked elbows with water protectors by the gate
and when 12 ripped us apart

When we were released over 50 hours later
Our comrades were waiting with cigarettes and sprite

My body was visibly battered
one bruise a distinct handprint
from the cop with no name or badge number

The medics approached me
and helped me take pictures
They gave me compassion and Arnicare in a pink Ziploc

Months later, when my arrest comes across my FYP
when my comrades' screams are stuck in audiation
I miss the smell of smoke and the moments we healed together

I try to remember all the times we shared cigarettes •

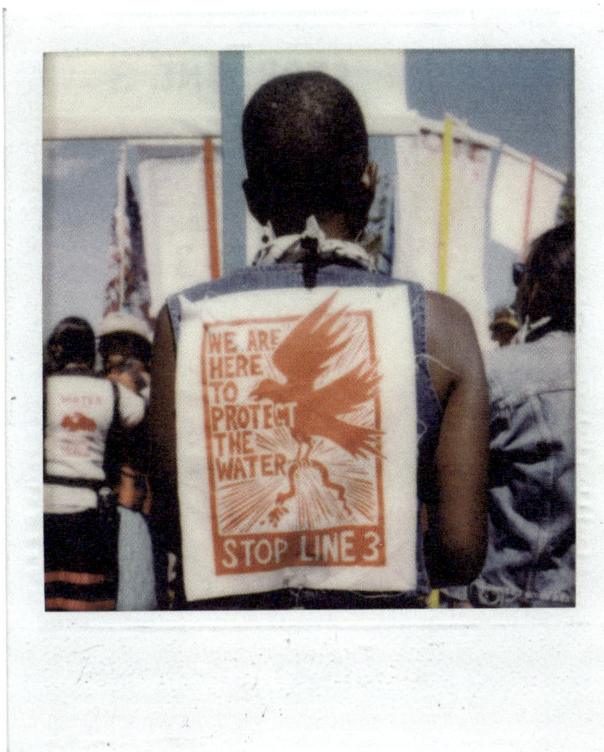
WE ARE
HERE
TO
PROTECT
THE
WATER
STOP LINE 3

Dear Pennington County Sheriff's Office and Minnesota Governor Tim Walz,

My name is not important right now. I am 20 years old, Two-Spirit, activist and street medic for an Indigenous led street medic collective. I was among those arrested during the Sun Dance ceremony at the Red Lake Treaty camp. On Friday, July 23, I was in sacred ceremony and peaceful prayer with many others on unceded Treaty land of the Red Lake Nation as protected by our article 6 and first amendment rights, declaring treaties as the supreme law of the land and protecting religious practices.

Ceremony started at dawn, and by noon riot police had surrounded those in prayer on all sides. I saw no riot. I saw no disturbance of peace. What I saw were water protectors from all walks of life and from all over coming together to pray for our Mother Earth, for the water, for the future of all the Creator's creatures. Despite this, I watched as law enforcement violently grabbed, assaulted, and detained those dear to my heart and then eventually myself as well. We sat in jail for four days. Many of us were denied repeated requests of emergency medical treatment, prescription medication, changes of clothes, and menstrual products.

Police showed a blatant disregard for constitutional law, human life, and Mother Earth. This is a disregard that will not stop with reform, it will not stop with new laws or optional standards. The police are in Enbridge's pocket, receiving exorbitant amounts of money to fund riot gear and encourage arrests. This traumatic encounter I and multiple other water protectors had is far from unique, you do not have to try hard to find them. None of us wanted to be arrested, but when the land, water, and our way of life is under threat, what else do we have to lose? Where do we draw the line if not here? Our entire existence is on the line, and we should not be deemed criminals for trying to protect Mother Earth and the living beings on her. Hundreds of water protectors are facing criminal charges for engaging in peaceful protest, dissent, and prayer. I am just one of those, I am not the first nor the last. I know firsthand the devastating effects that being put through the criminal "justice" system has. I see no justice in the persecution of those saying, "we care about Mother Earth, we care about the water."

> *Do not make us criminals for fighting for a future worth living.*

Tim Walz and the Pennington County Sheriff's Office, the damage has already been done. However, it is not too late to do what is right. I am writing this letter to tell you to drop the charges. Drop all the criminal charges against the water protectors of Minnesota. We have put blood, sweat, and tears into trying to give all of us a future on a livable planet. We have put our freedom on the line because we are in a state of climate emergency across the globe. Do not make us criminals for fighting for a future worth living.

Sincerely,
One of many •

Embroidered on the skirt:

The
7" Fire
Throbs like a
Drum beat in our
Heart.
Guiding our dance.
We will not give up.
Our resistance is ceremony.

This skirt is the one I was wearing while arrested.

My friend & I "watched the line" buzzing around Northern Minnesota all winter: windows down, masks on, taking photos, documenting pipeline construction/destruction. The pipeline workers, mostly from out of state, knew they were being watched. We kept our eyes on animals and plants and kept our courage. •

Author's Note: Fragments from journal entries —
November 2020 to November 2021.

I'm up at camp, sleeping in my car, learning about direct action with people who care about creating a sustainable & just future…

—

The permits for this pipeline were approved much too soon — I have years of learning to do still if I want to know how best to act now. This is combined with a deep feeling of necessity — I must do something & I must do it now. Anything could happen — I might spend days in jail, or years. We might stop construction, it might be finished by summer's end.

—

The police put up yellow tape in a twenty-foot radius around the tree sits, & Enbridge proceeded to tear out all the surrounding trees with a feller-buncher. We watched it all, worried about our friends & feeling the need to do something. One guy, B., said he would lock down to the machine. So, we charged the site…

—

There's clothes strewn about in the trailer, & graffiti on the wooden makeshift bunk beds: "Smoke weed for days!" "Stop Line 3 FOR FUCKS SAKE," "ACAB."

—

Tomorrow I'm going to clean out the meat coolers. They smell really bad.

—

The landscape is so beautiful here, especially after very cold nights when every tree branch & evergreen needle gets covered in a white sparkling frost. The result is a glimmering, breathtaking mass of trees that shimmer under the opaque sky. Crystalline flecks of ice patterned themselves crisply on the top layer of snow today. And the rivers are all frozen over — with tracks left behind by rabbits, foxes & deer crossing over the banks.

—

It's sickening how quickly they can tear through the forest.

—

Sometimes, the construction of this pipeline feels like the end of the world as we know it. I let it feel that way, sometimes.

—

S. texted me saying her car spun off the road, about 45 minutes from camp. R. has a truck with four-wheel drive, & we drove together to pull her out. He was driving way too fast on the icy roads, then correcting when the wheels of his truck slid out of control. He was blasting 2000s RnB, smoking cigarettes, eating Peach-O's, & choosing songs on his phone while driving. He was boisterous & quick to share…

—

I realized today that I'm not sure what an HDD even looks like.

—

They've moved in a pipe-bender, a vaccuworks suction pipe lifter, & some long segments of pipe (four trucks with three segments each). We also scouted the X. site, first by foot & then with a drone…

—

Workers have brought in a lot of pipe & they're laying it out. I cried this morning when I looked out at the bulldozers & excavators. I realized that I've been so focused on trying to organize against this pipeline that I hadn't let the emotional weight of all that I was experiencing hit me.

—

The group drove it in and tried to flip it over at the entrance, but it was too heavy, so they decided to slit the tires instead. Between the two blocked entrances were six access roads, & we stopped work on that entire segment of the line for the whole day…

—

I've been parked outside of the county jail since yesterday afternoon, besides driving to a Walmart parking lot at midnight to sleep for a few hours in my car.

—

There are lots of dead pheasants in the garage. D. is coming to pluck them tomorrow.

—

It's going to be strange when I'm no longer camping in the cold, surrounded by beautiful organizers & water protectors, having these meaningful conversations around the fire & dedicating myself to this resistance work.

—

His snoring is so bad that last night I had to get out of bed to find earplugs.

—

A big group came to camp this week & we planned an action that flopped on us. We've been under 24-hour surveillance here. Two big actions happened today.

—

Not a whole lot has happened that I can see. Jailers arrived for their morning shifts, a mailperson came, an elevator repair van idled in front of the entrance for an hour or so, a nurse brought what looked like an oxygen tank in on a dolly, & two people were released from the jail, both women. Not a whole lot of in & out. A whole lot of people inside who aren't allowed to leave.

—

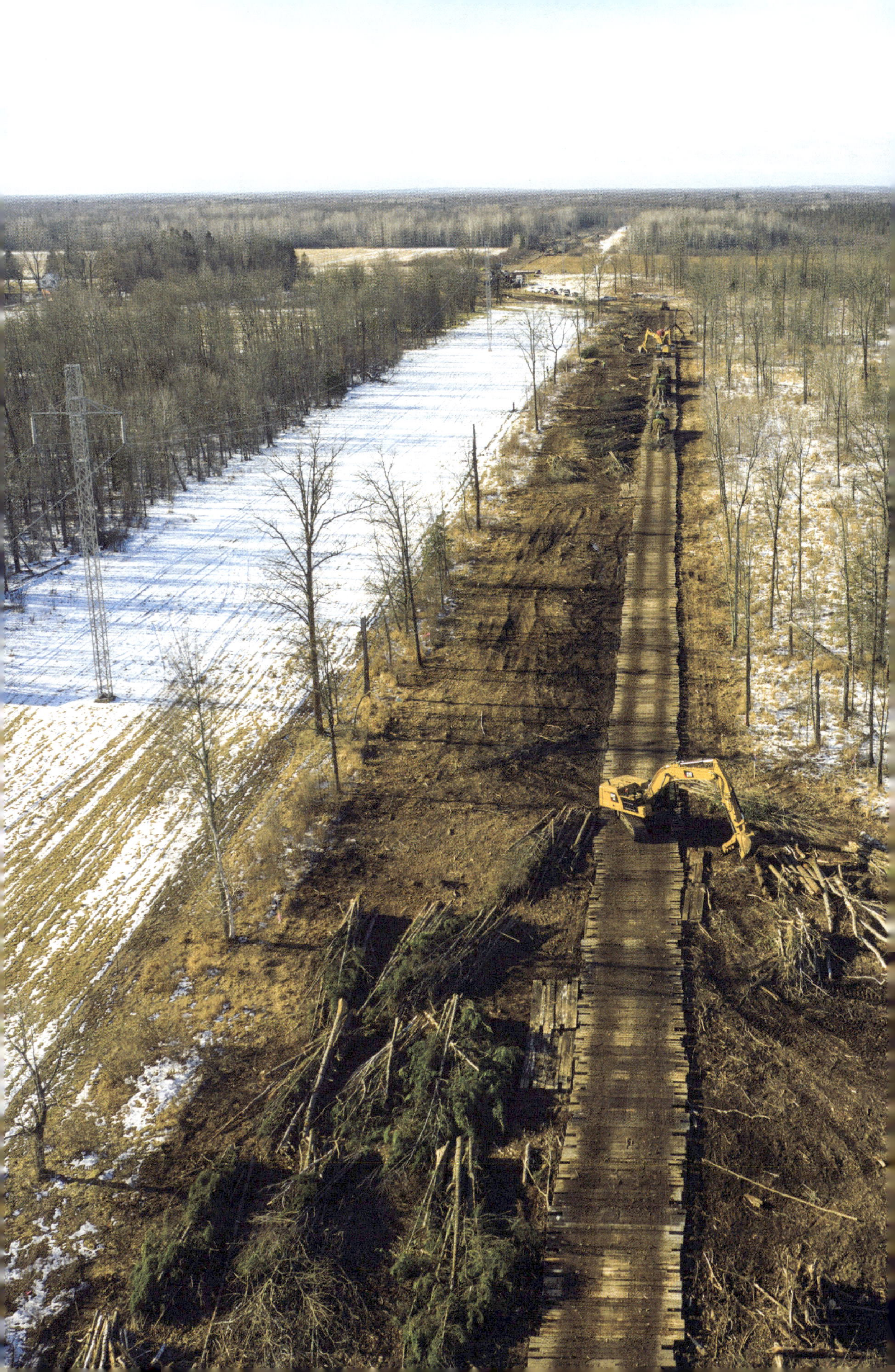

I stood on that hill, the wind whipping my hair into my face, & looked at the thawing ice that is slowly sinking under a layer of lake water. At the shoreline the ice has disappeared completely & you can see the mud & the leaves below — a tapestry of browns & grays.

—

I get so caught up in everything. I don't give myself time to process & grieve. And now I'm processing the fact that we're losing the pipeline fight, & the frontlines are disorganized & don't have a coherent plan, & this pipeline will likely get built & start to pump 750,000 barrels of oil a day across Minnesota & Fond Du Lac, & I spent the whole winter effectively watching this happen…

—

I should probably go to therapy.

—

The action today was all the things again — stressful, exciting, inspiring, a bit of a shit show all wrapped into one. It's 10:30 pm now, folks are booked & the jail calls are trickling in. It's going to be a Democracy Now headline tomorrow.

—

I had the jail support phone from 12 to 5 am. I was already pretty sleep deprived from the action, & I started to get full body aches, fever & chills from my COVID vaccine. I found someone's half-finished kombucha by the wood stove. It was pretty damn gross but I had been awake for 23 straight hours & needed any caffeine I could find. Then G. called from the jail — she needed her ID, & asked me to find it in her yurt & bring it to her. I was in a fugue state for the whole two-hour drive…

—

I watched someone trot out of the jail in a metallic silver track suit that flashed undertones of purple & green in the sun. He had his belongings slung over his shoulder in a trash bag, freshly returned to him. We were miles from the nearest town, but he skipped across the jail parking lot & past the trees until he was out of sight, a smile on his face…

—

I've been thinking about how I do love my life. I love being alive, & there is so much that I'm able to experience that brings me joy & happiness & pleasure. And how sometimes that feels wrong or unfair while the world is falling apart around me.

—

Today was extremely hazy & the air quality is horrible & I couldn't even tell you which fires the smoke was drifting in from but I know that one of the fires burning in Oregon right now is the size of L.A., & how the fuck am I supposed to do my part to fight the climate crisis? What does that even mean? I spent all winter helping organize & execute direct actions against fossil fuel infrastructure — it was really empowering & eye-opening in many ways. But it hasn't stopped Enbridge.

—

The skies were even smokier today. The landscape is draped in it. You could even taste the smoke: the trees consumed to dust, thickening the air in our lungs. As I drove to the COVID testing site I felt like I was driving through the end of the world.

—

It's raining. It's a big deal right now when it rains, & a storm is on its way tonight. It's 10 pm, & I'm sitting out on the screen porch. The air is thick & humid — I can feel it cooling as the rain intensifies.

We fought with petitions, rallies, marches, banners, graffiti, lockdowns, blockades, camps. We fought in the courtrooms, at the banks, on the construction sites. Enbridge built the pipeline anyway, & just today they started pumping the thick sandy bitumen though the buried pipe.

—

We're planning this big rally & action at the state capitol next week. The pipeline is moments away from being finished. This event feels like one last dying spasm of a movement in mourning, shock, horror. The capitol just put up security fencing in preparation for us.

—

We fought Line 3 throughout the permitting process & the construction process. We fought with petitions, rallies, marches, banners, graffiti, lockdowns, blockades, camps. We fought in the courtrooms, at the banks, on the construction sites. Enbridge built the pipeline anyway, & just today they started pumping the thick sandy bitumen though the buried pipe.

—

The oak leaves on the lower branches of the trees have wilted & fallen to the forest floor. The goldenrod has gone to seed, sending little tufts across the ground. The weather is sunny, practically windless. Comfortable. Ripples dance lazily across the St. Croix River. Canoers paddle by, children shriek with joy, crows caw — all these sounds bounce off the sandstone rocks at the edge of the water, where D. & I write in our journals next to each other.

—

It's been a year since I first moved up to the frontlines. •

Author's Note: Written December 2020.

Aitkin County Jail Song

(G) Donuts for breakfast
One hundred dollar (C) bail
(D) Such is the life at
(D) Aitkin (C) County (G) Jail

(G) I saw that feller buncher
My friends were in the (C) trees
(D) Ran to give that blade a hug
Cops (D) threw me (C) on my (G) knees

(G) Sheriff Dan, he lumbers up
Says "trespassin's a (C) sin!"
(D) Pulls off his mask and takes his aim
And (D) shoots me (C) with a (G) grin

They (G7) slammed the (G) door
Cell (G7) forty (G) four

(G) Donuts for breakfast
One hundred dollar (C) bail
(D) Such is the life at
(D) Aitkin (C) County (G) Jail

(G) Barrels filled with concrete
Cars flipped on their (C) head
(D) Enbridge we won't let you by
Gotta (D) go a(C)round (G) instead

(G) Now they got me booked in here
Who'll pay to get me (C) out?
(D) I've always got my comrades
And (D) this is (C) why we (G) shout!

(G) Donuts for breakfast
One hundred dollar (C) bail
(D) Such is the life at
(D) Aitkin (C) County (G) Jail •

That was a hug like no other. Held in our arms was a weekend of being held alone in our separate cells, of not knowing what to expect, before the advent of the jail support team. It was the rhythm of "Solidarity Forever" tapped through the wall that kept us apart. It was crying into the cinderblocks, being pulled out at the worst moment for booking and looking really, really sad in the mugshot. It was pressing our ears to the door to catch any snatches of a C.O.'s conversation that might give us news of the world, the frontlines, each other. It was how much we didn't know and how much we learned. Forgetting how bright the world is. The start of a ritual of laughter and stories that we'd repeat again and again and again.

Editors' Note: This story was developed from an interview. It has been excerpted and edited in collaboration with the interviewee.

I live in Bemidji, where I've lived for the past 25 or 30 years. And my family is from the Red Lake Nation here in Northern Minnesota. My mother was born there. My grandmother was born there. And then my father is Italian from Argentina. I feel my mixed heritage, and it informs the way that I walk through the world.

I've been trying to keep my eye on what's been going on with Line 3 over the years and wanted to be more involved. But also trusted that there were people working really hard on it. And that I couldn't do everything. That I had to do my own work at the time. But there was always that piece of me that was really feeling the need to be involved. This is my homeland.

Water means everything to us, and to me. I dream about water all the time. I dream about living in water. I could swim before I could walk. My mom's given me lots of different water teachings, and we do full moon ceremonies with Grandma Moon. So, water's really, really important.

The drill pad was really significant for me, because it was where they were going to drill under the Mississippi River. And there's something about that that is so apparent to me, it just — it's like an assault upon everything that we love, our soul. It just hurts.

I was looking at the river the last time I was there and it's just sitting there, you know, just being a river. My understanding from my parents is that our responsibility to creation looks something like this, which is that we all take our risk. We all agree to something. The spirit agreed to something we agreed to uphold. An ethic of taking care of all of creation. And so, animals give themselves to us for food, and water gives of itself. And our wild rice gives of itself. And we as humans, we also made a pact.

When I looked at the river that day, I was like, "This river is holding up its end. It's nourishing us, taking care of us, all the animals. Everyone's doing their part except the humans."

So, I just felt really called to make as much of a stand as I could. And sometimes you have to give up your favorite things or the things that mean the most. That's what we're asked sometimes to do. And for me, being incarcerated is one of my greatest fears. I have family members who are locked away, and it's really, really hard to think about them. So, that was also part of the reason why I thought that I'll have to give one of the hardest things to give, which is my freedom for a little while.

I don't like being in the front. I don't like having attention. I don't like anyone hindering my freedom. I don't like being tackled to the ground by two large men. I don't like having my hands tied behind my back and standing out in minus 2-degree weather.

It was a sacrifice. And it was a small sacrifice in the overall scheme of things, honestly. But it was really hard for me, and it's also just a small part in comparison with what other people are doing. And in comparison with what Mother Earth is doing, it was a small, small thing. But it was the best I could do right then. •

Paddle for Nibi to Stop Line 3, Mississippi River Headwaters, June 2021

"A Different Kind of Ministry"

When I came to Line 3, I knew I wanted to become an ordained Lutheran pastor. What I didn't know would happen was that the fight against Line 3 would change everything I knew about ministry and what it could mean to be a pastor.

When we hear the word "ministry" we often think of people preaching, about whatever version of God they believe, seeking to convince others that their God is the right version of God and that you must believe to be "saved." I, at least, also think of white pastors and priests converting colonized people to their version of "the right religion." This is the same sort of ministry that robbed my family of any knowledge of Black American Folk Magic. This is the same sort of ministry that facilitated the colonization and genocide that happened on the continent we live on. Despite feeling a call to ordination, I wasn't quite sure how ministry could look like anything except for the white Lutheran pastors I had seen at the front of my church my entire childhood. I had read and heard of the Black pastors who fought for civil rights and faced brutal beatings or death for their work; of Dietrich Bonhoeffer, the Lutheran pastor who attempted to bomb Adolf Hitler; of the priests in Latin America who fought against US-backed dictatorships that oppressed people and allowed for colonial extraction to take place.

It is one thing to know the history of such alternative forms of ministry, and it is another thing to find what that means today, in your own life. I knew that I came to fight the pipeline because it was an act of colonial violence that threatened the land of my Indigenous neighbors, and a desecration of the Earth. But I did not know that for a time this would become ministry for me.

After being arrested in January, my subsequent trips up north were to do jail support. Helping people fill out jail support forms, organizing them, trying to answer questions about what jail is like and how the process goes, answering phone calls, and doing on-site jail support, trying to keep track of arrestees, as well as the both loved and hated release parties. While part of me still feels this was out of cowardice, another part of me focused on jail support out of wanting to challenge myself, moving from a directly confrontational role in struggle to doing care work, something men like myself often ignore. So far, my understanding of ministry and its relationship to struggle was simply confrontation, those images of pastors risking their lives, facing violence "so that others may live." But this began to change.

I remember the second or third time I did jail support; I was there when a close friend of mine who had just been released from jail was talking to a more experienced jail support person about their experience of mistreatment and abuse. Talking about mistreatment is of course important for jail support to keep track of for the lawyers, but this conversation was more than that. We sat together by the unlit fire on that chilly afternoon, and despite sometimes taking notes during the conversation, my JS colleague was mostly focused on being comforting and affirming of my friend's experience. They didn't force out information, would ask if they needed to wait again before talking about their experience, and made sure to affirm that what happened to them was fucked up and part of why the carceral system in this country is so evil.

As I sat beside my friend listening to the conversation, I began to think: Perhaps this is ministry. A ministry that doesn't involve belief, or overt spirituality, but rather relationship building, community, and healing in the name of liberatory struggle.

Ahead of actions where folks thought there was a risk they could be arrested, I answered dozens of questions:

"What does booking look like?"

"Will you call my mom?"

"Can I get my medications in jail?"

"Is it normal to be scared?"

I don't remember all the conversations, but I tried my best to address their concerns. I didn't really have much to say to comfort folks, beyond: "Yes, jail is scary, and it can be and often is a really shitty experience, fuck the police and fuck prisons." Despite not having the greatest answers, I began to see that people walked away feeling somewhat relieved. Not because I had answers, but because of the relationship built between us as human beings, and the mutual vulnerability shown. Sometimes we would talk for five minutes, sometimes I'd spend 20 minutes with them. However much time it took for the person to feel confident enough about what they were about to do.

After the actions and arrests, as folks were being released, we'd gather in jail parking lots for "release parties." While now I question the celebratory nature of the release parties, many of the small conversations I was able to have with the recently released comrades taught me so many things.

As we would sit on the grass together, and often smoke a cigarette, a great deal of folks talked about how much the jail support process and the conversations were very helpful before going into jail. Some said it made them feel empowered, and many said that it was comforting to know that there was a team of human beings on the other side committed to watching them and making sure they'd get out. Of course, many folks also had a lot of intense emotions, whether anger or sadness, about what they had just gone through. I don't really know if the conversations various jail support team folks had, including myself, made a huge difference. But to hear the few people thank me and other colleagues of mine later in the day for sitting down in the grass of that parking lot to talk with them made me think a lot about what we were doing here as jail support. I don't think I really said much in either conversations before or after folks got arrested. But I now realize it wasn't what I said that made the difference, it was the presence of another person who cared and listened deeply that made the difference.

As the last arrestees were finally being released, I talked to a new friend who was also involved in the jail support/legal side of the movement after sharing my lighter with them. I found out that they also knew a bit about Bonhoeffer, and I shared my desire to be a pastor, but also how I was unsure about how I could do pastoral ministry and still be active in struggle and social movements beyond merely the figureheads I had read about. They told me something foundational to what I do today. They told me that what I had been doing *was* ministry, even if it wasn't the overt preaching that I'd previously defined as ministry. Ministry is as simple as being there for and with others. Ministry is the relational work we had been doing as a jail support team.

We talked for no longer than 30 minutes, but that moment has stuck with me since. Everything that all of us had done during the movement to stop Line 3 was our own personal ministries in our own traditions — spiritual, religious, or perhaps the lack of either. Ministry isn't simply preaching; it's making love known to others through our actions and through our relationships. To pull off effective actions, we had to form relationships with each other. To keep camp running, we had to form relationships with each other. We built a community together, one that not only resists the forces of empire, but also one that takes care of each other. And that to me is the greatest ministry, the same ministry that I read of on Sundays, of a poor colonized carpenter who built a loving community to take on the Roman empire and eventually die for the sake of others. But I know now that ministry doesn't need to be overtly religious, it doesn't need to include preaching, but it absolutely *must* include building relationships and building a resilient community that cares deeply for everyone in it. When we show vulnerability to each other, when we share hopes and dreams, when we lament together, that is ministry.

Sometimes, ministry is as simple as sharing a cigarette and a coffee, listening. •

The Movement to Stop Line 3 as a Series of Numbers

12/14, 3/3, 3/25, 5/6…
Time goes, and I go with it.
I started smoking cigarettes again in 2021.
I'd quit drinking on New Years,
and without those vices
something had to give.

6/2, 6/7, 6/8, 6/14, 6/15…
If anyone were to claim the role of starting fires,
it was my role to put them out.
But the fire starters didn't know me.

6/21, 7/1, 7/6, 7/10…
To some, I was just a keyboard warrior.
To some, I was an impossibility.
To most, I didn't exist.
To a few… well,
a few of us fell in love.

7/19, 7/20, 7/23, 7/29, 7/30…
What they don't tell you is fires don't die
when they're put out — they leave smoke
and ash
and embers.
What they don't tell you is legal proceedings
don't end with arrest — they cost time
and freedom
and can last for years and years.

8/3, 8/11, 8/20, 8/23, 8/26, 8/28…
Of course, these are not the only arrest dates.
Just the jigsaw puzzles;
the ones that pulsed in my nervous system
when I laid in bed at night.
The only thread distinguishing the events of summer.

9/7, 9/9, 9/14…
For what it's worth, I don't smoke cigarettes anymore. Time goes, and I go with it. •

Author's Note: This piece was performed on October 30, 2020, at the house of Laura Bishop, the former commissioner of the Minnesota Pollution Control Agency (MPCA). At this time, the MPCA was deliberating on Enbridge's final set of water crossing permits, which were needed to officially begin construction on Line 3. The MPCA granted these permits just two weeks later, on November 13, 2020.

Editors' Note: This is an excerpt of the full performance.

This day's the eve of Hallow's Eve,
When goblins, gremlins, ghosts, and thieves
Come out to play for just one night
And leave us all in fits of fright.
It truly is a scary sight.

But wait! There's more! The fright enhances
With truly scary circumstances.
Far more than witches, worms, or weevils,
Haunted suits of armor: medievals,
Here take root much darker evils.

If seeking a true source of terror,
Look no further than over there-rrrr.
What!? You say. It cannot be!
This paragon of civility?
The house of number seven three…?

…One one! That's right! You've cracked the case!
Yes, this is Laura Bishop's place.
And in her hands rests total power
(I say this plain though't makes me glower)
To turn our very water sour.

Now not to broadcast idle gossip…
But Laura's pipe drips like a faucet.
Oh! Have you heard? Like the Black Sea!
Black as the hearts of bourgeoisie!
That putrid, polluting Pipeline Three.

And wo! Behold! It gets much worse,
For more than water has been cursed.
This pipeline breaches treaty rights
Only to profit greedy whites.
And all enforced by Northern Lights…

Alas! We're doomed! I curse my fate!
If only we were not too late!
But wait. That's right. It's still October.
Construction hasn't begun, moreover,
There's still one permit! This fight ain't over.

Therefore, we plead this Hallow's Eve
Dear Laura, hear the people grieve!
Stop this environmental slaughter.
Act for your great great granddaughter!
Do not let Enbridge cross our water. •

I've been a street medic for two years now, and medicing at Line 3 was a truly humbling experience. When I first became a street medic, I had no idea how drastically it would alter my life, how it would change nearly everything I do. I did not know it would bring me back to my roots, that some days it would bring me to my knees. I've had the honor through this work to meet people from all over, from all walks of life, and to help heal them and teach them how to do the same for others. The medic shack has been a physical symbol of this for me, just a small, modest shed filled with the materials and will to get aid to whoever may need it.

It was eleven in the morning when we slipped from the pipeline easement, four dirty kids with three water bottles, two oranges, and one compass between us. It was two in the afternoon when we saw her, the owl, soft and white and round as a poorly packed snowball, head swiveling expectantly as we swept past her, our steps soft and even. It was seven in the evening, the end of eight impossible hours spent crawling and sinking and whispering and wading, when a tan Prius pulled into a dusty driveway to carry us home. I stepped into the car and the driver handed me a Gatorade. I downed it in four gulps, and when we returned to camp, I learned that we were not the last group to make it out. There were others in the woods, still, as the sun slid behind pines.

I could have known this, I believe, had I asked the owl. When our eyes met, two pairs equally dark and unwavering, she told me that we would escape to the place beyond blockades and barricades, back to our aching, muddled world. Owls don't wait in the afternoon sun unless they have something to tell you, I've learned, and she told me her secret wordlessly, dangled it somewhere in the air between us. We would be free.

I remembered this as I sank to my knees, elbows to the Earth, scratched and torn by unseen nettles as I crawled through the grasses of a stranger's yard. We couldn't allow these homeowners, residents of the river's edge, to see us, lest they call the police and bid the state patrol extend the road blockade a few miles further. Somewhere, on the far side of the blockade, our friends waited in Priuses and Tahoes to drive us to safety; we only needed to reach them. The man crossed first, long red hair pulled tight, and upon reaching the cover of cattails he turned slowly on the balls of his feet to address us. A flattened palm turned in our direction: wait. A pointer finger curled inwards, towards him: come, now. The brunette followed, slithered through dead grass, whispered "Ow!" beneath her breath. The man placed his finger flush to his lips: not a sound. I moved next, seeing on my left the abandoned back porch of unwitting strangers and on my right the river, the water, the reason for our fight. When I reached cover the blonde woman crawled after me, sleek and subtle, and joined us before continuing in silence.

I remembered the owl's promise again when we pulled off our shirts, dank with sweat and soil, and tied them around our heads like bandanas. We had consulted the compass and the maps (the blonde woman's phone still held some charge) and we reached the conclusion that, in order to arrive at the place beyond the blockade, we had to cross the river. Most of the day was spent trekking through wetlands, ankles occasionally slipping between patches of moss into the peat that lay beneath, and there was little question of preserving our shoes. For many days afterwards, I worried that I had contracted athlete's foot, my skin stiff and scaly from hours soaked in muck. Our pants, too, we agreed could not be saved, blue jeans turned brown from the hem to the knee. Shirts, however, and whatever precious goods we might have tucked into our backpacks, might make it across the river unscathed if we only fastened our tops tightly around our slick foreheads and hoisted our sacks above our heads. We waded upstream until the river turned and we emerged from it — cool, refreshed, drenched from the waist down.

I thought again of the owl when our water bottles ran dry and the brunette passed us each segments of her orange, a gesture of kindness and faith that we wouldn't need the fruit to carry us through the night. She had rehydration salts, too, and poured them into what little remained in our water bottles, the saline taste covered only by the bits of citrus we popped in our mouths after every sip. Earlier in the day we had sat in the shade and talked, thinking that if we only waited long enough the cops might leave of their own accord. In those times, before we lost such hopes, we drank too much too soon, gulping water and sharing stories freely. In the hours after, our drinks grew increasingly rationed, but some strange comradery carried us through; the only other food to pass between our lips in those fateful hours was the occasional wild raspberry that grew between the ferns and the skunk cabbage.

Once more I remembered her, the owl, little more than a baby, still mottled with downy fluff and feathers that jutted at odd angles. We neared the point in the road where our friends could find us at last and an unfamiliar voice shouted, "What are you doing back there?" Three of us dropped to the ground, crouching in weeds and mud. The red-headed man remained standing. "We're just hiking." The voice, a woman walking her dog on the side of the county road, barked, "You're not part of the protestors, are you?" He said no, but even as the words left his mouth we crept backwards, disappearing into the woods from which we came before the police on the other end of the woman's phone could prove otherwise.

Some hours later we escaped, the sun still high above the mid-summer sky. I began to recount the story to friends — the gruesome parts, the gunshots, the parts I didn't disclose here. My phone died minutes before we passed the owl; when we saw her, I asked the blonde woman to take a picture. The woman was logical, disciplined: "No, we need the maps on my phone. It can't die." We continued forward, the owl occupying only a minute of our eight-hour venture.

Still I see her, though, in sleep and in daydream. She grows hazier with each recollection but her eyes remain, dark and unwavering, gazing into my own. •

For 12 days, beginning on December 3, 2020, water protectors slowed construction of

the pipeline by occupying trees that were slated to be cut in the path of construction.

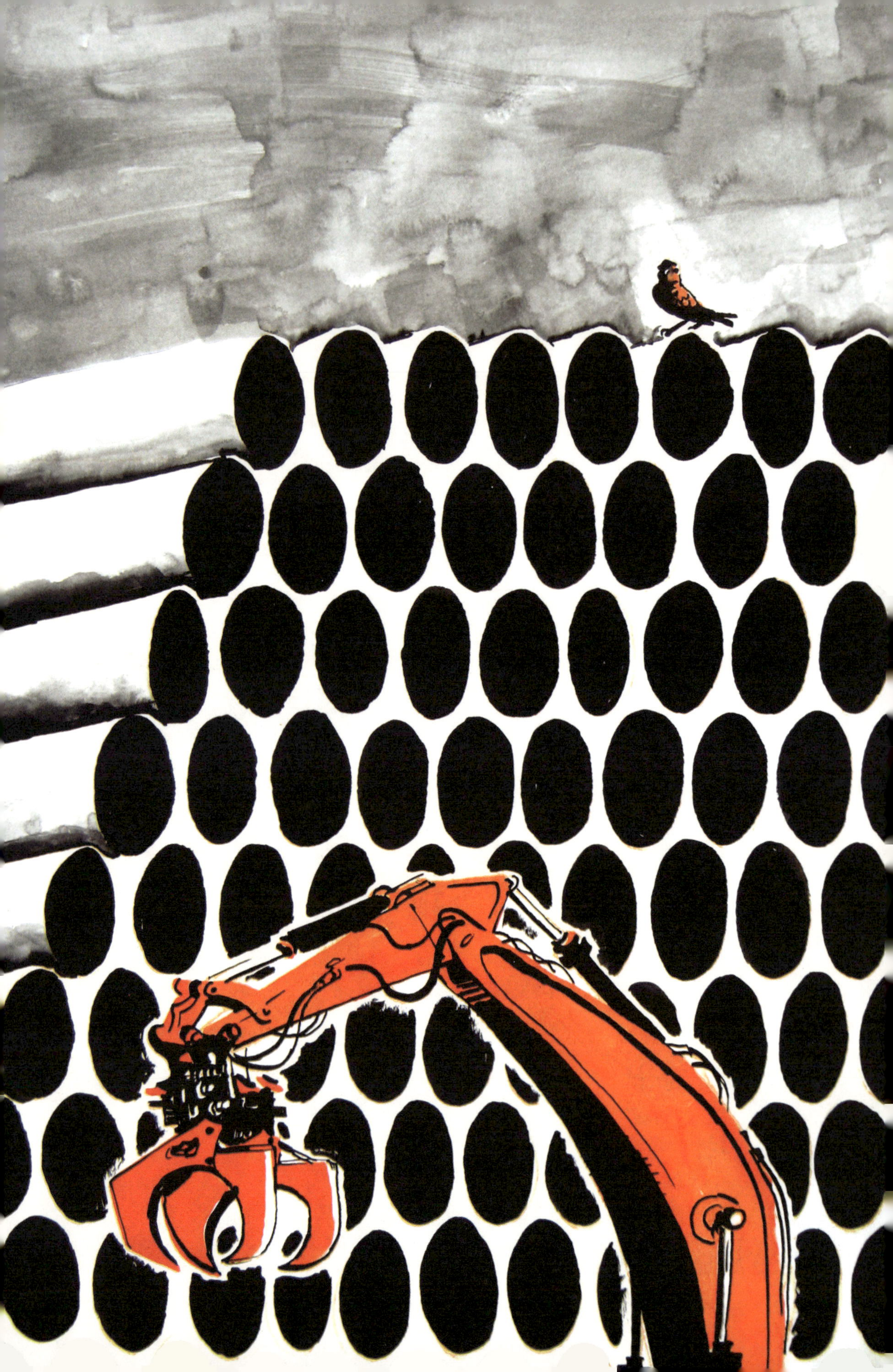

In summer, I began to suffer from an affliction that I refer to as "pipeline brain." The pipeline construction and our resistance occupied all of my brain space. There was no room for anything else.

My days at camp were filled with frantic one-on-ones, as my comrades and I confided our sadness and fear to one another. It felt evil to give up hope. But really, we weren't giving it up, it was being forcibly taken from us. Nothing we did felt like enough. I went weeks without showering, days without feeding myself properly, because my focus was tied up in how I could be most effective, useful to the movement at any given moment.

Our nights bordered on complete sleeplessness. We stayed up, on shifts at the camp gate or dispersing ourselves for intervention along the route. When I finally did let myself crawl into bed, I would lay awake, racking my brain for any conceivable way to make construction stop.

One night, I found myself deep in the woods. Although we were close to the pipeline easement, the trees helped me to feel cut off from the outside world. Due to drought, the earth was so dry that clouds of dusty, fine dirt rose up around our ankles with each step. The nearby river was running so low you couldn't even paddle a canoe without getting stuck.

> *When I finally did let myself crawl into bed, I would lay awake, racking my brain for any conceivable way to make construction stop.*

I woke up in a tent to a loud, unending sound. It sounded like high-pitched, powerful machinery. Whining, whirring, *drilling*. They were bringing the pipeline under the drought-stricken river.

With the noise came an unignorable vibration of the ground. It was insidious. It was in the earth. My body shook. My brain was strung out. My heart broke.

A few days later, I was napping in a friend's van because I had been up between 1 and 4 am, scouting the line. The sun was hot and the air was still, but I was so exhausted that I fell asleep immediately. It was a cursed sleep, in and out of foggy dreams of failure, and I was inescapably hot. I woke up because of a very loud, repetitive banging noise. It was obviously the construction, but for the life of me I couldn't figure out what they would be doing to create that noise, let alone why.

Bang! Bang! Bang! Bang! Bang! Bang! Bang! Bang! Bang! Rhythmic, unending.

I had a splitting headache; it felt like the pipeline itself was drilling into my skull. Not unlike a mechanical possession.

Another friend found me inside of the van. He asked what was wrong, and I began to cry. *"It's not working. Nothing we do is working."*

My father gave me a call, "What's this mail from court? Did you get arrested again?" In the past several months, I had received court mail from Hubbard and Hennepin counties, notifying me of charges and zoom hearings, and now I had mail from my home county, Ramsey. I had not, to my knowledge, broken the law there. I asked him to open the letter and it turned out to be a jury summons for the first week of August.

Although my comrades had been trying to get me to take a break for weeks, the only thing that could pull me away from the frontlines was my civic duty.

When some friends and I finally did pull up in the Twin Cities, I was shocked at all the lush green lawns, the tidy streets, the huge homes. These people were not living in the world I had been living in.

For months, I had only known dirt roads, heavily patrolled by cops. We lived mostly in tents, tipis, tiny houses. I had been sleeping in my car. I had been trespassing frequently but driving around in urban neighborhoods made me feel more out of place than anywhere else.

Occasionally, I would pass a house with one of the iconic blue "Stop Line 3" yard signs. *Do they know? What we've been through up north, what's happening to the people and the earth?* I would ask myself. *How could they possibly know?* The answer I gave myself was wholly cynical: that no one actually cared, that the lawn signs, as with bumper stickers proclaiming various candidates, were just for show. Everyone had resigned themselves to lack of change long ago, even when we needed it most desperately.

That night a friend and I smoked weed. I thought it would help my nerves. I was wrong. Throughout our conversation, my attention drifted again and again to the five-foot fence that bordered my friends' property. The image of the fence panicked me, because it reminded me of the proximity to the drill pad at Red Lake Treaty Camp. Over the past several days many people at Red Lake had been sprayed with tear gas and shot at with pepper bullets. At that moment, several of my friends were sitting in Pennington County jail, skin still burning from the "less than lethal" weapons.

This fence was not ten-feet tall or topped with barbed wire. There weren't cops with K9 units equipped with chemical weapons guarding a drill on the other side, but it was still a fence. My brain couldn't detect a difference in the fences, and so this harmless fence put me on guard. As if I were still there, at Red Lake.

Each morning of jury duty, my shock was still fresh. People live in houses? They have running water? And air conditioning? They sleep on beds!

The cognitive dissonance of modern American lifestyles frequently proves too much for me to handle. It seems that nearly everything we are surrounded by, phones, fans, cars, lumber, paint, food from industrial agriculture, even your toothbrush, is made from violent extractive processes that poison the planet, ourselves, and especially the peoples whose labor is exploited and land is taken to make it all happen.

I don't want to live so alienated from the Earth. Sometimes I want to hide in the woods forever, but then I remember that the snake is there, too.

I began suffering from pipeline brain because of my commitment to resisting the fossil fuel industry. My salvation comes from knowing that simple resistance is not enough, we must create something together, remind ourselves that a better world can exist, will exist, does exist the second we start building it. When the ground shakes, let it be from our doing, not the drill. •

Drop the Charges! • Stop the Pipeline! • Water Protectors Stand Together!

The Line 3 story I want to tell is about an earring. It's a small, purple stud. Titanium. Nothing too special. Back in September of 2020, just after I got involved in the Line 3 fight, actually, someone stabbed it through my earlobe with a little white gun. And then its sibling on the other side. It was a 21st birthday present. And yes, it was at Claire's. What can I say? They were my first piercings.

After the piercings healed, I started being able to use other earrings in my new decorative holes and I really got to liking this whole earring thing. So, 10 months later, my friend used that same little purple stud to pierce a new hole in my right ear, just above my first piercing. This time it was in the parking lot of a resistance camp up North. With an apple and some hand sanitizer and the sheer brute force of a strong they/them. I remember feeling the gristle and cartilage of my ear as the stud tore through it. This was very different from Claire's. And although I chickened out on getting the second double piercing on my other ear ("Oh! Boy! Um, well I think that's enough!") in the end, it worked out and I loved it. And then, a few days later, I went to jail.

It was my first time being arrested, and I was prepared to go to jail, but not for the way in which it happened.

I remember crouching on a hilltop. There had been a furtive meeting. Somehow, the plan had gone askew. But I didn't know how because I didn't know the plan, I just knew my role. There were tons of cops and it seemed there was no hope of success. But suddenly, another team began to deploy, and someone made the call. We slunk down the hill towards the imposing barb-wired double fences of the drill pad. Closer, closer. Staying low. Only five feet away, we set into action. The rugs were thrown, ladders deployed, and as we began making our way over the fence, I started to notice these harsh popping noises all around us, and these little stings up and down my arms. A smoke began to rise from the grasses. Then it started hurting to breathe. The air was sour and sharp, and my nose began to run, and that's when I understood what was happening. "We're being tear gassed."

I remember seeing my friend's face dyed completely orange. The tear gas had gotten underneath their safety goggles and was swimming in their eyes. It was underneath their respirator and they were inhaling it with every breath. I reached for my med pack thinking, "slow is smooth, smooth is fast, slow is smooth, smooth is fast" and used all the saline solution I had brought on the first person I treated. I remember repeating, "I am not resisting," just as I had been taught, as the cops dragged my limp body down the hill towards the drill pad. I remember the odd thrill of feeling them heave and slip on the uneven ground. I remember the feeling of scissors on my shoulders as the cops cut the backpack off my arms. It was the only time any of us made it inside the drill pad that day. I remember sitting on the concrete floor in the jail, waiting to be booked, and looking at a stack of chairs lined up against the wall. "Hey, can we get some of those chairs to sit in?"

"No."

And that's when I started being able to think again. I had been warned by my friends that when you go to jail the cops make you take out your piercings when you're getting booked. You have to strip down, put all your stuff in little plastic bags, and also take out your earrings, supposedly so you can't hurt yourself or anyone else. Sitting there, all I could think was that I really didn't want to do that, because the piercing was so new that it would just close up right away if I took out the stud. And somehow, this piercing had taken on a greater meaning. I wanted it to survive this experience. I needed it to make it through Pennington County. Maybe I just needed a win amidst so much defeat.

One by one, they called us out of the room to get processed into our cells. When it was my turn, I got up, followed the cop, and was led to a little room where I traded out my clothes and personal belongings for an orange jumpsuit. That morning, I had specifically chosen to wear these turquoise studs that my mom had given me, because they made me think of her, and I wanted to have them with me during the action. Those, I put into the little plastic bag they provided, but I left the purple stud in, positioning my hair to hang over my face and conceal it, crossing my fingers that the guard hadn't seen my what-felt-like-monumental deception.

Before I knew it, I was being led to my cell, piercing intact, and feeling like I had just pulled off a major heist. When I got to my cell, the first thing I did was look at myself in the mirror, a polished-metal-lunch-tray-looking-thing bolted to the wall above the sink… and it was there. The little purple stud. And I felt that somehow, everything was going to work out.

With that little victory under my belt, or my loose orange waistband, I should say, I thought I'd better take a shower to wash the tear gas off myself. After a hot, painful shower, where my pores opened up in the hot water and reabsorbed all the tear gas, I put back on my clothes, made my bed, got settled, and at some point, my hand drifted back up to my ear… the earring back had fallen off! I sat bolt upright in my bed and nearly hit my head on the ceiling. There's no way the stud will stay in without the back. Where'd it go? It must have fallen off in the shower. Did it fall down the drain? After a minute of frantic visual search, I finally found it, between the cracks of the bathmat on the cell floor. With a huge sigh of relief and shaky hands I picked it up and walked over to the mirror. I found the pointy back with my thumb and pressed the backing onto its point. But as I pushed, I forgot to hold the stud in place and accidently knocked it out of my ear. And so I watched the stud fall, right in front of my eyes, directly down the drain of the sink.

I breathed in. I locked eyes with my warped reflection in the mirror, and I laughed, looking hopelessly down at the earring back feebly clutched between my shaking thumb and pointer finger. Defeat.

By that night, my piercing had closed up. And even though we were arrested on a Thursday, we ended up being held until Monday. When we were finally released, I found myself again undressing back in that same little room I had been in the first night, putting back on my tear-gas-soaked clothing. But wait! Checking my pockets, I realized I didn't have my earrings. The little clear bag with the two turquoise studs. The ones from my mom. I called the jail, but I was told "they weren't in your personal belongings, and I'm sorry but there's nothing we can do."

In the end, I lost three earrings, and four days, and four nights, to Pennington County. •

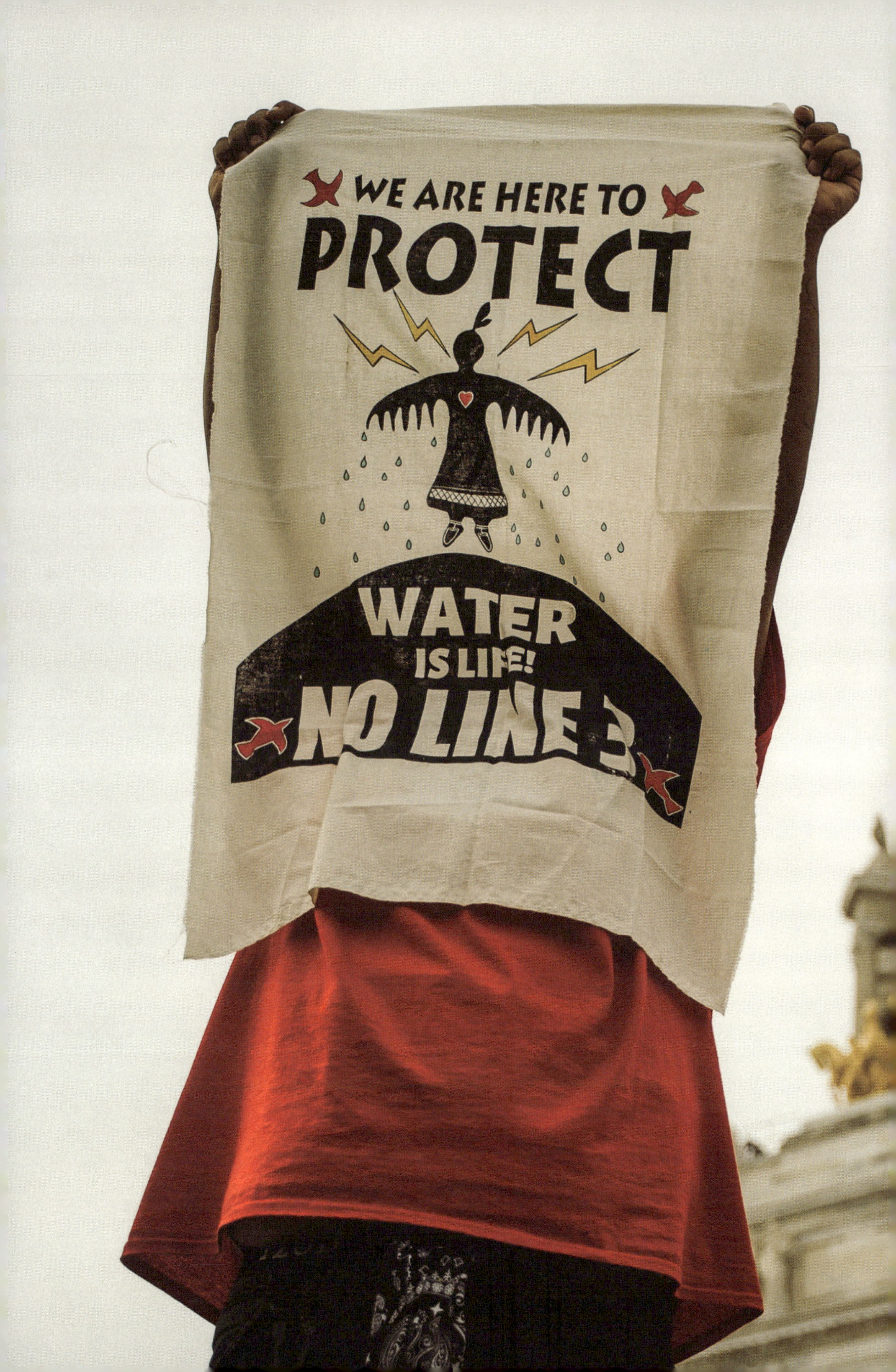
WE ARE HERE TO
PROTECT
WATER
IS LIFE!
NO LINE 3

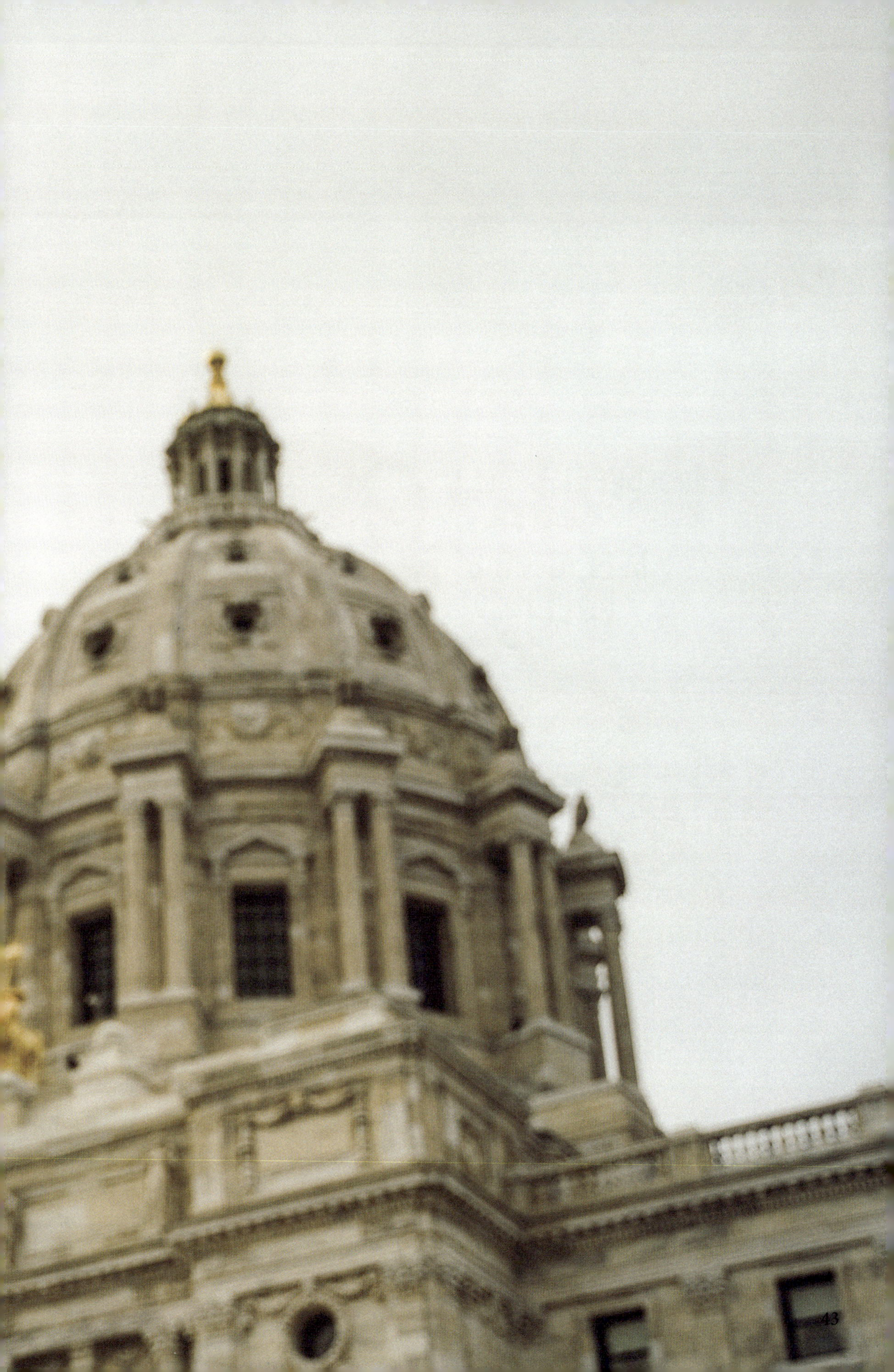

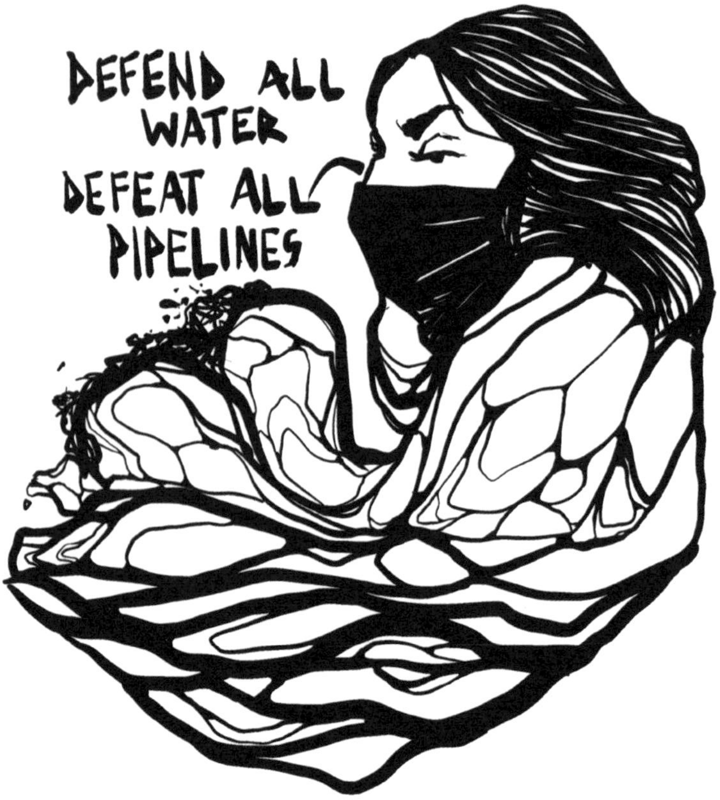
DEFEND ALL
WATER
DEFEAT ALL
PIPELINES

Editors' Note: This story was developed from social media posts. They have been compiled and edited in collaboration with the author.

Gitchi-gami felt the Spirit of billions of heartbeats today. Those who came before. Those here now. Those who have yet 2 come.

For Nibi, trees, four legged, winged, swimmers, and for us pitiful two legged. We as humans in my teachings are said to remain pitiful and humble. Humility to all others before ourselves.

We knew without knowing how important it was. Ditch-living, monitoring, and truly believing in the prayers of Our Grandmother's ceremony, but mostly for giving that Nibi what it truly needed. It needed not to be hurt in silence but to be loved and for it to not go unnoticed and again we filled it with love, laughter, song, dance, and for a moment our feelings truly did not matter, just the Nibi.

For those still missing, for those who have survived, we say

No More
For youth that are screaming
No More
We want Our Future 2

We have showered our relatives with their gifts, the colors of the Medicine Wheel. We have led you back to taking care of Mother Earth. We will stand up. We will shut down business as usual. We lay our bodies on the line to fight Enbridge.

For our youth we can do this. They are screaming for us to do this. They want their future too just as we wanted one. I've been listening to my elders and our youth. I see our toddlers and our women. I hear their calls. We as sovereign nations have had enough. With all our relatives walking next to us, I also heard songs, singing, laughter, hugs everywhere, and drums going in the distance from every direction. I felt love and good life everywhere. I felt healing for all my family and for more than just the people. We rocked that lake.

We learned to find our voices, our gifts.

We overcame shyness, anxiety, and collectively we did more than just stand. We unconditionally loved, cared, supported, and encouraged each spirit to soar above and let our gifts flourish. Above all, we believed in each other unconditionally with compassion, understanding, and patience.

We are, we are, we are so much more to us than just being Water Protectors. One also must take time to reflect, heal, comprehend, and live to fight another good fight.

It's never over. Just another chapter. •

The first beats of the blades of the helicopter didn't come as a surprise. Living in Minneapolis I had become accustomed to the familiar pulse of government surveillance following the murder of George Floyd. The circular flight paths of helicopters and planes flown by forces of asset protection under the guise of public safety wound to a constricting tightness, choking and spraying citizens with dust and rocks from all directions. I shielded my eyes and pointed my camera back at the smiling passenger recording the antithesis of his agency's mission from above. Video of the mechanically induced tornado of debris usually reserved for victims of American imperialism went around the world. The brief storm of internet outrage and FAA complaints did little to stem the excuse of a statement explaining the so-called incident. The circles get tighter, the winds get stronger, the blades get lower, and no matter how many pictures are taken, America finds new ways to forget.

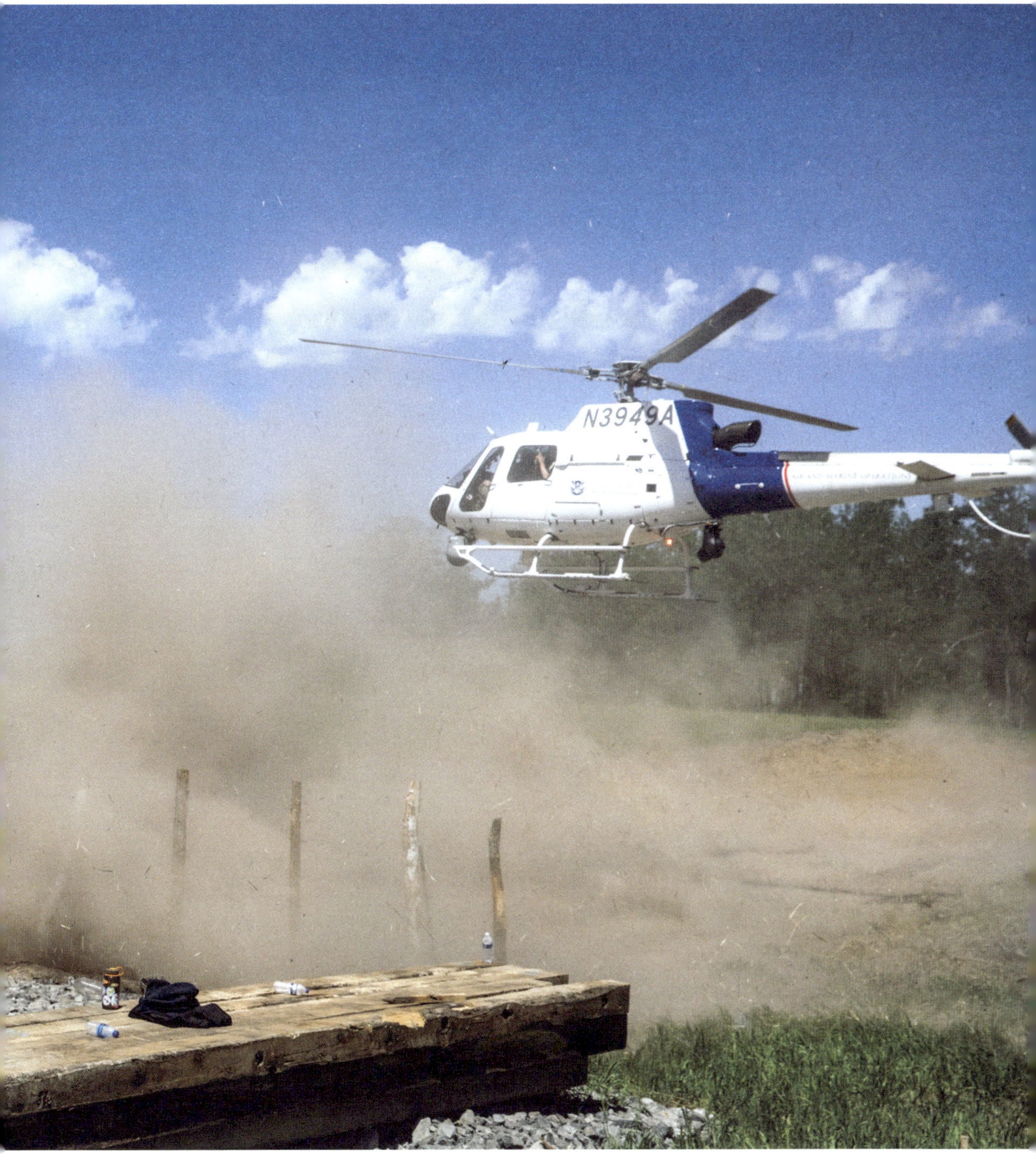
N3949A

Going into the Treaty People Gathering, I knew two things for sure: people would fall in love, and people would get heatstroke. I repeated that, a lot, to anyone I crossed paths with in the week leading up to it. I repeated it because it was a fun, silly sentence that didn't take much time to say and could get a laugh out of someone, which was easier than saying the truth: I was dreading it.

Nothing has ever felt worse than the days leading up to TPG. I had several moments of just sitting on my couch, unable to go to bed, because I knew if I went to sleep, I'd have to wake up and I'd be one day closer to it. The endless meetings, the side-meetings after the meetings, the arguments and meltdowns and long drives. The moment spent on site with my supervisor, a week before, where we hung our heads and admitted that we really couldn't imagine how we were going to pull it off. How awful we felt. And then, we got there.

It was so hot. It was unbearably hot, kicking off what we didn't know would be one of the worst droughts Minnesota had ever seen. The river provided so much relief, a stark reminder of why we were there fighting. There were thousands of people there, so many I knew, so many I didn't. My legs felt like molasses and I walked over 30,000 steps one day, just in circles around the land. Fights broke out and tears were shed. The things I thought would be our biggest problems turned out to be blips and the things I hadn't even considered nearly ruined the whole event.

> *The endless meetings, the side-meetings after the meetings, the arguments and meltdowns and long drives. The things I thought would be our biggest problems turned out to be blips and the things I hadn't even considered nearly ruined the whole event.*

People got heatstroke. I helped at least two, although there were likely many more. We ran out of electrolyte powder and I took refuge in the air-conditioned trailer we had set up as a makeshift office. We didn't put up the rain fly on our tent properly and it hung over the frame limply, sealing our hot breath and sweat inside. There was basically a hurricane the third night and I slept through it, grateful for the cooler air of the storm and the knowledge that it was almost over, while others slept on the easement, at the pump station, in jails spread across the state, in the crowded barn on site to protect themselves from the wind.

People fell in love. Before the crowds arrived, I said my little joke to an organizer and we laughed together. I pointed to my outfit, the uniform I was planning to wear during our sweltering days, athletic shorts and a baseball hat, and said, "Other people might fall in love, but look at me. It's not gonna be me!" I ran around the grounds not noticing anyone, willing people to not talk to me while I placed phone calls to Walmart to inquire about their tinfoil selection. I didn't want to meet anyone, I wanted to get the fuck out of there.

We realized that we hadn't adequately prepared to close down the event at all. There were still people occupying the easement, and there were approximately 1,000 loose t-shirts, boxes of granola bars, and broken umbrellas left behind at the event site. I went home, because I had to drive a friend to the airport, and then I came back to the easement, where my colleagues and friends were living for a time.

I was there for three days, three of the longest and best days of my life. I wasn't responsible for anything except having my body be there, willing to be forcibly removed. I swam in the lake, participated in ceremony, froze my ass off at night with the inadequate clothing I hastily brought, more athletic shorts and baseball hats. When we were asked to leave, less forcibly than expected although the forces were lying in wait, I cried a lot. I got a wicked sunburn that shocked me in a gas station mirror the next day.

And I fell in love. With someone I met the night of the hurricane, who was asking me where the burritos and pastries were, who was waiting up to greet people when they got out of jail. I didn't register them at the time, far too immersed in my stress-haze. I arrived at the easement and there they were.

I decided I had a crush and through a series of events completely out of my control, although I certainly took advantage of the circumstances, I ended up giving them a ride to Minneapolis. That was the longest day of my life, waking up in my cold tent to learn that we had lost in the court of appeals, then spending the day cleaning off the easement so we could all leave with dignity. When we left, I got the aforementioned sunburn along with my citation for trespass. We jumped in the lake after and I asked if they wanted to drive back to Minneapolis immediately or go to the feast. "Drive back," they said. I paused and recanted, and said I needed more time before I went back to my life.

I thought about what the day had meant — likely, the completion of the construction of Line 3 due to the shitty court decision and the fact that this incredibly special action was over — and thought about how I could distract myself for a moment. What would it mean, for me, someone who refuses to allow themselves a moment of joy most of the time, to let go?

So I asked if they knew I was flirting with them, and they said they knew, but that we had a long drive back the next day and they didn't want to ruin anything. I told them I didn't think kissing would ruin a car ride. Afterwards, I wondered if we would ever talk again, but told myself I didn't kiss them in order to see them again. I did it to prove to myself that I was okay, that I was human, that I could make good things happen in the worst moments.

We did talk again, and again. And then they were in Minneapolis again, down for a visit from living at the resistance camp where they never meant to stay. And then again and again, until it was no longer a surprise, a coincidence, but a plan, a need. I wondered why, a lot. We didn't know where it was going, only that it went, that we tried, until we couldn't anymore, worth our time nonetheless.

I don't know how many other people found someone at TPG. I know many people in this movement have fallen in love, simply due to proximity, or the need to feel good about something for once, or because there's no good time for love like the end of the world. All of 2021 felt like the end of the world. The people I met, the people I love and loved, are the ones who make me want to keep living through it, side by side, for however long we have, for however long we can be with each other. •

I didn't think I'd find myself sleeping on the lawn in front of the Minnesota State Capitol, surrounded by cops, taking my pants off to put on pajamas belonging to someone I'd only met a couple hours ago. Even after a year and a half of a life-changing pandemic, the uprising the year before, and another summer of the Line 3 fight, it wasn't on my bingo card. Those of us who were staying the night gathered just across the street from the Capitol and gradually posted up on blankets after a couple hours of ceremony and song circles. It felt a little like a middle school sleepover, but with crust punks and water protectors of all ages. And cops looking on from afar.

I stayed up late talking with the comrade I'd just met. I was exhausted from the afternoon's rally in the scorching August sun, but I knew I wouldn't sleep for a while. I was on edge being around the militarized response to our pretty unthreatening action; the armored personnel carriers on the Capitol steps dragged back the memory of the same vehicles driving through my neighborhood the summer before, with a cop sitting on top aiming a semiautomatic at my neighbors and I right and left as we sat on our porches and the convoy rumbled down the street. It was sobering to see many comrades still carrying bruises from rubber bullets and batons up north, and all too many just weren't there, after the trauma and horror of the actions they'd been in.

But I also felt safe, and cared for, and connected to the people around me. In the midst of what looked more like a defeat every day, with Enbridge racing toward completion and the Mississippi headwaters cloudy with drilling mud, the evening felt like a small accomplishment in movement building. The group was small, maybe a hundred and fifty from what I remember others saying, and there were familiar faces from the movement as well as many

> *I was exhausted from the afternoon's rally in the scorching August sun, but I knew I wouldn't sleep for a while. I was on edge; the armored personnel carriers on the Capitol steps dragged back the memory of the same vehicles driving through my neighborhood the summer before.*

new ones. Spontaneous conversations broke out, friends were made, cigarettes were shared. There was tension and fear and disagreement over tactics, to be sure, but by the time people started going to sleep we knew nobody would be left behind that night and everyone was looked out for.

The sky was tinged with wildfire haze and light pollution as I laid back on the blanket and looked up. Singing drifted gently across the lawn. I smiled to myself as I saw the cops change shifts in the distance and remembered I had no pants on. My rage and hurt at the pipeline took the back seat as I thought of everyone else lying there with me, understanding more deeply now how our fates were tangling up with each other by being here, and how powerful we could be together. •

What Landback Means to Me

*In my understanding, one of the most important tasks for the Landback movement is to do away with the false narrative of **scarcity**... of homes, of meaningful community and work, of privacy... Landback must wrench all these things and more from the grip of the ill-logic of capitalism and bring them **back** to the people directly. From the hands of one directly into the hands of another. In other words, we must do this for ourselves. Those who have more must provide for those who have less.*

And do this not because the people have "earned" these rights through years of suffering and servitude, but simply because we the people are the people, and this planet is our home. If we cannot live and be here, then where can we be?

Landback means that the concept of privately owned large sections of the earth is dismantled. It means that stolen lands will be liberated and used to form new villages, stewarded and enriched by those who have made a commitment to do so.

Landback could be the resynchronization of our human nature with the rhythms of our planet home again.

Last summer, land-and-water protectors built an encampment near the Line 3 pipeline route, on a site that had once been home to a people who had lived there for many generations. The people of those villages had been driven out, their families had been splintered and destroyed and their homes had been taken away, by a heartless *enemigo*.

The land-and-water protectors had been invited there by a movement called Stop Line 3.

For weeks we held our ground in that place. We fed and sheltered other activists from many different resistance camps. We learned to keep small children and pets off the dirt roads because enemy vehicles were circling the camp at dangerous speeds — white knuckled and grim faced, often yelling obscenities, their only concern was to intimidate us into running away. When gunshots resounded in the woods, we made sure all land-and-water protectors were present, alive, and intact. We extinguished the flames from enemy firecrackers that nearly set the surrounding woods on fire. We monitored the water levels on the river as they sank lower each week, and we held protests at drilling sites and at the offices of the enemy.

We marched, we taught, we resisted. We went to other camps led by other organizations and joined them in their initiatives to raise awareness about the pipeline. We learned the facts and talked to pipeline workers, trying to convince them to expand their sights and stop working for the enemy. We shut down drilling operations. Some of us were arrested and jailed. Others were merely beaten.

As the summer was drawing to an end, many of us at camp realized that it had been weeks since we had received any direct communication from our leadership. We wondered whether we would continue to hold our ground by the riverside and begin to winterize the camp for resistance against the soon-to-be-completed pipeline, or move on to other projects within the same vein of resistance and Landback. Some people had suggested that our encampment would be moved onto another land where we would be sheltered and able to winterize. The procurement of this land was confirmed and celebrated.

A few days later, folks returned with instructions from leadership to begin to break down the site. They took away our food and broke down our teepees. They forced land-and-water protectors out of the half-dozen camper vans that had become home to many. The leader of the breakdown activities admitted that there was no plan for these shelters other than to be repossessed awaiting further notice.

We wanted a chance to make Landback real, even in a small way. We wanted to model something for other camps, and invite people from far and wide to join us, just as we had been invited there. If we had stayed together, we could have used the winter months to summarize the experience of our riverside encampment and deepen our understanding of leadership and survival. We wanted the space to do the real work, to challenge our personal flaws and become new people, to collectivize and commit to one another and to the land. We wanted to hold ceremonies, and raise our voices in song and prayer. We wanted to build a new society with our hands from the ground up, and we wrongly believed that this context would give us the opportunity.

> *We wanted the space to do the real work, to challenge our personal flaws and become new people, to collectivize and commit to one another and to the land. We wanted to hold ceremonies, and raise our voices in song and prayer. We wanted to build a new society with our hands from the ground up, and we wrongly believed that this context would give us the opportunity.*

I believe that those whose hearts truly beat for the planet will be inspired by what Landback could be. They will fight to open spaces where capitalism can be challenged and rooted out even from within and among the people. It is long-overdue that those who have been acquiring resources unclench their fists and release some of the land back to be re-indigenized and taken over by small communities and villages once again.

We must practice our activism with *discernment*, as though we were actually *serious* about remaking the world in the image of love. We must subject all who claim the mantle of leadership to scrutiny. What we are looking for is unwavering goodness of heart and a wisdom rooted in the possibility of an existence free from harmful hierarchies, unchecked greed, and bloodthirsty desperate competition. •

Requiem for the Dish Pit

A moon (waxing gibbous) illuminates
all that your too-dim headlamp cannot.
Dishes, mostly,
pots and pans and sheet pans,
an abundance of cheese graters (1, 2, 3, 4)
and mason jars you can never quite clean
and your favorite vessels to eat out of,

> tin bowls
> that look like they're
> made for dogs.

Today is Shabbat,
which appears to have been
the reason
for (seemingly?) all the kitchenware
in the kitchen
to be used. It's cold for mid-September
tonight, and you're two elbows
deep in soapy water,
and your sleeves won't stay rolled up.
No matter—the dishes must get done
(you tell yourself),
and no point feeling
bitterly towards them
(you curse each dish inside your head,
imagine tossing each mason jar into the recycling bin,
those motherfuckers you can REALLY never clean,
and why aren't more people
talking about that?).

> The dish pile
> wanes,
> but slowly.

Finishing them feels like overcoming
insurmountable odds. In an
alternate universe (you imagine)
perhaps the dishes are already done;
perhaps camp's acquired

    a high-speed
    solar-powered
    dishwashing machine;

perhaps this pipeline was stopped forever,
or never built at all.
It's nice to think about, for a minute or two.
But your friends live in this universe,
and they're doing these dishes with you.
Sometimes the revolution looks sexy
and other times it looks like this.
You can't be an anarchist
without doing a lot of anarchist dishes,

    making each other
    laugh like you're
    all in a fever dream. •

In the earliest months of 2021, I acquired six pairs of socks, at no personal cost. Perhaps this is too subjective — maybe some would consider a winter spent in army tents, heated by logs that we packed tightly into too-small wood stoves and potatoes that chilled minutes after they left the cast iron, as a great personal cost. It never felt that way. That winter, tucked into sleeping bags that bore holes where we'd curled too near to the stove, it felt like the only option.

Some socks came from the Pole Barn, from the shelves with the cardboard boxes that spilled over with unopened packages of gloves, fleeces, hats. Others were donations to the Welcome Water Protector Center, where, a Water Protector myself, I grabbed socks from time to time on the basis of need. And I did need them — the toes supposedly pushing at the end of my Sorels felt uncomfortably like pebbles when the air dipped below zero, as it often did.

If I were to recount each of my cost-free socks to you, I would tell you first of the two identical pairs of black Bombas, the ones with the gray bees printed on the sides and a swathe of gray honeycombs hugging the arches. Another pair is brown with an orange line circling the calves; these used to gather loosely at my ankles. A year later, however, after 12 months of washing and drying, of soaking them in sweat, and mud, and river water, and blood, and later laying them to dry across tent poles on the days when the sun came out, they fit snugly. Then there are three pairs of gray wool socks, thick, each a different brand that I had neither known nor needed to know two years prior. In fighting a pipeline, I learned much about tar sands, and just as much about which brands of socks are best suited to combat them.

Maybe all of this description is unnecessary. Maybe you, too, spent the early months of 2021 in a tent or trailer or cabin, scattered somewhere across Northern Minnesota in the hopes of bringing a pipeline project to a shuddering, sputtering, world-saving halt, and you, too, have already seen these socks. Look down; perhaps you're wearing them now. Perhaps you visit a friend, a friend you haven't seen in weeks or months or days or hours, and you say, "Oh look, we're wearing the same socks." You each extend a leg, giggling and bumping ankles and remembering the time you slipped these socks onto frozen feet some morning when the sun had yet to rise, and then you stood on a pipeline easement until the police escorted you off of it.

I don't know if I can say that I miss the cold, or hand warmers like stones tucked in coat pockets and car seats, red and blue lights forever whirring in the rearview mirror, but I can say that I'll miss this. I'll miss the people who wear my same socks, and sometimes, I'll miss the times we wore them. •

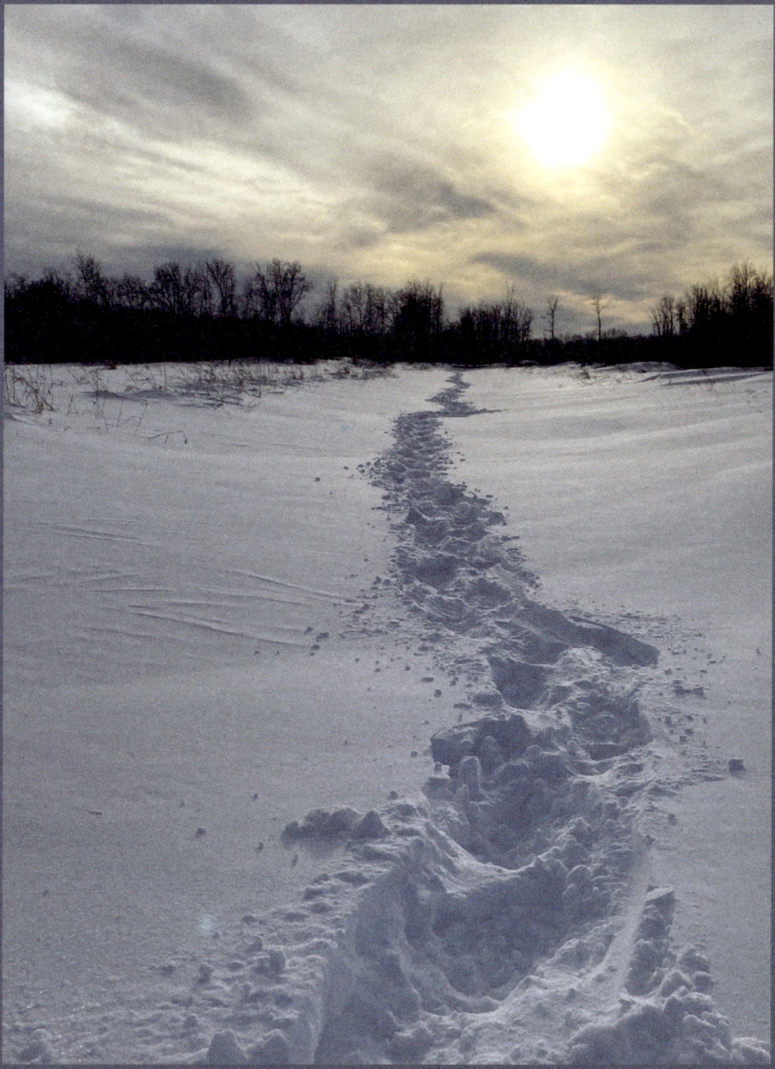

I was in 6th grade, eating a bagged lunch on the capitol lawn, when someone tried to tell me the gold horses on top of the capitol building were supposed to be beautiful.

I thought about the bus ride, the people along the way who held signs made of cardboard boxes, living on the city street, asking for a bit of change.

But the horses. Yeah, the horses.

(Apparently, they were beautiful.)

Sitting atop a dome made of marble.

(Apparently, that was beautiful too.)

Hungry mouths, looking up at horses made of gold.

(I didn't feel convinced.)

—

Now I am 27, lying on a tarp on the capitol lawn. Rain is pouring down, an occasional strike of lightning. Bats are flying over the golden horses. They're beautiful.

The bats are beautiful. The rain is beautiful. Fuck the golden horses.

(I still don't feel convinced.)

Tarps for mattresses, tarps for blankets, surrounding a ceremony much more important than any dreams I could have had tonight.

(It's hard to dream anymore.)

I am sleeping next to people whose government names I may never know. But I love them.

And I trust them. Far more than those who win dry seats inside domes made of marble. A comfortable spot from which to sell the river.

(It's hard to vote anymore.)

There are 37 cops lining the steps of their apparently beautiful building.

Despite all their darkness, light still comes back into the sky. The morning comes. The rain keeps falling.

(You can't use pain compliance on a storm cloud.)

—

I am 27, rising from a tarp on the capitol lawn. Standing tall, soaking wet, staring down 37 cops.

In the middle of this drought, it's finally raining hard. The steps have become a rushing waterfall.

And I'm singing. To myself. To this new waterfall. To the people whose government names I may never know but who I love.

(Certainly not to the golden horses. And certainly not to the cops.)

Six in the morning, standing tall, soaking wet, and I'm fucking singing.

Singing!

And for a moment, I am convinced this place could be beautiful.

(Because, for a moment, we made it that way.)

I am singing! Knowing! Seeing! Believing!

Beautiful. I am convinced.

(Fuck the golden horses.)

Beautiful. I am convinced.

We will make it that way. •

Sun setting over the Mississippi headwaters the first night Water Protectors occupied the pipeline crossing.

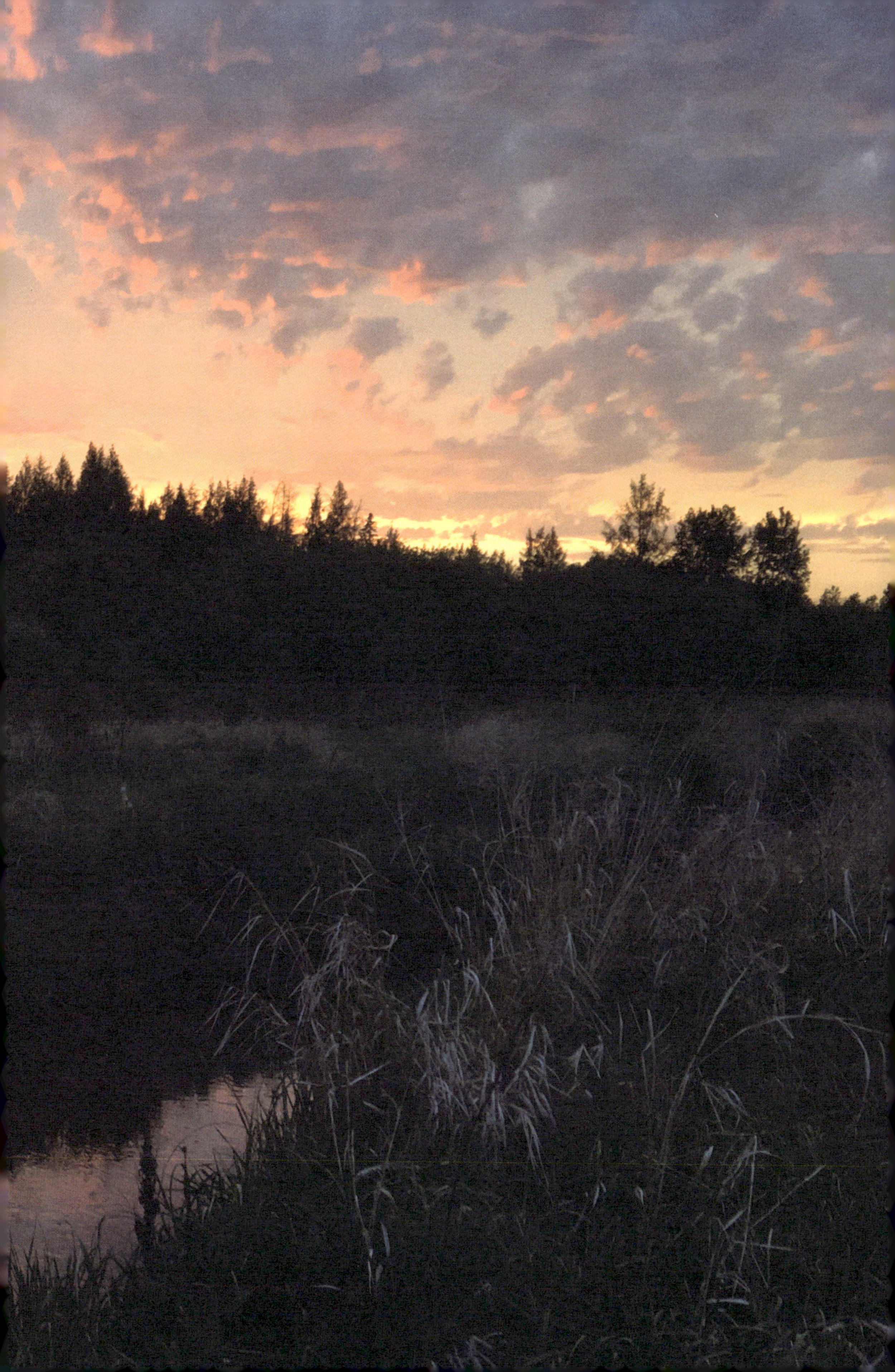

"I don't want to hear a whole long thing about global warming."

The bored, young judge in a pink blouse was a mixture of disgruntled and bemused at the parade of wannabe-citizen-intervenors in her courtroom. From a gray-haired woman arguing she had a direct stake in whether Line 3 was built because her Minneapolis residence got water from the Mississippi, to the irascible owner of a parcel of hunting land along the proposed pipeline route, one person after another, who looked nothing like the usual suited-up lawyers, had made their way to the lone microphone in a windowless hearing room to tell this judge why they deserved a formal seat at the table in the permitting process for Line 3.

By far the most unusual was the gaggle of young people, age 25 and under, that I was standing with. Drenched from sprinting through the rain from the parking garage after a series of carpool mishaps, we had all just barely managed to assemble ourselves to make our case: that an unlikely group of 13 young people calling themselves the Youth Climate Intervenors would each be directly and uniquely impacted by the climate cost of Line 3 and deserved the right to go toe to toe with Enbridge.

We didn't know yet that six weeks later we would be one of the only citizen intervenors this judge accepted into the process. We had no lawyer, clear in our conviction that we were the best advocates for ourselves.

We didn't know yet that we would go on to assemble a team of 10 expert witnesses, including Anishinaabe elders and world-famous climate scientists, to help make our case.

We didn't know that we would go on to write over 300 pages of legal argument, or that after pouring over thousands of pages of filings, we would spend nine days incisively cross-examining Enbridge's witnesses.

We didn't know we would find ourselves in a pizzeria researching how to write a legal brief on wikiHow.

We didn't know that some of the Youth Climate Intervenors would end up on NPR and in Teen Vogue, or that some of the Youth Climate Intervenors would speak to crowds of thousands, or that some of the Youth Climate Intervenors would collect tens of thousands of public comments against Line 3.

We didn't know that by the end of the hearing process, this judge, who was initially so skeptical, would evict hundreds of Enbridge employees from her hearing room to make space for the public, or that she would vehemently recommend against giving Enbridge what it wanted.

We didn't know that, like us, she would be wholly ignored.

We didn't know yet that in June 2018, the five uninformed Minnesota Public Utilities Commissioners (PUC) — who hadn't participated in any of the public or evidentiary hearings — would unanimously approve Line 3, going against 94% of the public comments, four sovereign Ojibwe tribes, the Minnesota Department of Commerce, the judge in the pink blouse, and us.

We didn't know that we would be some of the only members of the public given the chance to speak to the Commissioners before they made that decision, in a single 10-minute opening statement; we didn't know that just that brief exposure to our voices would so move the Commissioners that two of them broke down in self-pitying tears as they cast their votes, apologizing guiltily directly to us.

> *We didn't know yet that in June 2018, the five uninformed Minnesota Public Utilities Commissioners would unanimously approve Line 3, going against 94% of the public comments, four sovereign Ojibwe tribes, the Minnesota Department of Commerce, the judge in the pink blouse, and us.*

We didn't know that, despite finding lawyers to sue the PUC and take our case to the Minnesota Court of Appeals, the tie-breaker judge would waffle and decide against us.

I didn't know yet that I would find out we had lost that last court case, almost exactly 37 months after we first set foot in the hearing room, while standing on the banks of the Mississippi where the river is only knee deep, surrounded by a beautiful marsh that feeds dragonflies and wild rice and sandhill cranes, where Enbridge was poised to send a huge drill under the river.

On that first day, I just knew that we had made it as far as this windowless hearing room, having banded together because the process was too daunting to take on alone. We each held unique skills and stories essential to our whole. We believed that ordinary people are worth listening to, and that the wisdom and brilliance of our communities deserved to be carried from the streets and the rivers to echo in the ears of judges, governors, commissioners, congresspeople, reporters, and neighbors.

"Your honor, you asked why we are here to intervene, why we each have a unique stake in Line 3 and how it will impact us. You need to hear from all of us." •

In the summer of 2018 — just after a key vote allowed Line 3 to proceed — a group of us blocked an intersection in Bemidji, an effort to draw media attention so we could talk about Line 3's harms to the waters, wild rice, climate, and treaty rights. A group of tech-savvy young people live-streamed the event into the sitting room outside then-Governor Mark Dayton's office.

We took over the intersection of Beltrami Avenue and 3rd Street Northwest, not a main artery, but not a side street, either. Supporters gathered on the sidewalks, including a group of young Indigenous men drumming and singing. One local business owner was upset we were deterring customers.

About 50 people started the action. Some 25 or so of us broke into four groups, each taking a corner. We held long banners between each corner to block traffic. The group included members of many organizations. Some were there with no affiliation, including a person who owned property near the pipeline route.

It was a warm summer day. Supporters were bringing us snacks and things to drink.

The police tried to wait us out. We ended up occupying the intersection much longer than we expected. It actually got a bit boring. After a while, some of us began questioning the need to stay. Hadn't the media already been here? Hadn't we made our point? The four groups were told we were autonomous and should make our own decisions about whether or not to keep occupying the space.

At that point, an Indigenous movement leader called us all to the center of the intersection. She said when this action ended, we all would go home to our safe homes and neighborhoods. The Native people in and around Bemidji didn't have that luxury. They would be on the Line 3 frontlines when the cameras weren't there. They wouldn't feel safe, or be safe.

"What message are we sending them if we just walk away now?" she asked.

We stayed. •

On the Willow River — where two weeks ago we had discovered a frac-out (spill of drilling mud) — we placed 100 kinship flags created from natural materials in the river channel as drilling began again. Workers had to stop to watch us wade in the water, eventually calling police, who came and stood with them. My cousin who lives at this drill site (the one who denied my grandmother access to see the place she was born, where Enbridge is working) was there too, standing with the workers. I said hello, and we acknowledged one another over the water — it was a moment I'd been imagining for a while. Our camp is mostly empty now — everyone is at other camps or actions on other rivers that are also being drilled as I type this. I'm with the kids and a handful of others — we will keep praying and sending resources and people where they're called and will be joining where we can. Resistance is never wasted.

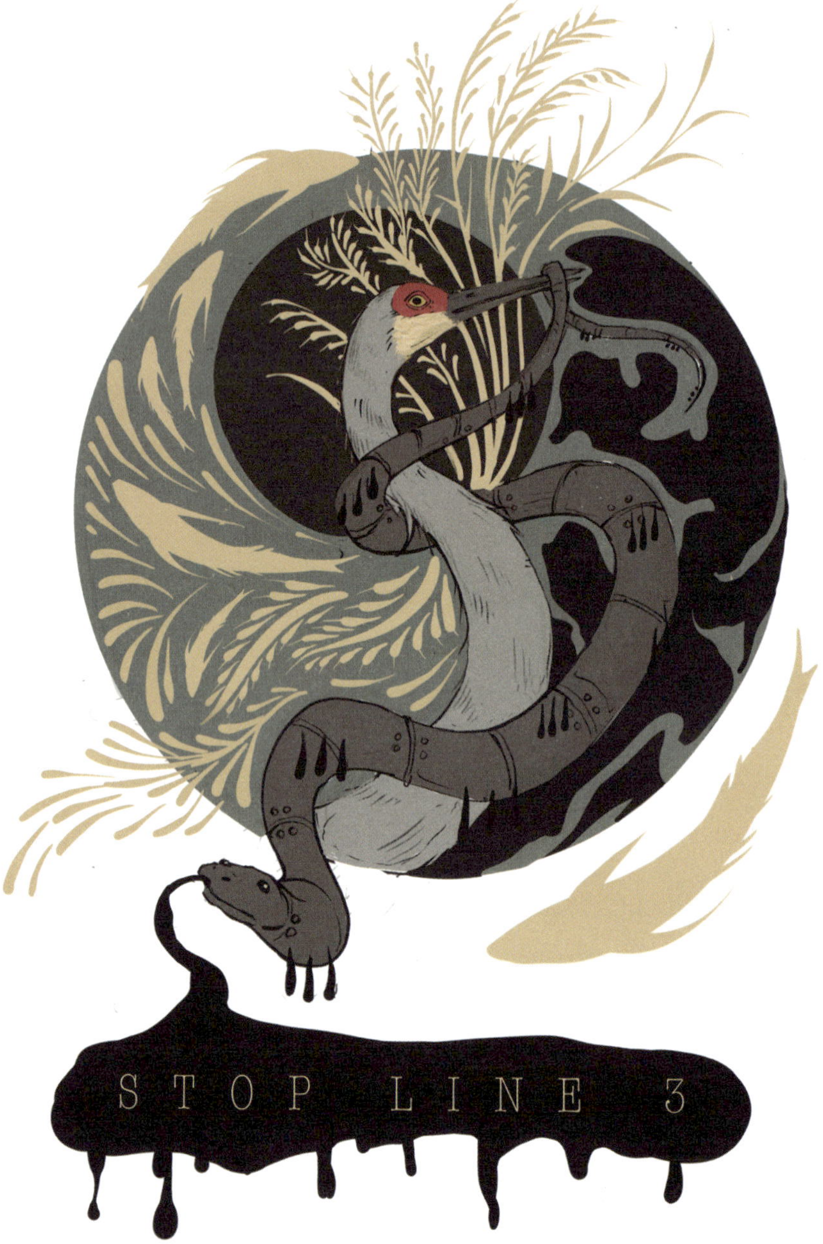
STOP LINE 3

Editors' Note: This story was developed from an interview with a 10-year-old, a 12-year-old, and a 14-year-old. It has been excerpted and edited for clarity.

We came up here mostly every single day. Like every day over the summer, and then I'm pretty sure we came up in the winter too. Cause we all did distance learning for, like, a year or two. So, we'd come up here.

Our first time, I remember we came here, and then we went to go see the people up in the trees. It was scary. I thought: They're going to fall down.

I said, "How's it going?" And then I said, "Is it cold up there?"

I heard that Line 3 was going under the river and I was just like, "How is *that* going under the river?"

We went swimming in the river over the summer when they were building the pipeline. The water was so low, like, you could tell that they kept taking water out of it. But it was fun. One time we went all the way up there, and then there was a current, and we had tubes and we went down it and it was like, deep and stuff. It was fun though.

And we made, like, a *lot* of artwork. I made a circle and it said, "We are water protectors," and stuff like that. And then we painted flowers.

There was also a lot of food and stuff. We made food for the camp for a little while. We made, this like, bread thing. It was like, bread, bread pudding. And it was nasty and soggy. We made a lot of it. •

I sing "Dear Wormwood," the length of which is exactly 5 minutes and 16 seconds, silently to myself in the backseat of the police SUV. When eventually allowed my phone call, I'll tell my emergency contact that I don't know where I am, but I know I'm half an hour, or six Dear Wormwoods, away from him.

I track street signs & count turns, including the loops we take when the officer laughs, "Let's lose your friend on my tail." I wonder what my elementary school teachers would say, the ones who taught me to call 911 if ever tied & forced into a car, to track street signs & count turns if being driven to an unknown location.

This is my first time being arrested quietly & alone on the basis of policemen recognizing me, rather than arrested as one of many in a disruptive crowd, on the basis of being one of many in a disruptive crowd. First time in metal handcuffs instead of zip ties. First time being asked on the intake form if I'm queer.

"Don't say yes," I'd been warned 72 hours ago, "or they'll put you in solitary." Up until this moment, booking was a piano scale I could rehearse in my sleep & recite without a script. Name, birthday, ID, approximate height. I'm on cruise control, but still speaking calmly when spoken to. C., sir. 1995, sir. Passport, sir. 5'1", sir. Our bodies try to protect us, often switching modalities without our consent. Today, after I'm handed the intake form, autopilot makes a screeching pivot into a new tactic: flight/freeze. The clipboard & I glare at each other until an officer collects it. Breathe, I think. She didn't notice I left it blank.

As privatized, militarized, armed, uniformed police go, she is remarkably amicable. She turns me into a smaller, tiled room & instructs me to undress. As the chill of the room tingles on my bare skin, she says, "Wait. You didn't finish this. Are you LGBT?"

We stare at each other; my ears ring. She repeats the question, then rephrases it. Finally, she sighs, her tone flat with impatience, "It's for your protection, okay? It's so we don't put you in a room with someone who would hurt you." It sounds logical enough, believable even, despite being warned differently. I can't help but notice there is no question on the form asking if I would harm someone like me. I'm asked if I'm a sexual assault survivor, but not if I have a tendency to sexually assault. If I've been a victim, but not if I've made one.

Many non-impacted folks hear statistics about missing and murdered Indigenous women yet doubt that Enbridge's hands are bloody. We mutter to survivors, "That's terrible, I'm sorry," yet are reticent to name or confront perpetrators. But if we can't eliminate the cause, we will never eliminate the effect. I'm stuck in a microcosmic moment of a much larger, more violent machine. Oh, I realize. *Is this how they do it?*

My cinderblock-stiff body language and panicked silence answered the question for me at this point — so much for keeping my mouth shut — and I'm starting to shiver.

She drops her shoulders, steps in, and holds my gaze. "Listen. You're scared. Maybe you're questioning. Maybe your parents, your church, told you different. But I just need you to know," she inhales, soft and fierce, preparing to deliver the heroic script she's correctly assumed my own mother never gave: "You should *never* feel ashamed of who you are. You should be proud of your identity. You are good. There is nothing. Wrong. With you. Okay?"

> *It wasn't a trick, but I couldn't write a sitcom this satirical: two women, stuck in a brick box, one naked, one uniformed & armed, the latter assuring the former not to be afraid.*

In days of training, in years of education, absolutely nothing has prepared me for this situation. It wasn't a trick, but I couldn't write a sitcom this satirical: two women, stuck in a brick box, one naked, one uniformed & armed, the latter assuring the former not to be afraid. I wonder if my childhood church friends, who vehemently condemn queerness as demonic & repugnant, yet vehemently support police arresting protestors, would recognize the irony.

There's a proverb that if children can't eat honey off spoons, they learn to lick it off knives. Occasionally, I'm amused by this — an agent reeking with the power of a multi-billion-dollar paramilitary institution, telling me only after I'm in her territory, undressed and under surveillance, that I should be proud of the part of me that gets me in the most trouble. Even against the backdrop of her industry's well-known gender violence against Indigenous folks and other water protectors, she's the first mother to offer me this, so the starved child in me is tempted to accept, to lick the knife. Holding the cognitive dissonance is like holding a handful of broken glass.

I wonder if my mother will ever passionately give me the queer child acceptance speech. But I'm fairly certain she won't have a gun if she does. •

Editors' Note: This story was developed from an interview. It has been excerpted and edited in collaboration with the interviewee.

Well, I don't know if you know about the Shell River, when Marisa Tomei showed up — I didn't know that Marisa Tomei showed up. And I wasn't introduced or anything like that. Marisa Tomei showed up, and I wasn't aware who that was. I just thought it was another ally or something like that.

They were riding with W., in a canoe, we were getting ready to go to the action. T. had met them though and was really kinda uptight that day, and I didn't know why and didn't ask why. Here I am, we're paddling down the Shell River, to the easement, and I'm having a good ol' time, laughing around, telling stupid jokes. And W. and Marisa Tomei are in the canoe next to us, and T. is looking at me like stop, stop, stop.

And then, we get a little ways further down, and all of a sudden the horses come into the river you know, and like rear up, and it's like a scene from a movie, just loving it. And I'm like, get this on video! This is like from a freaking movie! Holy shit! And I'm telling dumb jokes, like, Canoe Collective instead of Giniw Collective, you know, just dumb shit. And we get down to the easement, and it got serious after that, but I mean it was just like that pivotal moment, where I'm just making an ass of myself, being my dumb joking self as we're paddling down the river.

And, just like everyone's all uptight around Marisa Tomei and I'm the only one acting up and acting rezzy as hell. T. told me afterwards Jesus you're embarrassing! And I was like what? And she was like that was Marisa Tomei, and I was like who's that? And then I was like oh wait, they're in those movies. •

This piece, titled Determination Through Limbo, is made from white turkey feathers, acrylic paint, thread, and seed beads. This piece represents the strength to persist with your community, even when the emotional lows feel as brutal as the temperature lows of a Minnesotan winter.

Broken Hearted Tales of the Water Wars

Native Queers

We are driving fast
Along frozen lake roads

We are passing a smoke around
We are free in the loudness
Of the homie's fire playlist

They look back
We make eye contact
They nod at me
Affirming this time
This place, is it.

Native queers
Shelter each other
Lift each other up
Hold each other
In a way that our white partners never can

It's that Indigenous love
Black, Brown and Red
We are all here now

Give each other permission
To be fully
Who we are
Big beautiful mouths
Dripping our ancestor's languages
Sharing the smiles

We were forbidden for so long
We survived I tell them, the ancestors
We made it

And I pray for the next 12,000 years
300 generations to come

Things I Miss About Mni Sota

That feeling of purpose
Like we were really fighting something
Every day

The look of the forest
In grey morning light
Smoke trickling skyward

Your dimples

Mother Earth Death Squad

The machines
Were lined up
In neat rows

My heart
My eyes

The message
The meaning

Mother Earth Death Squad

I said

And then we bought a roto tiller
    Because we were the Mother Earth
        defenders

Pass it down
Pick it up

Do what we would do
But don't do what we would do
Do what you would do
But don't

Be like the cedar trees
Give yourself as medicine
Especially to those that offer

prayers •

An Ode to Car Caravans

One skill I never thought I would have so many iterations to practice in the movement was the art of the car caravan.

In 2018, I got my first try at it. In the caravan was a mix of White Earth elders, faith leaders dressed in full regalia, and university students… you know, just a typical assortment of aspiring and seasoned water protectors going on a Sunday afternoon ride. At the beginning, my car-mate had brazenly claimed their love of paper maps and eschewed downloading Google Maps to their phone (how many of us made that mistake). You can see where this is heading, while I obviously didn't. The back-half of our long line of cars ended up across the reservation a full 80 miles from our destination. Meanwhile, half the university students on their school-sponsored trip were being visited by the fledgling Northern Lights Task Force. By the time we turned our long train around and joined up with them at the pipe yard, they were surrounded by flashing blue and red. It was quite time to pack up and head out.

As it got warmer, these car caravans started to attract more company, and not the kind we exactly wanted. I was on a radio as the caboose of a tour across Fond Du Lac, and from my view it was like a scene out of Smokey and the Bandit. There were a dozen cop cars at every intersection along the route. I counted over 100 squad cars and another 50 Enbridge security vehicles for whom the most interesting part of their day was watching us drive by waving our little "water is life" flags. They even had a dozen squad vehicles pull up to the rest stop to watch us all wait in line for the bathroom… I wonder how they filled out their punch cards at the end of the day to bill Enbridge.

I continued organizing car caravans, mainly because it is usually more pleasant to organize a car caravan than to participate in one. That is, except for the caravan from Pure Bliss Ranch to Firelight. I would have rather not have known how absurd that plan was. I was the second car that day, and I truly wondered if our vehicle would reach the action site before the last car left camp. Everyone in the organizing meetings knew it was a completely ludicrous undertaking to get thousands of people to the site, parked and in formation to march in 95-degree heat with an unknown police response. But it wouldn't be the wildest thing we had tried to stop a pipeline, so on we went. The radio team calmed my nerves with radio banter about leeching, which was the vibe I needed.

The last and perhaps most memorable car caravan I ever helped organize was at the Shell River in July. There were three modes of transit possible to get to the drill site — by car, by boat, and by horse. With a little morning-coffee ambition at camp we said, "Why not all three?" The problem, again, was parking. It partially helped that there was a large coach bus coming from the Twin Cities which could drop 50 people off at once. I always assume the best of people, so it was actually quite last minute when I asked the commercial bus driver about the plan. I asked if he could, well, "follow a car caravan to an undisclosed location, at which point could you please drop off a bunch of passengers, some of whom will return and others who may find a different ride back home, with a quick stop at jail?" He was down for the cause.

We still needed more parking, so we headed out to scout the area. A friend's white truck got us past the Enbridge security, and all it took was wearing a couple hard hats and bright vests from Walmart. However, we did arrive to find the Hubbard County Sheriff duct-taping together a little makeshift "no parking" sign, which looked like it was also purchased that same day from Walmart.

We were not to be defeated, and so we proceeded to go door-to-door along that street, asking, "Could we host a sizable party in the area and use your yard for a parking lot?" A certain close relative of the Sheriff reportedly lived right nearby and was a bit annoyed at hearing the drilling under her land while her brother arrested water protectors on the daily, so she was happy to host.

And so, the next day, the water protectors rolled in, by horseback, canoe, kayak, coach bus, and my comrade's little Prius at the front waving a "Water is life" flag and hollering for everyone to turn into this nice lady's drive. When the Sheriffs surrounded our caravan, this homeowner walked right up to them and said, "These are all my party guests, could you help them park?" They begrudgingly obliged, and our party continued with drumming and dancing right on down to the river.

Much love to all the water protectors who know how to roll in, in style. •

These protest signs were held at direct actions along the pipeline route.

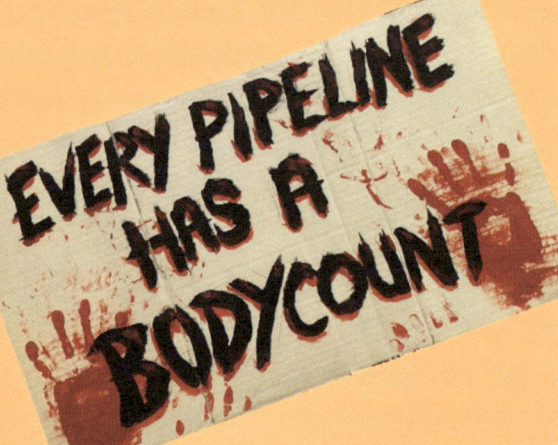

STOP LINE 3

NO MORE PIPELINES
NO MORE STOLEN SISTERS

KILL THE BLACK SNAKE

TAR SANDS KILL
PIPELINES SPILL

EVERY PIPELINE HAS A BODYCOUNT

FOR FUTURE GENERATIONS

Despite our best efforts, Tim Walz was elected to be governor of Minnesota in November 2018. During his inauguration, three of us snuck our banner into the capitol building by folding it up and putting it under one of our shirts. Then, as casually as possible, we walked amidst the crowds of water protectors disguised as Tim Walz fans, waiting for the new governor to make his first appearance. While I had been slowly building up my confidence at actions, this was the boldest action I had done at the time.

Walz left the senate chambers and took a victory lap around the capitol before addressing the public. We stood against the rails of the overlook, watching as the governor walked past, his team of eager staff and press following right behind. I saw how excited he was, grinning from ear to ear, holding his wife's hand. For a second, I almost felt sorry for him. I almost thought we shouldn't ruin his big day. Maybe we should give him a pass this time. But then, right as he passed, us he stopped, looked right at us and said, "Don't you ever forget — this is your house! This is the people's house!" Then he was rushed downstairs to make his remarks.

J. turned to me, shrugged, and said, "Well isn't that nice. I kind of feel like hanging a banner in my house today." •

Editor's Note: This story was developed from an interview. It has been excerpted and edited in collaboration with the interviewee.

It was my first time going to the Shell River camp, which was on 1855 Treaty territory, over towards White Earth. A friend of mine canoed me down to the easement. It was like two or three miles in river miles, which is different from regular miles, I think, because of how the river bends. It was a trek, about 10, 15 minutes. We got out there and we saw the "No Trespassing" signs, but I was like, this is Native land, there's not really any trespassing that's gonna happen. So we climbed over, and we just walked up the easement because it was up on a hill. And we got to the top and we looked and we paused, because there was a mother bear and three of her cubs. Nimaamaa makwa and makoons. These little baby cubs that were crossing the easement. I was thinking, oh my gosh, they're reclaiming that space after it's been clear cut to make room for Enbridge to come and do their destruction. It was powerful seeing that. And also kind of frightening, because those bears were only, like, a hundred yards away. •

Author's Note: This poem was written collaboratively by approximately a dozen and a half people in September 2021 by passing around a small, battery-powered word processor at a morning circle gathering at Namewag. Someone would write a line or two and pass it on. Nobody saw the poem in its entirety until it was finished.

A Rather Loud Cacophony of Cackling Queers

In so-called Minnesota,
there was a rather loud
cacophony of cackling queers
mincing about the Northwoods.
Suddenly, in the dead of night,
millions of ticks emerged from the brush,
clickity clacking their tiny pincers.
Nonetheless, his bare golden plumps shone
brightly as ever, translucent under crimson
moonlight revealing the pattern of her
desire violently scratched and etched,
gently spooned into their mouth; his words
echoed in ripples: "I must have you my
ripely goblin blossom, I savor the juice
that does leak from thine brain." I would
rather my brain juices remain in my brain if
it's no different to you, thank you very
much. The trees called on the water and the
water called unto me so I came then I came
to you and we went together to the others
and they said that anything is a sleeping
dragon if it is not awake. But now the
morning call has come, my tea is not hot!
But my corporeal form sure is. •

Saying No to Direct Action, Then Saying Yes

I knew that no matter what happened, I would always remember that long line of geese flying into a brilliant orange sunset over our heads. Our group had faced off with an even longer line of cops for close to five hours in the hot, sticky sun. As it grew dark, they finally started making arrests, and all I felt was ready.

In planning for this action, I had prepared myself for fear but not for boredom. Not for the listlessness and exhaustion that came with hour six of sitting, waiting, occasionally rallying to sing the same protest songs again and again. I didn't expect the persistent hunger that yet another granola bar could never satisfy — otherwise, I would have packed a sandwich.

My experience of direct action was decidedly unsexy. I was dressed head-to-toe in sun-protective layers now caked in dust and sweat. When two state patrol officers pulled me from the ground and led me away, I hoped they could smell me.

—

The year before, I walked away from a different opportunity to risk arrest. I was part of an affinity group that was planning a high-risk action to delay construction, one that asked a lot of me, including quitting my job.

> *I spent weeks agonizing over whether to participate. I weighed the consequences of leaving my daily life behind with the potential to make a real impact on Line 3's progress. At the same time, I scrutinized my own decision-making process, wondering what saying yes or no to this action said about my commitment to the cause.*

I spent weeks agonizing over whether to participate. I weighed the consequences of leaving my daily life behind with the potential to make a real impact on Line 3's progress. At the same time, I scrutinized my own decision-making process, wondering what saying yes or no to this action said about my commitment to the cause.

Eventually, I leveled with myself: I simply didn't want to do it. After days of rationalizing how I could say "no," I admitted that I wasn't ready, for whatever reason, and whatever that implied. In the end, I chose to say "yes" to my improv class, time with my family, watching TV and driving my car and I was still good.

I wrote a few things down that day that I try to not forget:

1. "No single action can determine who you are"
2. "Simple answers are never the answer"
3. "You can't really be bad, but even if you could, you need to be okay with that"

Our power comes from our self-worth. Acting out of guilt or fear lacks the force of our will that comes with conviction and a sense of groundedness. Especially for white activists, our privileges can hold us back from taking risks. But the personal transformation that movements spur in us can't be forced or faked. And direct action is serious stuff: getting into a situation I wasn't ready for could have put myself and others in danger.

—

After many more months in the movement, I was ready to risk arrest. I had formed an affinity group with two of my closest friends and was participating in a large-scale event that I'd been well-prepped for. Going into the action, I felt scared but I also felt supported and strong. Participating in the action, I felt for the first time my full potential to affect the world around me.

Just when the cops started pulling people away, that's when I saw the geese. The skein called out from up high, drowning out the threatening announcements of unlawful assembly until the last drop of fear I was holding onto evaporated. I knew I was supposed to be right where I was, and the birds did, too. •

When they look back at this moment in time a few years from now, will they:

...thank you for your **courage?** or...

..hate you for your **cowardice?**

A Phone Call, Allegedly

As an adult, I have learned not to answer the phone.

It's telemarketers. It's the dentist's office reminding you of your appointment. It's news about an illness or death in the family. It's about loss.

Most often, it's not the person you were hoping would call, so there's that, too.

Anybody who knows me knows, pretty much, not to call: very likely, I won't answer, and I probably won't call you back, nothing personal.

Here's something else I know: any letter from the State, from the government, is bad news. You owe money. Someone wants to speak to you. Someone with a great deal of power is about to reach into your life and, very likely, make it worse.

Two things I distrust: phone calls and the State. The news is almost always bad.

So, when the phone rang one afternoon, I wanted to ignore it, but it was a Minnesota number. Too coincidental to be somebody trying to sell me an extended warranty for my vehicle or house? I answered because, at some level, I knew — possibly — what the call would be about: my child, for many, many months, had been deeply immersed in anti-Line 3 protests and had — perhaps — been living on the frontlines, in the camps, had — perhaps — been organizing, had been trying to tell people about the ongoing damage to the land, the air, the water, to life on the planet due to the burning of fossil fuels. In roundabout ways I had — perhaps — been warned that arrests were possible.

The news: my child had been arrested for, allegedly, trespassing on Enbridge property. An action. Allegedly.

This is a word I've learned over the last couple of years: allegedly. Other things I've learned: on the frontlines, nobody uses their real name. In the movement, folks watch what they say and to whom they say it. Communication will not be straightforward, might be encrypted, might omit specifics. Phone calls might come in the middle of the night.

Here's what else I've learned: our children, having taken a long, hard look around, have realized that the State will not save the planet, will not seriously try; our children have realized that they are on their own, that no one is coming to help them.

I have also learned: the State will not gear up much of its energies and resources to protect life, to protect the environment, but it very certainly will gear up its considerable energies and resources to punish young people for trying to protect our water, land, and air.

The State will arrest your children for the sin of trying to do the right thing, the necessary thing, the good and moral thing, while also doing its best to ensure that the rich get richer and that the planet burns.

Here's something else that I heard, something that I had to have explained to me: Fuck 12.

So, I answered the phone, because I knew what the phone call might be about. Later, when I saw the videos of these giant police leading my child away in handcuffs — several of them, some in tactical gear, to lead away one small, non-violent, non-resisting human being? — I knew what it meant to be deeply angry: the State will arrest your children for the sin of trying to do the right thing, the necessary thing, the good and moral thing, while also doing its best to ensure that the rich get richer and that the planet burns.

Here's what makes me ill: strangers, in the employ of Money and backed by the State, put their hands on my child, put them in the back of a police cruiser, took them to jail. My child went into the system, and there were lawyers and judges, court appearances and terms, and a record, something that will follow them for life.

Yet here's what fills me with pride (and not inconsiderable anxiety): my kid and their buddies live their values, sleep in tents on the frontlines, share communal meals, dumpster dive so that there will be less waste, talk and think things through, organize and act, and they are not afraid. •

A Reckoning

We walked for the water from the headwaters to the falls, a steady shuffle of steps taken in a single-file line coursing like a river through the land. On the outskirts of another pioneer town, someone veered off from the group ahead, shooting diagonally past and behind, laterally in time, towards a construction site, a sort of roadside shrine. As a hummingbird to nectar, the water protector went. Not to take, for the taking had been done, but to give. Something hidden, unbidden was placed with uncanny reverence upon a pile of lumber there. An offering made to the humble 2x4, head bowed gently and aggrieved to the cleaved and naked boards, to the extracted and machined but still noble trees. I watched. I saw. I saw the forest through the trees. I saw the trees. I saw the quaint knots as whole dimensions lost from the settlers' view. I saw the forest, whole forests reduced to the math of profit and loss. But not forgotten. The hummingbird moved back to her place in line in the fluid of the we. My set view open like a stream in spring. It was then that I heard a voice and turning around saw a pair of eyes twinkling, wisened and keen. She said, "She's like that," sounding pleased. Pleased with the wise hummingbird and perhaps with the watching squirrel alike. A reckoning with the not-so-humble 2x4, an honoring, begins with seeing them as trees. We walked for the water from the headwaters to the falls. •

The Forest Calls Me In

Today, March 26, 2022, there is an event on the west bank of the Mississippi. I've been back in Palisade at the Welcome Water Protectors Center for a week but haven't gone down to the river, yet. I walk down in the late afternoon. The remnants of a winter sun throw light to the opposite shore and the forest to the east. Across the river, only the very top of the blue letters spelling out "Stop Line 3" are still visible above the swollen, frozen Mississippi. I remember my arrival here in February of last year, the frozen river, a pipe not yet laid.

The river, slowly melting, groans. A deep grief rises; a slow end to winter, and a loss not yet met.

Last year, we ran this trail to confront the workers, the cops, and the DNR. We ran through snow, then mud, then waist high ferns as the struggle intensified into the summer. The sounds of the machines as they moved down the easement, treads rumbling over the matting, the constant beeps of the backup signal, haunt me. This path was our supply line to the prayer lodge, built on the easement where the pipeline crosses the Mississippi. The drill passed directly under the lodge. Some felt the rumbling under their feet. The land this trail bisects, this land we protect, called Akiing, the Anishinaabe word for "the land to which the people belong," has had runners on these trails forever. I remember. The summer heat in the fully bloomed forest. The ferns, the trees in the wind, the wildflowers, the paths narrowed from ground cover. The aspens across the way bear witness to all that went down. The weight of knowing the pipe had been pulled under the river. This battle, the first of 22 crossings, was lost before midsummer. Tears fall to the melting snow, to be returned to the river.

> *Sitting by the Mississippi, I feel the collective grief of failing to stop a pipeline.*

There is a lot to grieve.

Sitting by the Mississippi, I feel the collective grief of failing to stop a pipeline. The trees, the water, the creatures on this land will suffer. The lodge remains. The LandBack sign is faded but still waves in the breeze. It's difficult to accept that a tar sands pipeline flows beneath me and a nickel mine is on the horizon. The forest, deeply quiet, calls me in. I go. •

STOP LINE 3
NO DAPL
water
RESPECT THE TREATIES
is
DOOM TO THE PIPELINES
life
PROTECT THE EARTH
NO MORE STOLEN SISTERS

How it was

How lovely to have a friend make the long walk down the driveway to bring you breakfast during your 6-12 security shift.

How sweet for the baristas at the coffee shop to give you a free coffee lemonade after you expressed interest but ordered something else.

How special to get out of jail and for three friends to say they want to make out with you, and for two of them to kiss you, and then for everyone to go jump in Lake Superior.

How dear to have a friend send you voice memos of her singing to lighten your day. Oh, how it lightens your everything.

How silly for the policeman to think there was a real Animal Farm episode in the middle of St. Paul when your friend alerted him of a piggy infestation over yonder at the capitol.

How scrumptious to have a brunch of sausage, french toast, hash browns, and fruit served in jail.

How "generous" of the cops to bring a peace offering of plastic water bottles after they destroyed the Tipi and arrested your comrades in ceremony.

How warm to huddle — 11 of you — hiding in the trees at one in the morning, uncertain if anyone will come to pick you up. And then how relieving to hear "Cacaw Cacaw!" when they do come.

How exciting for your appendix to burst and to be healing in the hospital while your comrades are blockaded into camp as a distraction as they drilled under the Mississippi.

How sexy for your friend to ask, "do you want to make out?" and months later for their partner to say, "I guess I want to kiss you" and in between for the Reverend-in-training to walk in on four of you making out all at once, crossed and cross-legged on the kitchen floor.

How lucky, how forsaken by spirit, for a tree to fall on your friends' tent the one night they were in jail.

How dramatic to run around the streets of St. Paul barefoot in the rain, dancing with the thunder, with nothing to fear but the future. •

I lived at camps off and on during most of Line 3's construction. I dealt with the unpredictability of my days using the one area of my life over which I had full control, my backpack. These are the things I always carried with me.

The Northern Water Alliance's opposition to the Enbridge proposals started with the Sandpiper Pipeline in 2014, proposed to run from the North Dakota Bakken oil fields to Clearwater, Minnesota, and then south, opening a new pipeline corridor to Superior, Wisconsin.

Was it really eight years ago? As we got involved with resisting the Sandpiper Pipeline, it became apparent that several local and not-so-local organizations were also strategizing about this issue. Each from their own perspective and ability, but not coalescing into a unified movement that could have significant impact. What to do? With leadership from Honor the Earth, we called a meeting around our kitchen table. In those meetings of lake association leaders and others, we decided to coalesce into an alliance to address *water* issues: pipeline routes, aquatic invasive species, and aquifer contamination. We named ourselves the Northern Water Alliance of MN. Meetings continued over several years as word spread of the potential for the Sandpiper to contaminate our wetlands and waters. We hosted Water Conversations in churches and lake association meetings. The energy in those rooms fueled our resolve.

Later, Enbridge added a second proposed pipeline, the Line 3 replacement, to follow the same proposed corridor. Initially, the Administrative Law Judge hearings about Line 3 excluded any testimony or public comments having to do with "climate change." However, during those hearings we pushed for several significant changes to the process:

> "Climate change" became a consideration in the proceedings when the Administrative Law Judge approved the Youth Climate Intervenors as plaintiffs in the hearings.

> Six of the Minnesota Ojibwe Bands became intervenors for the first time in a Public Utilities Commission (PUC) process.

> A total of nine or 10 intervenors in opposition to the Enbridge proposal were approved to have official status in the process, including the Northern Water Alliance of MN.

This background gives you the measure of how much the combined opposition to the Enbridge proposals has changed the process of pipeline review.

Although the PUC finally approved the Enbridge proposal, it was a lesson to all of how powerful corporate capture is in these deliberations. It should also be noted that the proposal was not unanimous as almost all PUC decisions are. While the outcome was a disappointment, the actual construction of the pipeline showed how inadequate the State's oversight was of the process. Damage to aquifers and frac-outs were only reported months after the fact.

We now can look back on our efforts and know that our opposition shed more light on the opaque process under which the PUC operates. Let us not forget that we have paved the way for a more equitable outcome in the future. •

ENBRIDGE TAR SANDS
STOP LINE 3
PROTECT
NO TAR SANDS
CUT OFF THE HEAD OF THE BLACK SNAKE
NO MAN CAMPS NO MMIW
PROTECT OUR SISTERS! STOP SEX TRAFFIC ON THE GREAT LAKES.

Stop Line 3 with pen embellishments (added by my children for a demonstration outside of Palisade and car caravan action).

Waiting in line before sunrise,
for the hundredth hearing on the fate of a pipeline project
before the PUC
before the people
beside the river
trying to find the words,
which they would inevitably cut off
again and again
coming from so many beautiful bodies

What warms me in this frigid dawn
is the reminder that so many seemingly consequential words are just
metaphors
passing things

even if they capitalize them
words like

Public Utilities Commission
Department of Commerce
Pollution Control Agency
Corporate Rights
Evidentiary Hearing
Northern Lights Task Force

all metaphors
passing things

But when I speak I will try to avoid these
I will say
"We are the River"
there is no metaphor there •

Editors' Note: This story was developed from an interview. It has been excerpted and edited in collaboration with the interviewee.

When I first quit my job working on the pipeline, T. asked me to do a short little video of me on the easement drumming and singing the bear song, in order to invite other workers to be courageous and brave enough to quit their jobs. And ask the police, who were doing us a disservice, to quit their jobs. And, because T. knew I knew some of these songs from before, from a different movement, a sobriety movement, and she asked me to sing some of these songs, and I just stuck around drumming. •

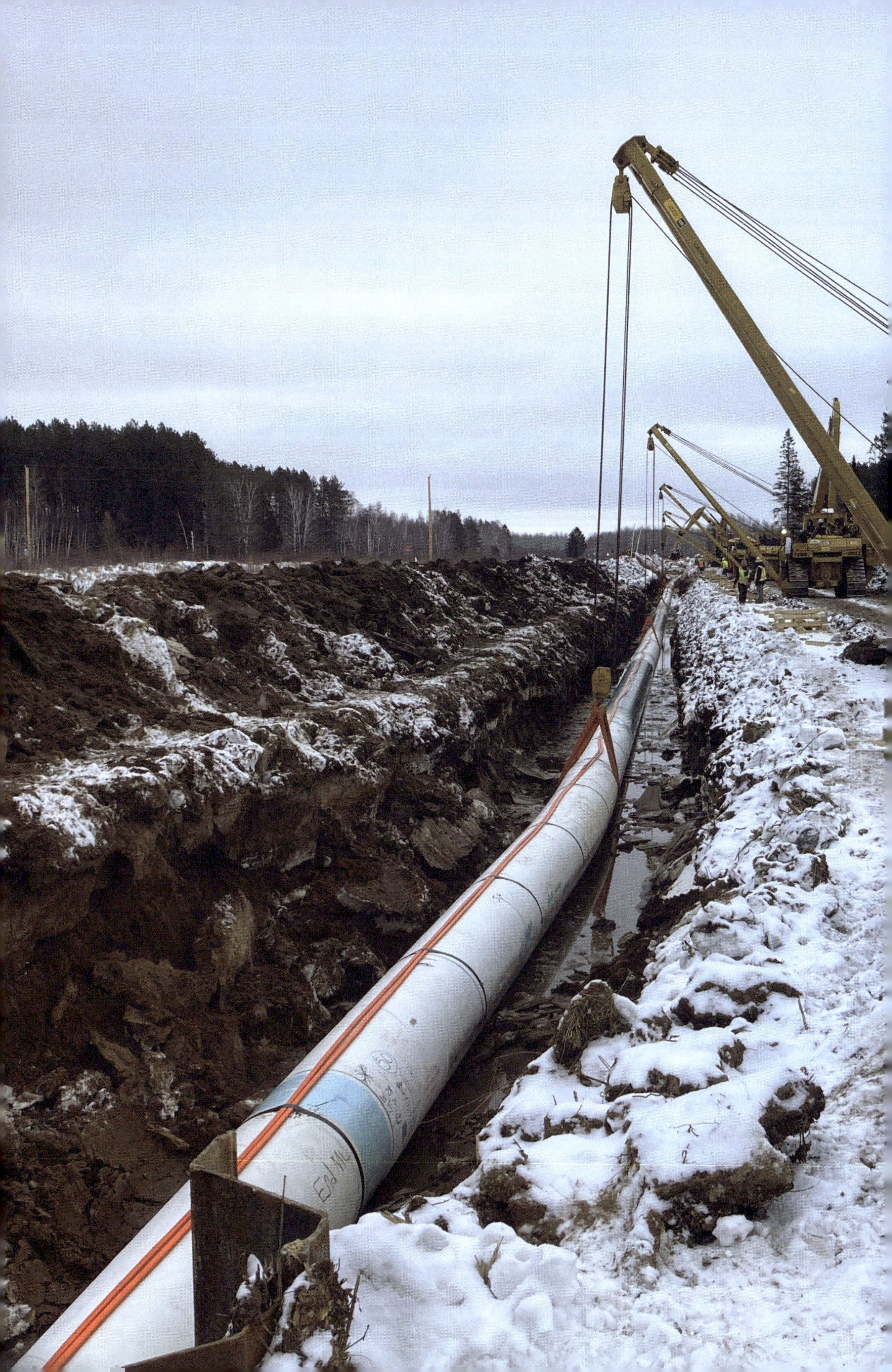

To Stop the Flow of Oil, Stop the Flow of Money

May 7, 2021. I wake up in Seattle, some 1,500 miles from Minnesota. Yet, all these miles away, we've been plotting our own resistance to Enbridge's monstrosity, spending the last two weeks planning this action. The plan and the target are clear. JP Morgan Chase is not only one of the largest funders of Enbridge — providing the company with $3 billion in loans and underwriting since 2016 — it is also the largest funder of the fossil fuel industry, period.

As I get ready for the action, it's made more exciting by the fact that we're not alone. We're expecting actions at the banks funding Line 3 in around 100 cities today.

Along with a couple of friends, I drive to the Chase branch in Ballard, arriving around 9:30. I park, leave my friends behind, and walk over to the bank. All is clear and quiet. I pull out my phone and open up my Signal.

I type into a thread called Deployment Team: "Ten minutes to deployment. Everyone in place?"

One-by-one the team leads confirm that they're in location and ready. Traffic Team 1. Traffic Team 2. Banner Team 1. Banner Team 2. Human Mural Team. Tarpee Team. Police Liaisons.

I check the time. It's now only a few minutes until ten. I'm sitting outside the bank. There's a single security guard lingering inside, a car drives up to the drive-thru ATM.

"Coast still clear," I type. "Deploy in two minutes."

Deployment is smooth, running exactly as we rehearsed. The traffic teams — wearing high-vis vests, working boots, and hard hats — run "Road Closed" signs and traffic cones across the street. With all the proficiency of a professional crew, they redirect the oncoming traffic.

The road secured, other teams move into place. One crew places a ladder against the bank and begins to deploy two banners. One banner looks like oil and is left dripping from the Chase sign above the front doors of the branch. Another reads simply: "Chase Funds Climate Disaster." At the same time, another team erects a tarpee — a structure, created by P., a member of the Saanich Nation, which is modeled on a traditional tipi. The tarpee is about 10 feet high and before long it stands proudly in the middle of the street. P. stands on top, his cedar hat on his head and his drum in hand. He sings and drums, as we begin to lay out the human mural.

Person after person lies down on the street, creating an image of an oil pipeline being washed away by a series of onrushing waves. The words are spelled out large and bold, several dozen people making up the huge letters: *DEFUND LINE 3*. It's beautiful. Our drone pilot makes sure that we get an image of it from the sky, the words standing out stark and clear against the street.

We hold the street for hours. There are speeches and songs. The police show up and watch from afar. With one hundred of us on the street and our traffic team doing a good job of directing traffic, they seem to think that we're not worth the fight to clear the street. A TV camera shows up and an interviewer starts asking questions: What are we doing here? Why are we protesting an oil pipeline outside of a bank? We're happy to answer his questions, to tell him all about the obscenity that is Line 3, about the complicity of those funding it and profiting from it.

After we've been there for around two hours, it appears that the branch has closed business for the day. Not long later, we decide to call it. We pack up the human mural and bring down the tarpee. We leave the banners on the Chase branch. If they want those down, they can do it themselves.

A TV camera shows up and an interviewer starts asking questions: What are we doing here — in Seattle, some 1,500 miles from Minnesota? Why are we protesting an oil pipeline outside of a bank?

That evening, after I am back home, I sift through the images from other actions across the country. Oil vomited outside of bank headquarters in New York; oil smeared on the windows of a Wells Fargo branch in DC. All evening, I swipe through the images. From coast to coast, in nearly 30 states, people have been in the streets, shutting down bank branches, demanding that they stop funding this horrific pipeline. There was a second Defund Line 3 human mural — in the financial district of Zurich, Switzerland. There were people on the streets in London, England.

As I watch the images pouring in, it begins to feel, for a moment, as if we have a movement. And maybe even a movement that — if we play our cards right, if we're bold enough, if we're willing to take enough risks and pour enough of our full selves into the fight — might just be powerful enough to not only stop this damn pipeline but bring the whole murderous industry to its knees. •

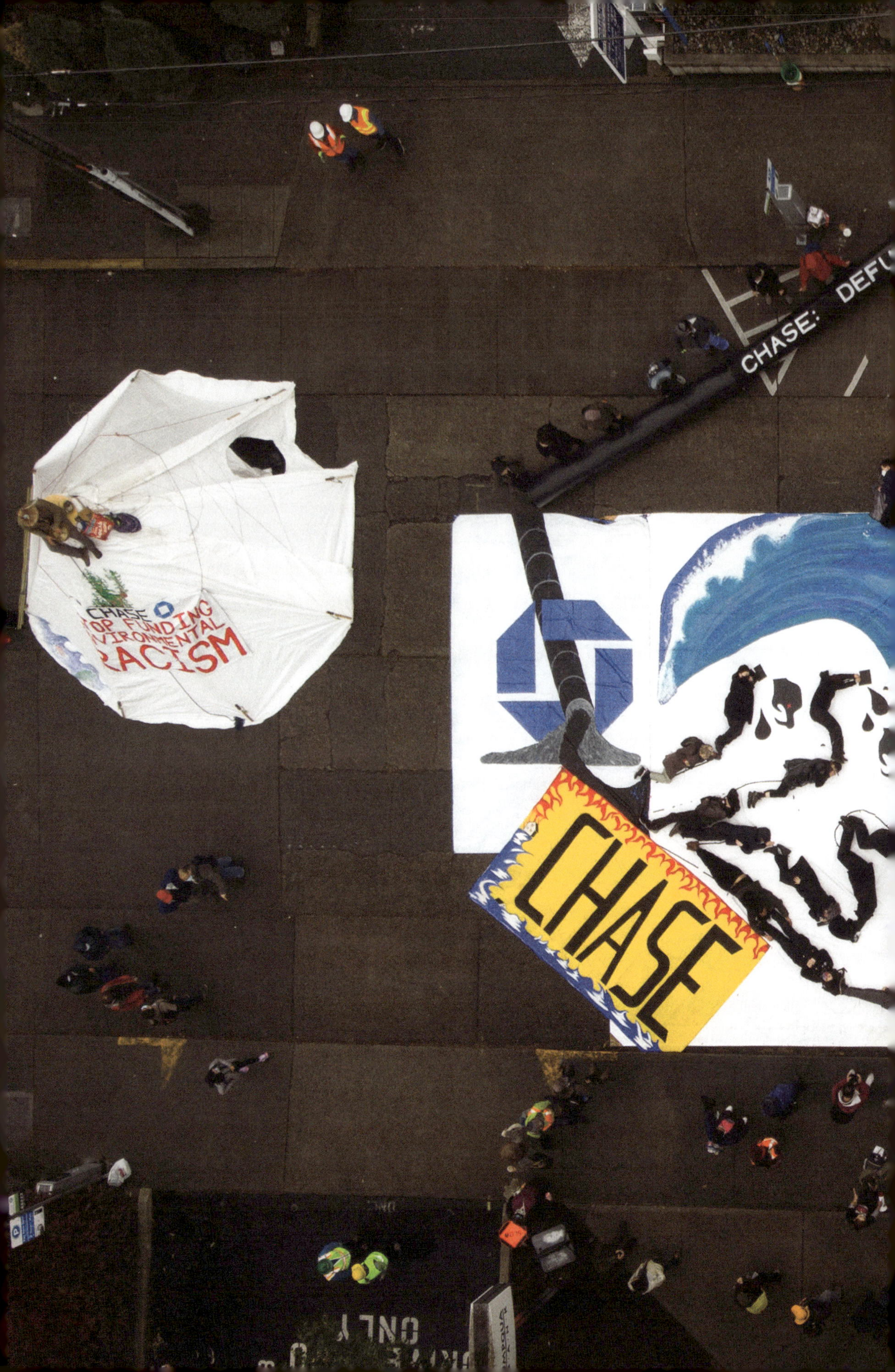
CHASE
RACISM
CHASE:
CHASE

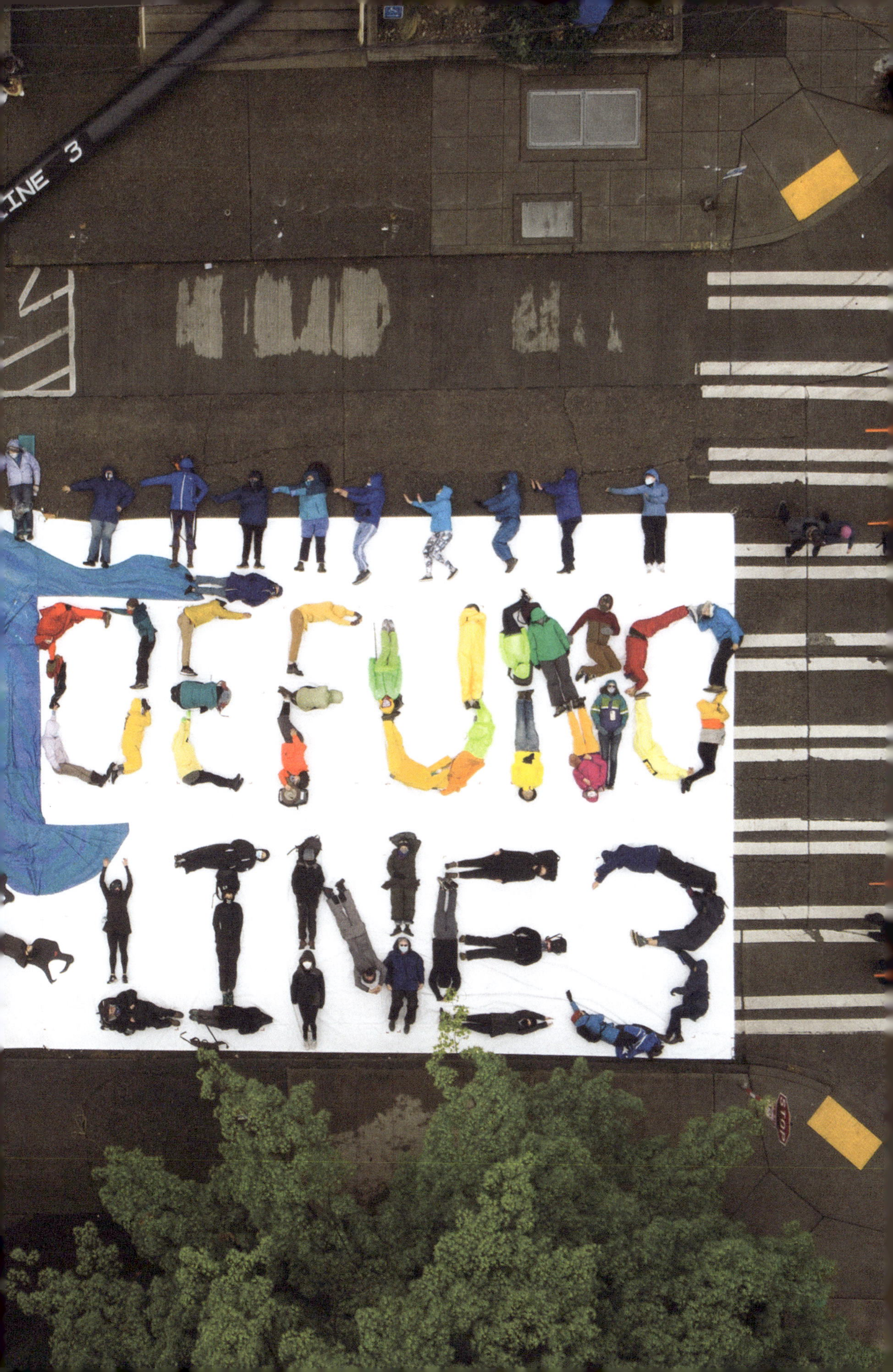

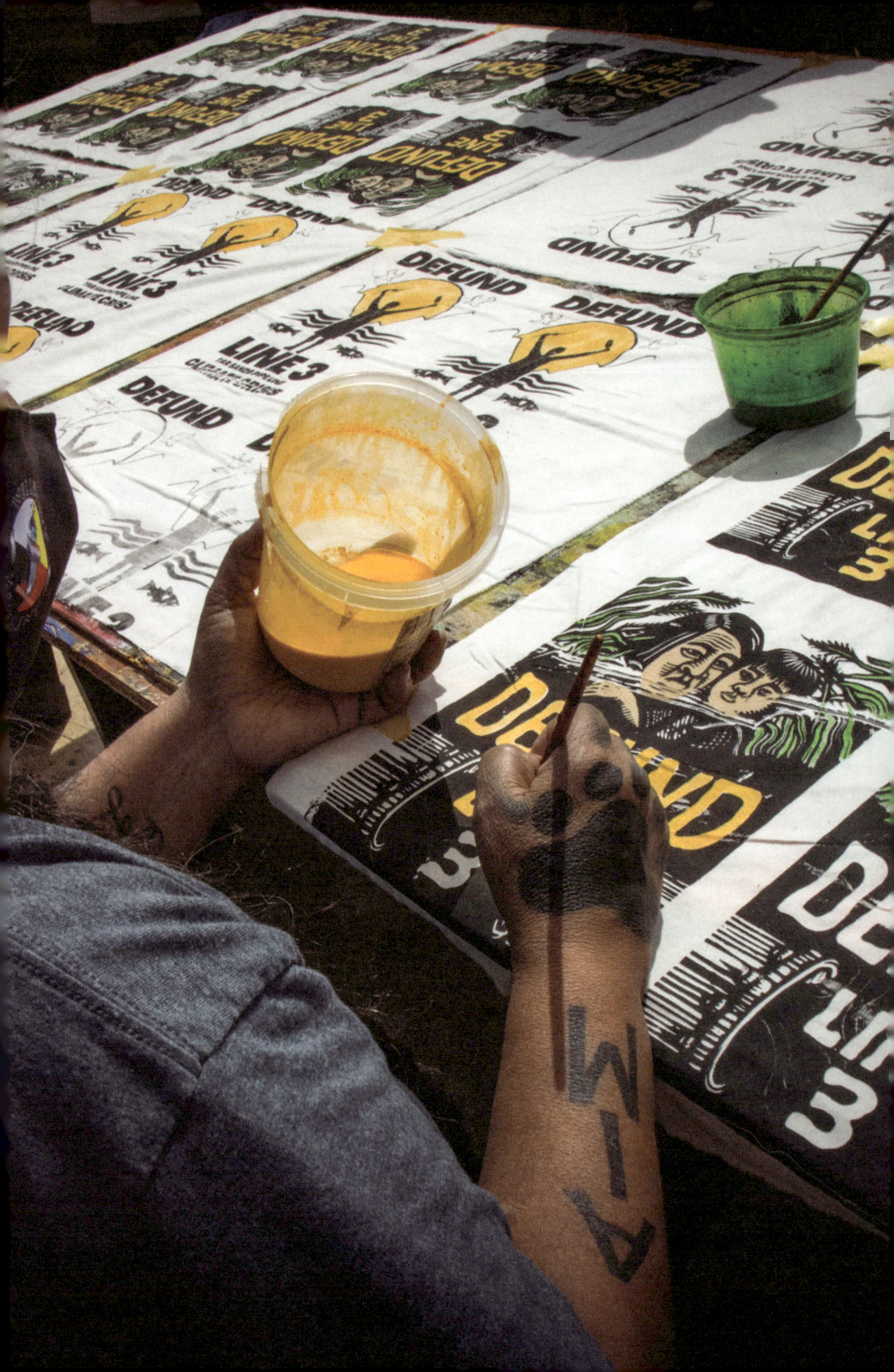
DEFUND
LINE 3

2,324 Files

It's past 11 pm. My phone lights up with a text from S. "wanna make a graphic tonight?" I've only heard snippets of the breaking news from friends on the ground — a camp is being raided. A blurry picture appears on my tiny phone screen and the text "we need a call to action" floats below it. I spit out my toothpaste, pull out my computer, and drag the photo into my design program as the scattered follow-up texts arrive with more details to be included. All caps feels fitting for the urgency of this situation. I'm worried about all the people standing off with the cops. I wonder how many of my friends are there. I scan the blurry photo for recognizable faces, but it's impossible to make anyone out. Good for security culture, bad for my anxiety.

I send back an Instagram-sized graphic a few minutes later. S. suggests some changes, and I send back a new version. I call the Governor's office using the call script I've just typed while waiting to hear back from S. I text my people and religiously search for updates from anywhere that might have more details. No new information is showing up on my phone, and now it's midnight. My friends are both hours and hundreds of miles away. "I'm going to sleep but call me if you need changes," I text S. I turn the volume up on my phone and fall asleep with it on my pillow.

An hour later, I jolt awake, roll over, and pick up my ringing phone. It's S. There is a new script that needs to replace the old one. I grab my computer and make some more changes to the previous graphic. There is too much text on each slide, but not much to be done about it. I send S. the new images, now a series of three. Fuck! There's a spelling error. I delete the message, fix my mistake, export the file, and send it back.

The folder on my laptop called "Stop Line 3" has 2,324 files.

This has been my life since Line 3 construction began in December 2020. I've pulled over on the highway to make urgent graphics, stepped out of work to answer every signal call, and updated my phone hotspot plan to build websites from the backseat of a car. I've felt incredibly honored to contribute to crucial moments of resistance, and incredibly guilty for resting while my friends were standing up to the state. I've memorized graphic file sizes (1080 x 1080 for Instagram and 1920 x 1005 for Facebook events, in case you were wondering) and woken up to numerous anxiety dreams about digital file management. I've typed out "urgent call to action" enough times that I often feel numb to the actual urgency these situations demand. I've become addicted to my phone and can't turn off the constant sense of emergency that active construction forced on our community.

We do what we can with the tools that we have. This digital hellscape was my personal toolkit, and has ingrained a sense of urgency in me that hasn't resolved in months. I don't know if it ever will. •

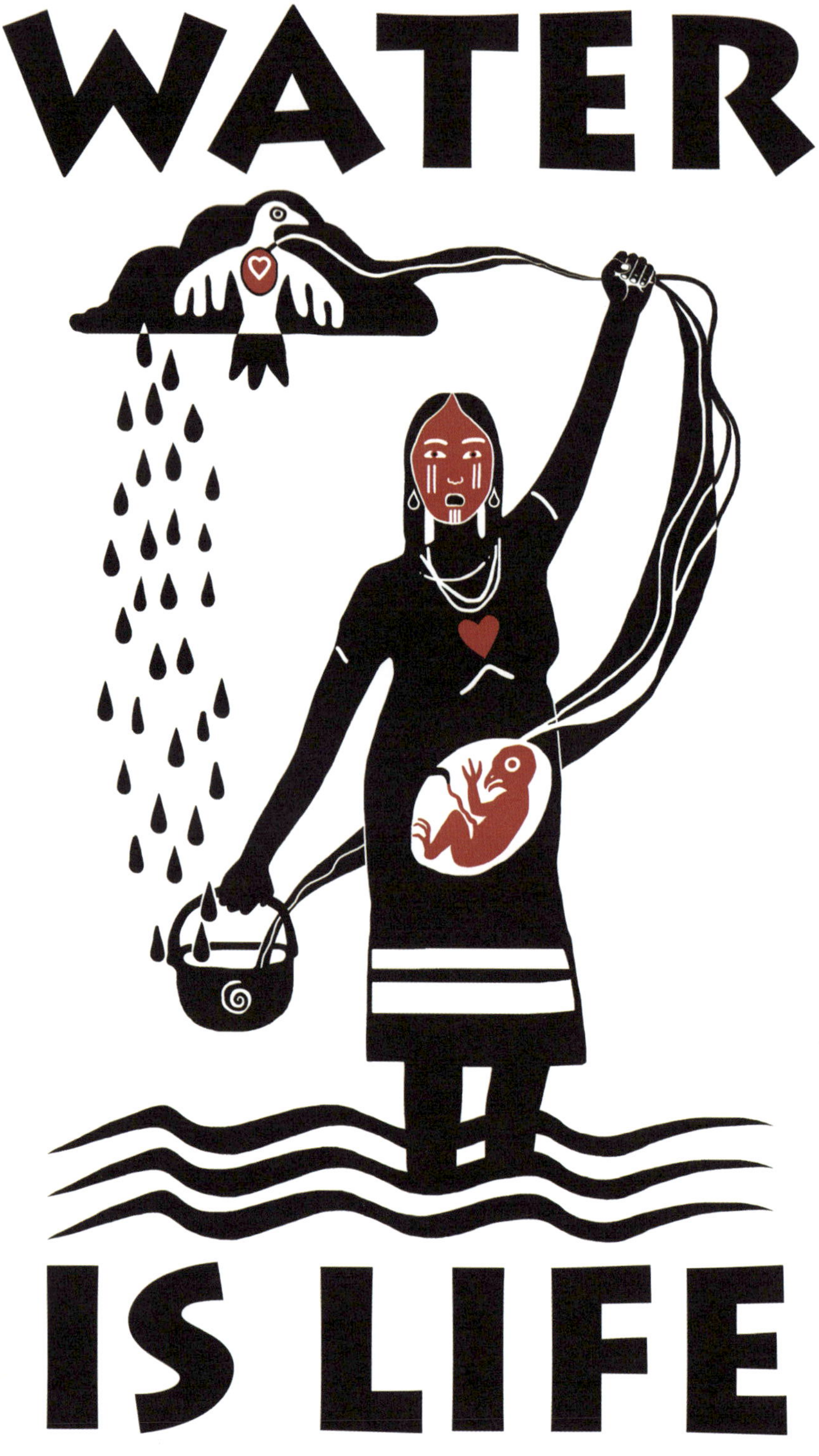
WATER
IS LIFE

Silence

Standing at the corner of Marshall Avenue and Mackubin Street in St. Paul on August 25, 2021, the Grandmothers asked for silence. They gave these instructions to the thousand-some people prepared to journey the final mile of the Treaty People Walk. To remember the Missing and Murdered Indigenous Relatives, we would walk in silence.

Growing up, I internalized silence as cowardly and unhealthy. The Rage Against the Machine lyrics still reverberate in my head, "silence, something about silence makes me sick."

I discovered that day that a thousand people walking in silence is power. Silence said something louder than our voices could shout. Passersby froze, mesmerized by the quiet. My body tingled, actually trembled, as we moved in unison.

Our collective silence called bullshit on the hollow political promises to protect the environment. Silence allowed attentiveness to the movement of our bodies and the wisdom within them.

We remained silent until we arrived at the State Capitol with fists raised. That day, silence offered resistance to oppression, another way to protect the land, the water, air, and each other. Another way to stand for all the things we are meant to care for and pass along. •

Feeding Your Friends: A Collaborative Food Journal

Recipes, Guides, and Tips to Make the Most of Your Time in Northern Minnesota

Entry #1: How to Make One Sandwich for your Horizontal Friend

When I first committed to lying down on back-country asphalt for seven hours with arms and feet immobilized in wrought steel pipes, my first 100 thoughts about the matter didn't breach the subject of what my body might need to remain operational all along that very stationary day. It's difficult to put into words the appreciation one feels for another while resting your head in their lap as you are fed what will certainly remain the best peanut butter and jelly sandwich you eat in your entire life.

When it becomes your turn to take care of a group of people lying down in a road at 5 am without access to their arms, you may not be able to predict exactly what they'll want, but perhaps, just maybe, someone will want a sandwich. The enclosed instructions may help.

1. To make one perfect sandwich, you will have to make eight sandwiches. Ask all eight people locking down what kind of sandwich they would like to be fed on the day of their arrest. From experience, their answers will almost certainly be:

    - Ham, pepperjack, lettuce, and mayo on white bread (NO TOMATO)
    - Two slices of provolone, lettuce, tomato, dijon mustard, and sliced bell peppers, on wheat
    - One slice of pepperjack, lettuce, on wheat
    - Turkey, lettuce, mayo, on white
    - Turkey, pepperjack, lettuce, tomato, mustard
    - Lettuce, tomato, provolone, on white
    - Extra turkey, extra mayonnaise, on white
    - Turkey, lettuce, tomato, mustard, on wheat

2. Disappear into town for hours trying to find ingredients for these sandwiches. You'll want to grab some warm potato salad for dinner since you're already at Hugo's and the sun disappeared behind the crest of the local skate park hours ago.

3. Stuff these very perishable meat and dairy items in your backpack (it's cold enough outside, right?)

4. Drive 60 miles to where you'll be sleeping the night before the deploy, prepare to make the sandwiches in a cramped industrial kitchen with a lake view.

5. Think about the people you're making these sandwiches for and what they're about to risk, this group a hodgepodge mix of the first friends you made after your lonely migration to this state and people you'd only just met who were about to change just-shy-of everything about who you are for the better. People who you'd fall in love with in all kinds of ways. People who you'd eagerly commit the rest of your life to.

6. Assemble the sandwiches! (As a general order: bread, then mayo, then lettuce, then tomato, then meat, then cheese, and bread again.)

7. Ignore the slow unyielding spread of that warm deli meat fragrance coming out of your bag as you pack everything back up before your departure.

8. Try really hard to hold back your stress tears sleeping in your friend's car at 2 am on yet another night below zero. Remember that you will have to be awake in two hours.

9. By 5 am you will have successfully deployed your friends and you'll find yourself separated from the line of riot cops by the barricade you helped construct made of metal and flesh, of concrete, and your friends.

10. There are about three hours before you're escorted away. Adjust everyone's hats and coats (they're lying down on fresh snow and will be until noon). Feed them cigarettes and water. Do your best to comfort them and yourself.

11. Once your own panic has subsided, you'll remember the sandwiches you worked so hard to make. It's only 7 am but they all have to be hungry surely? Grab the sandwiches (you've written everyone's action names on the ziploc bags in sharpie to remember who wanted what).

12. One by one, you'll ask, and one by one, each of them will look at you like you are the most insane woman on the planet. It is *7 am* and no one on this shitty bridge doesn't have a stomachache.

13. Once you have begun silently disparaging yourself for thinking deli-meat sandwiches were a reasonable request for an action that took place before sunrise, your thoughts will be interrupted by your roommate's partner — lying on their back with both hands in metal pipes and their beanie covering one of their eyes like the coziest emo kid in the world. "Hey… can I have my ham sandwich now?"

14. You laugh, someone makes a comment about how ridiculous it is to crave ham and mayonnaise before the light of day has reached your face. You'll grab the now pungently meat-odored bag and start to wonder how you're going to feed someone who can't sit up. You settle on imitating that image of the two lesbians where one is sitting on top of the other doing their makeup.

15. While straddling, feed your horizontal friend the ham sandwich. The sun has not yet risen.

Entry #2: Cass County Grand Slam

If you're like me, you travel through central and northern Minnesota. A lot. Which means, like me, you *need* food recommendations. That's why I'm excited to announce I'm starting a new series I like to call Minnesota's Diners, Drive-Throughs, and Dives. This week, we'll be visiting a lovely little town in Cass County called Walker, Minnesota. Here, I'll be giving you a play-by-play for the best breakfast and coffee money can buy.

1. The best way to enjoy a good breakfast is after an even better night's sleep. That's why I recommend you find somewhere cozy in town to spend the night. There's a lovely little motel just behind the detention center parking lot called, The Back Seat of a Subaru, But Only Half of It Cause the Other Half Is Full of Camping Supplies Inn. I checked in here at about midnight after having been up since 6 am the day before, so you better believe I curled up in the fetal position and slept like a baby.

2. Step two is an important one a lot of people miss — you'll need careful timing for this but it's important. You'll need to wake up in The Back Seat of a Subaru, But Only Half of It Cause the Other Half Is Full of Camping Supplies Inn at approximately 4:30 am — and you'll have to poop. Bad. Like really really bad. Like you'll wake up in a panic cause you've got to poop so bad. You'll need to frantically google the nearest gas station to see if any are open. There won't be any, the closest one is a Holiday that will open at 5 am. You'll need to play it cool in the backseat and hope nobody smells the farts. Your friend in the passenger seat will also wake up around now and realize they have to pee terribly bad. They'll ask you to walk with them so they can pee in the bushes without getting arrested. This step is ESSENTIAL — it will get you up and moving for the next step.

3. As soon as the Holiday opens, sprint there and shit your guts out. Go back to the Inn and rest a while longer.

4. Next, you'll want to wait in the Inn for the next shift to relieve you — they were supposed to arrive three hours ago but no one is here. You'll want to decide to just stick it out since you're already here.

5. Go to turn on the AC in the Inn and realize the battery is dead. This will make you decide to say, "fuck it," and go grab coffee and some breakfast.

6. Go to Holiday for coffee. Notice the employee behind the counter seems to be no older than 12. As you are putting the lid on your hazelnut gas station special blend, watch your friend walk out of the bathroom and say, "we need to leave, I took a huge shit and can't flush it." Leave immediately.

7. Decide to check out a little diner in downtown Walker — a lovely joint called The Outdoorsman Cafe.

8. Be seated and waited upon by a server who can't possibly be older than 13, maybe 14. Order the greasiest eggs benedict you've ever had. It will sit so heavily in your stomach that you'll have to poop halfway through your meal. You'll take the time on the toilet to reflect on your health and realize you almost definitely have IBS.

9. Go back to the table and finish your meal with your friends. Notice a 10-year-old boy washing dishes in the kitchen. What the fuck is going on in this town?

10. SUCCESS! You've officially eaten the best breakfast and drank the best coffee in Walker, Minnesota.

I hope this guide is helpful to anyone who finds themselves in the great town of Walker! And remember, the best way to follow up a good breakfast is with fun activities for the rest of the day. I personally recommend you try standing on the side of the road outside the County Jail desperately trying to wave someone down to jump your car, only to be passed by and ignored by like 50 people. Anyway, that's all for this week — be on the lookout for the next installment of Minnesota's Diners, Drive-Throughs, and Dives!

Entry #3: Schnapps & Cocoa, a Perfect Winter Drink

We've all been there — you're tired after a long day of D.A. 101 and Know Your Rights trainings and are more than a little apprehensive about the prospect of getting arrested a week from now. You sort through a small pile of long underwear and wool socks to put away your notebook, then pass by two of your nine roommates for the week on your way downstairs to the kitchen. Your back aches from sleeping on the floor, your toes are still recovering from hours in negative temperatures the day before, and you just want to unwind.

Well, do I have the drink for you. With only three simple ingredients, you can settle in to watch the snow, cozy up in your pajamas, and discuss your and your friends' deepest vulnerabilities.

Serves: 10 for a few days

Prep Time: minimal

Ingredients:

    1 large can Swiss Miss Hot Cocoa Mix

    Lots of hot water

    750ml Peppermint Schnapps

Instructions:

Weave your way through the tangle of people making tacos in the kitchen to put water on the stove as well as in the kettle. While waiting for the water to boil, line up 10 mugs and fill each with a few generous scoops of cocoa mix. You may have to wash a few mugs from the copious amounts of coffee consumed that morning. Dash to use the single shared bathroom if you get the rare chance. Once the water has boiled, pour some into each mug, leaning over someone chopping onions and avoiding spilling water into the bowl of cilantro. Announce that cocoa's ready, and everyone will crowd around the kitchen island. Add schnapps to taste.

Enjoy!

Entry #4: Recipe for Bean Burritos

Serves 150-200: Perfect for hungry activists stuck outside in 90-degree weather

Ingredients:

50 lbs dried ~~black~~, pinto, or kidney beans ~~(ESSENTIAL)~~

Cook time: 5 hours (best completed before noon)

Preparation:

1. First, wake up at 4 am — well-rested after less than two hours of sleep — and search for one 50-pound bag of dried black beans.

2. Frantically scour the food storage area only to find every kind of bean but the one the recipe calls for.

Chef's Tip (given angrily over phone): "Use your fucking eyes."

3. Grab a backup variety of beans: pinto or kidney will do.

4. Drive beans two hours to a secondary location. In the case that you have recently broken both of your arms, have someone else carry the beans.

5. Your part of the recipe is done — someone else will make the burritos. Next step: go to a tertiary location to sort 800 jail support forms into alphabetical order. •

Editors' Note: This story was developed from an interview. It has been excerpted and edited in collaboration with the interviewee.

We've Got a Long Way to Go for Freedom

A story that just like makes me smile to this day — because there weren't a lot of those, outside of the community and meeting people that were just as convicted to throw down and felt as strongly about social justice — that was a huge, like, strong point throughout my summer, but outside of that there weren't always a lot of reasons to smile.

So, there was an incident where we were holding an easement and we did a drag show. Yeah, it was just to that point in the summertime where we knew the pipe was going in the ground, we knew that we were not going to win this battle, and we just had to do something, something to change the fucking narrative for the day. And we were out there for many, many hours. They weren't able to unlock people, and they weren't able to get the extraction team down there right away. So, it was a lot of hours of talking to cops, we were up really early, so exhausted, we were up late the night before trying to, like, find our costumes.

And it gets to this point where it's hot, you're worried for your comrades who are locked down because they, you know, could be in danger. And there's a point where things are starting to shift, and the cops are gonna start taking actions, you know, that are not favorable to us very soon. And in that, a comrade came up to me and said, "Okay, I'm gonna make sure that the person locked down is safe. And after that, when I see the police tape go up, I'm gonna run across the field. Are you okay with that?" Because I was a person that somebody would consult with in terms of like, what needs to happen in an action and what's cool, as an Indigenous body. And I said, "Absolutely, you need to do what you need to do to stay safe. And if you are feeling green today, you need to stay green."

And *[laughs]* there was a point where — because it was like a while later, after we had that conversation — all of a sudden, I see this body stand up, and just fucking dart, dart through a field, a fucking field. They were a strong runner. They were in a schoolgirl outfit, butt cheeks flapping in the wind. It was such a beautiful sight, because there's five cops trailing them, not one of them is able to keep up or catch up. Our runner slipped in the mud and still got up and still outran them. And then you see the cops slipping in the mud in this field. So, it was just like, a visual moment of: We won that day. Even if we didn't win the pipeline, one of us got away. You know? Somebody wasn't arrested that day, you know, and somebody wasn't taken down by the state. And it was like a personal victory, to have a whole bunch of comrades cheering this individual on. And just to have a moment where — it was a lot of freedom and joy in that action, and it didn't feel, you know, as oppressive or as hard as just fighting with cops surrounding me, say, like, on the St. Paul grounds at the Capitol building, right, where a wall on every side of me is a cop, and I'm not getting out of there unless I can talk my way out and keep my comrades behind me safe who are protecting a lodge, a lodge *ceremony*, and there's almost definitely going to be police violence. Right. So, just to have like, that day of, of joy and celebration, and to know that we got our comrades, our comrade back safely, which was also a fearful event, but we did. It just felt like there was finally a day to celebrate something. And it didn't always have to be disappointment.

And the other story I would share is a day that I — I found my strength. Ooh — this is like, an emotional story, I don't know why.

It's just that — I know I'm a strong activist. I know I've talked to cops and put them in their place and made them feel like just absolute douchebags. But there was a day at Red Lake where we've been out there for hours, again, we were up early. We're all exhausted. It's hot. We're kind of wondering what's going on because there's not a big cop presence. And at one point, we realized it's because they were waiting to get all six counties up there. And there was a point where I'm detached from the crowd. And I'm very, very unguarded. And everybody else, you know, at least has comrade support. I'm up on the edge of the highway with a megaphone because I've been educating people for hours and hours, cops and comrades about Indigenous issues. And there was a point where they come out, you know, SWAT gear, fucking — like we're violent. And we're not. And they all form that line, you know, that police line, and they start to move forward. And I was by myself.

> *It was like — a terrifying moment in that I had to really quickly gauge who I was as a person. Do I turn around and run away? Or do I stay?*

It was like — a *terrifying* moment in that I had to really quickly gauge who I was as a person. Do I turn around and run away? Or do I stay? Or do I, I run towards the cops and definitely take a beating? And it was — the choice was to stand in my body and stay rooted right there in the ground. Completely isolated, but with the power of my ancestors. So, it taught me that day that you could have no weapon and you can have nothing but a megaphone. And the cops didn't do anything. I mean, they eventually arrested me *[laughs]*, they eventually took me down. And that was, you know, a brutal arrest. But it wasn't in *that* moment that they did it. It was in *that* moment that I found out that I would stand, I would stand against the enemy. I would stand up, and stand for, stand for us. And I wouldn't let them scare me, even though inside I was terrified. •

In the lead-up to the final decision meetings on Line 3 at the Public Utilities Commission, MN350's Pipeline Resistance Team was a big part of planning the Block Line 3 Party at the PUC, aka "the block party." This was a 24-hour takeover of 7th Place East, a narrow street which separated the blue glass Metro Square Building which housed the PUC from the granite street walls of Securian Tower to the south. The idea of the block party was to bring the community that opposed the pipeline together in a joyful show of solidarity right in front of the decision makers who were about to make one of the most significant decisions of their lives.

It is not especially easy, from a permitting and logistics angle, to shut down a downtown street for 24 hours. It is harder when you want to march into the space from the Capitol a mile away, set up a tipi, stage many vehicles on the street including the bus with Stop Line 3 painted on the side, do live screenprinting, serve food, pop up a stage and have an evening concert with amplified sound, invite the public to camp out overnight onsite, and then have a water ceremony and direct action training the following day. I think we gave ourselves just over a month to do all of this.

At the first meeting with the city, they said it couldn't be done — there wasn't enough time. We had to ask whether they meant that they couldn't handle this on their end or that they thought we couldn't do everything quick enough. They said it was the latter, noting that most events like this took about six months for the organizers to cross the Ts and dot the Is. With that established, we moved ahead like fools, committed to the vision and to the frenetic pace of organizing on deadline.

In the warm evening light after a storm, hard choices come into focus better. On a dark stage at 2 am in a blanket, the possibilities of the world we want to build felt so immediate, so tangible. How could you choose Enbridge when faced with that kind of beauty?

Luckily, the event generated a lot of excitement from organizers and allies in our network, the team put our full effort into it, and we got a signed permit approving our full vision, to the shock of the city, along with a myriad of sub-permits for things like food and generators and parking meter buyouts and barricades and a march route. It's always a choice whether to pull permits or not for any given event, but here we wanted to be fully legal and advertise the event as family friendly.

We did not know that the top cop who signed off on our plan was in a power struggle with a younger man in his department who absolutely hated him. Unfortunately, we learned — the top cop left on vacation right before our event, and during site setup, the younger officer came and introduced himself and asked to see the permit. When we showed him, he said that most of it would not be logistically possible and he would not allow it. We pointed out that it was already approved, and he agreed that it was, "But I'm here and he's not, and what I say is the law now."

After verifying that the Saint Paul Police Department did consider him in charge of the event and would not rein him in, we changed a couple things, negotiated others, adjusted the street layout plan a little, and didn't consent to his demand that we scrap the plan for people to stay overnight at the site — that was part of the whole point of the event. We shifted how we talked about the overnight to attendees since it now posed some legal risk and printed out "security team" papers for anyone staying. I am certain that many of us resolved to be less proactive about securing permits for events in St. Paul in the future. If the police don't care, why should we?

Despite the last minute rush, the event was so beautiful. About 600 people came. We rallied and marched, and there was art and screenprinting and tabling and great food. The concert was powerful and poignant, even with a freak thunderstorm (only a few city blocks in diameter but directly above us, not moving, not in the forecast) gracing one of the artist's sets. She sang us through the rain and for a moment 7th Place East was holy ground.

I slept in my car that night behind the stage, wired and cold, and happy. Everything was fine — the cops didn't show up; we won that game of chicken. One of the lead organizers parked her SUV across the street entrance to block any potential traffic and slept so well inside it that she got a full eight hours, midnight to 8 am, waking up and stumbling out of her makeshift bed on the folded-down backseat after night had turned to morning and people had started to gather again.

I wish I could say that the block party made the difference, but we know it did not. The PUC met some weeks later and approved Line 3 anyway. I wish they would have been there for those 24 hours to see what I saw. In the warm evening light after a storm, hard choices come into focus better. On a dark stage at 2 am in a blanket, the possibilities of the world we want to build felt so immediate, so tangible. How could you choose Enbridge when faced with that kind of beauty? We brought a glimpse of that world to a street in downtown St. Paul, and although the commissioners could not be bothered to see, I will never forget it. •

Camp Firelight

Camp Firelight was an 1855 Treaty People Gathering and Prayer Occupation on the banks of the Mighty Mississippi in northern MN, from June 7 to 14, 2021.

It began with the We Are All Treaty People Gathering. We convened for three days in Waubun, MN. Native culture and treaty knowledge were shared to build understanding and respect for Native communities. Treaties and our obligations as treaty partners were also discussed. Countless relationships were inspired and born. It was a beautiful three days.

Immediately following the Treaty People Gathering, we met at the Mississippi bridge near the La Salle State Park where we marched, sang, and prayed for the Nibi. Soon after, we followed our hearts and occupied the Line 3 easement in a prayer ceremony. We invited our treaty partners/allies and held space collectively in peace and prayer. We asserted our collective treaty rights along with our right to freedom of religion and together we held space for eight peaceful days. We stopped construction for those eight days, I'm sure Mother Nature thanked us.

Our non-Native treaty partners prayed with us and amplified our struggle and gave voice to our story. This story includes all of us: mitakuye oyasin, which means we are all related. We showed the world what it looks like to honor treaties and to live in peace as neighbors as the treaties intended. We followed our original instructions and became guardians of all that is sacred, we were protectors of the Nibi and keepers of the 1855 Treaty.

What those eight days accomplished… we controlled the narrative for the eight days, denied Enbridge's eviction notice with the sheriff's support, we also respected the sheriff during our occupation/defiance and held back the Northern Lights Task Force twice. We exited under our own terms under the sole jurisdiction of the Clearwater sheriff's department. Our occupation was in peace as we honored each other and the 1855 Treaty.

Fifty-one water protectors were cited with misdemeanor trespassing, some accepted a stay of adjudication, some cases were dismissed, and some of us are still waiting for dismissals. Asserting Treaties isn't a crime and should never be tried as one. Treaties are the Supreme Law of the Land, Article 6 of the U.S. Constitution.

We feel hopeful, win or lose. We'll continue to assert our Treaties, our sovereignty was never ceded.

The Firelight occupation was the beginning of what the new future looks like as treaty partners, a future we can all thrive in. The eight days spent together built everlasting relationships and continued We Are All Treaty People awareness, our good work continues as we continue to write our story. We hope you join us, we are a community.

> *We feel hopeful, win or lose. We'll continue to assert our Treaties, our sovereignty was never ceded.*

The 1855 Firelight Encampment will be forever in my heart, I'll never forget. Firelight was a loving and caring space I still hold dear. Miigwech for the courage and solidarity to those who stood with us and/or supported Camp Firelight. We couldn't have done it without you, when we stand together we don't stand alone. This is more than a pipeline, Treaties Matter and We Are All Treaty People. •

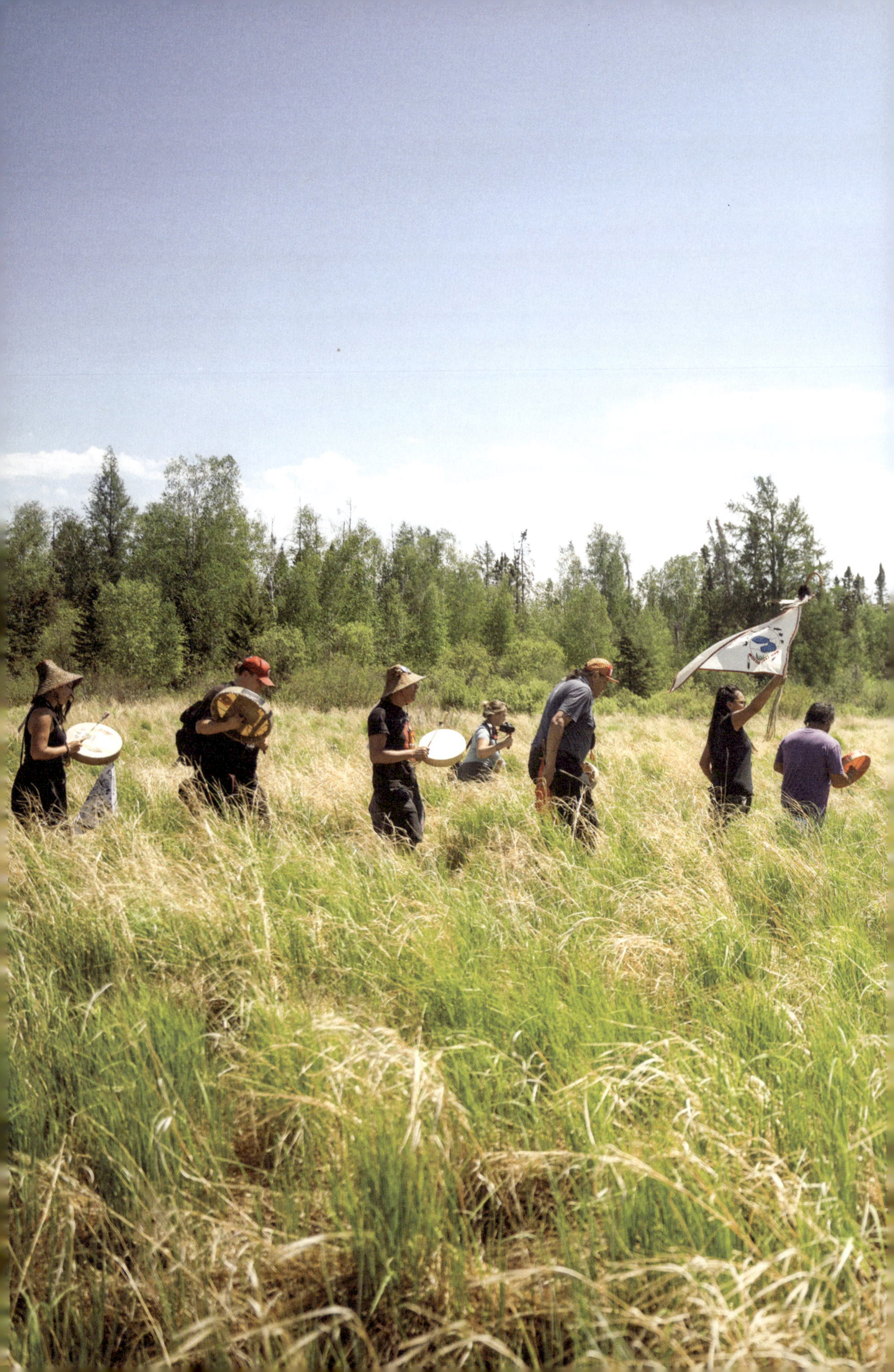

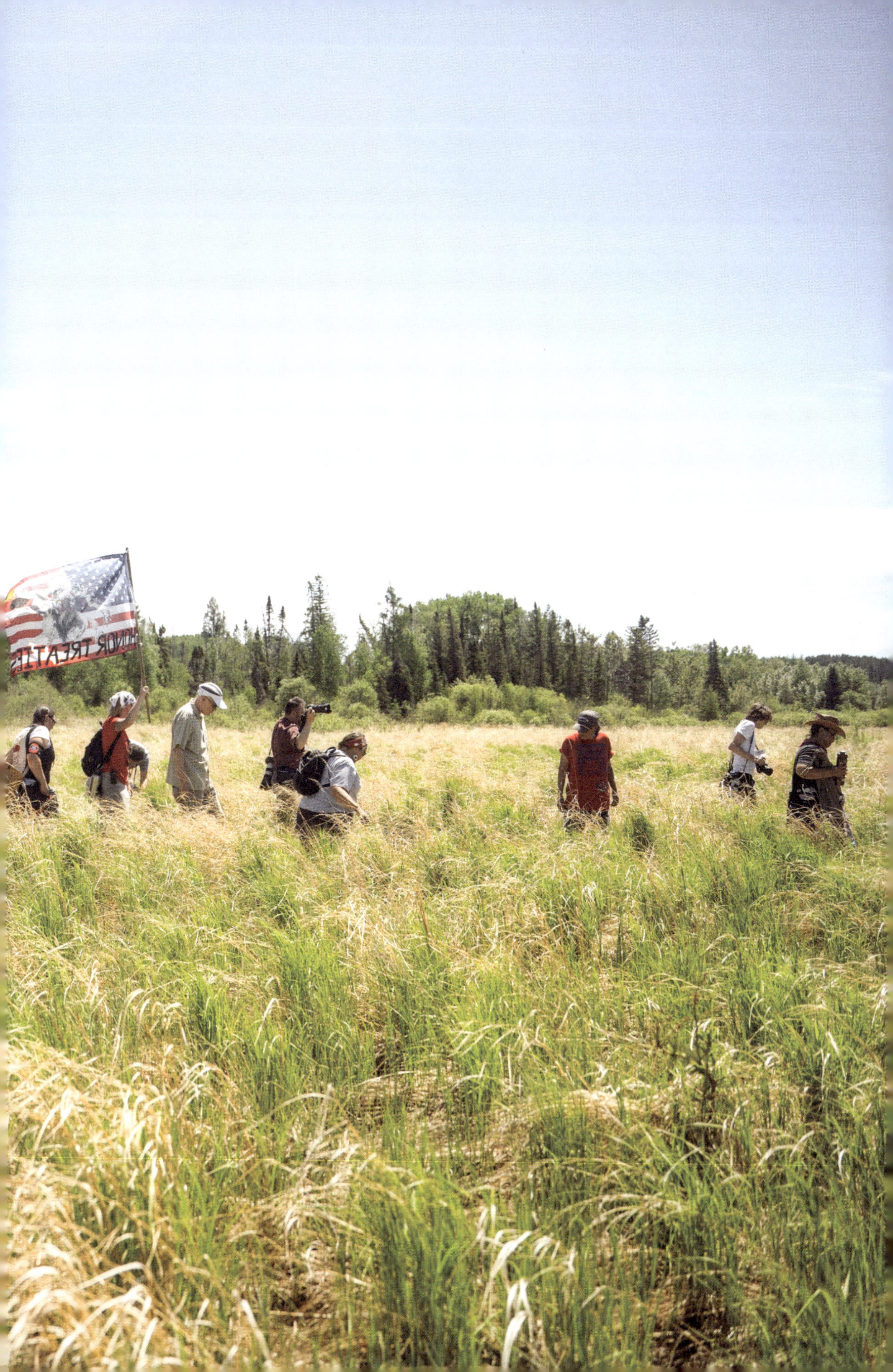

The Quiet Side of our Felonious Thievery

After many months of supporting the fight from afar, our week on the ground in Northern Minnesota started with a bang.

We arrived the morning the local sheriff, funded and supplied with intel by Enbridge, had laid siege to the Namewag action camp in a desperate attempt to stop the relentless waves of protests against the pipeline. So, instead of delivering supplies and making introductions as planned, we were thrust immediately into an Orwellian, 12-hour standoff of rolling skirmishes with the cops that ended with us all parking sideways and abandoning our whole convoy of vehicles to be towed off the remote dirt road as we retreated onto the private property of camp to save our arrests for another day of our choosing, not theirs.

The following week was chaos. Adrenaline, sleep deprivation, constantly shifting plans and emotional gut punches layered on top of each other as pipeline construction proceeded feverishly under the mainstem of the Mississippi, just below its headwaters.

Ready and eager to do our part to take a physical stand, we didn't know what form that was ultimately going to take until the early morning moment I was jumping out of a moving vehicle on the side of a highway with a 50-pound lockbox over my shoulder, joining a swarm of an active Enbridge construction site. Dodging security, workers, and welders, we clambered down into the freshly dug, 12-foot-deep ditch that the new pipe was being lowered into.

Searching quickly for the best place to attach ourselves, a previously unseen opportunity presented itself and we shoved our lockbox through a pump-house fitting, perfectly sized for our fortified steel device. As far as I am aware, of the nearly 1,000 people arrested for civil disobedience resisting this disastrous project, we are some of the only ones who have been able to lock down to the actual pipeline itself, which made the resulting Felony Theft charges we faced all the more sanguine — it was an odd sort of honor to be formally accused of stealing the Line 3 Pipeline.

While we did not, unfortunately, truly steal the snaking metal behemoth, we and our crew that day did shut down the construction site for over 10 hours, and between the feral intensity of the action's first hour or so, and the deeply uncomfortable extraction process of its final hours, it is the unexpected quietude and even poetically reflective moments of that day that I remember most.

It was the hottest July 1 in recorded history in northern Minnesota, so we were in a favorable position being placed deep in the sandy ditch shielded from the sun by the suspended pipeline.

After the initial hour of tension, with workers yelling and continuing to weld and shoot sparks just over our heads and our support crews being arrested and removed by the cops, there was an expanse of hours where it was just the few dozen of us who were locked-in still onsite, and there were prolonged moments where the experience was strangely… peaceful.

Monarch and swallowtail butterflies danced around us, probing with their proboscises in the moist, newly exposed sand. A Song Sparrow erupted nearby in emphatic song once an hour, like horny church bells keeping time.

An adult Bald Eagle appeared against the deep blue sky, circling us in broadening arcs overhead. Upon seeing her, one of our action partners, an Oglala Lakota water protector and grandmother who was locked down to the massive orange earth mover above us, erupted into an old Lakota song, invoking the support of her ancestors to our action. Her voice intertwined with the wind in a way that seemed to slow everything down for a spell, her words timeless amidst all our busyness, her voice both soothing and fierce in that way that can sear a moment of experience into one's memory forever.

There was also a deep and pervasive satisfaction to stop all the talking and strategizing and to just sit and say without words: this damn thing will go no farther until you cut my body off of it.

There had been so much preparation, anticipation, and uncertainty, dozens of press releases, so many hours of Zoom meetings and coordination calls, so much stress and so many sleepless nights, that after we were there, physically locked to the stupid pipeline, there was nothing left to do, nothing we could do, but sit there and wait, so it was sort of a forced, surprise meditation.

And even though there was grief and outrage at all the factors that led up to us needing to be attached to this violent pipeline in the first place, there was also a deep and pervasive satisfaction to stop all the talking and strategizing and to just sit and say without words: this damn thing will go no farther until you cut my body off of it. •

The new Line 3 was completed in 2021 and runs for 337 miles under land and water in so-called Minnesota. In 2019, I purchased an internal combustion engine vehicle for the first time to join the fight against Line 3.

The irony was not lost on me. I had hoped to never own one, but 337 miles is infeasible to monitor via bicycle.

Drive that back and forth 75 times and you've gone 25,000 miles. That's the same as driving all the way around the earth. 25,000 miles is exactly how much I drove over a year and a half of frontline resistance.

What was gained by driving around the earth? I transported many signs, banners, and bodies. I filled up the entire storage capacity of my phone with photos of construction sites. I transferred the contents of many full dumpsters into many hungry stomachs.

In driving around the earth (but actually back and forth across northern Minnesota 75 times), I used 1,250 gallons of gas.

The energy contained in that gas is 150 GJ (gigajoules). That's the same as 36,000,000 calories, which if eaten would provide 18,000 days of human food. This is approximately the same amount of energy that I would ingest in my expected lifespan.

Sometimes I wonder if my driving was worth using the energetic equivalent of converting a lifetime of food directly into gaseous CO2. Will future generations looking back at the efforts of me and my friends to stop Line 3 think we've done enough?

The new Line 3 ships 760,000 barrels of oil per day. That's 4.6 million GJ, or the equivalent of 31,000 lifetimes of food shipped each day it's in service. Did my driving do more harm than good? Not if it slowed down the line coming into service by at least 1/31,000 of a day, or 2.8 seconds. •

BLACK SNAKE KILLAZ

NO LINE 3   NO LINE 3

Wade in the Water

As a water protector from Standing Rock and Line 3, I was moved to write this piece as a rallying call to resist expanding fossil fuel infrastructure. For Black people in this country, spirituals like Wade in the Water have been part of a legacy of resistance to white supremacy. As a Black woman in this country, I see the environmental crises as one of the most pressing matters of injustice to marginalized communities. The rewritten lyrics tie both the resistance from white supremacy and the protection of sacred water together. They indeed are intersecting as environmental crisis after crisis have shown. Music has always been a pivotal part of cultures of resistance and this is my contribution to that tradition.

—

Wade in the water
Wade in the water
Wade in the water
Protectors gonna defend the water

See those pipelines coming round?
Protectors gonna defend the water
We're turning their plans upside down
Protectors gonna defend the water
The water's sacred like me and you!
Protectors gonna defend the water
And those who pollute the water are damn fools
Protectors gonna defend the water

Wade in the water
Wade in the water
Wade in the water
Protectors gonna defend the water •

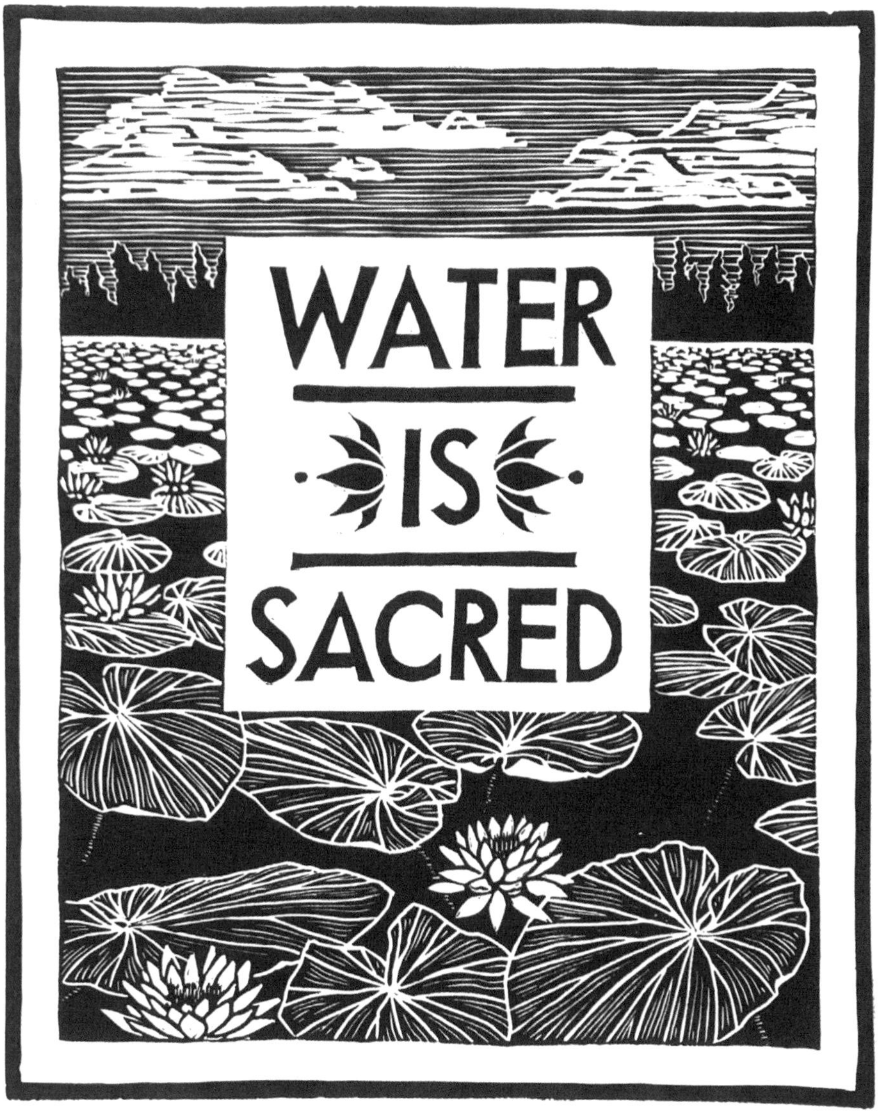
WATER
IS
SACRED

Every morning at Camp Migizi I woke up surrounded by slugs

After the capitol action
before build week
we needed to take time

to sear Spam
and sow seeds
to process

what happened to us   (trauma)
and how   (police escalate all actions)
and did we adhere to our values   (sometimes)
and what now   (we keep fighting, which sometimes looks like healing)

We sat in a circle by the garden
and listened

We heard each other
and the construction on the easement
and the wind in the waist-high grass

Sometimes the slugs would fall
instead of crawl
back to the ground

As I went to sleep
I could hear them smack the skin of my tent
when they lost their grip •

I drove to the action in one of the vans near the front of the caravan. We were driving to a small bridge which crossed over the headwaters of the Mississippi River, at a spot where you could almost jump across. We had the radio tuned to a pirate broadcast being produced in the van just ahead of ours. We listened to a young woman narrate stories of life in this region, stories of generations of families and neighbors, and what it's like to harvest wild rice.

The caravan stopped before the bridge and the march began. The banners were unfurled. Mobile art pieces were assembled. Signs were raised. Bandanas and flags were flown. Songs were sung. Chants were chanted. Marching behind the lead contingent of people from the Native communities of Minnesota, we made our way to the bridge.

The march was a beautiful spectacle. It was creative and inspiring. It was a demand. It was a release.

And it was hot. It must be said that it was really, really hot. It was an actual heat wave. It was over 20 degrees hotter than normal. During a climate protest. The average high temperature for early June is typically 73 degrees (I looked it up). As we marched on the asphalt highway toward the bridge, it was well over 90 degrees. The planet was helping us make the point that the burning of fossil fuel was unleashing perilous climate change.

I was excited to be part of the direct action. I was nervous about the heat. The crowd had a cooling effect. The banners created shelter from the powerful sun. We marched to the bridge over the brook labeled as one of the most northern points of the Great Mississippi River. One group continued their march out to the construction site next to the river to begin an extended protest. Our group stayed on the bridge which was being adorned by the creation of a street mural to demand action to Stop Line 3. This message was delivered in many forms with great creativity and enthusiasm.

When I needed some shade, I walked down under the bridge. I found respite under a guardrail. With my feet in the mud, my head peered out at street level. Fellow protesters sat along the railing, oblivious to me staring out under their feet. As I surveyed the carnival of action from under the bridge, I spotted a unique expression of protest. A corporate swoosh personalized with a message of the movement. A commitment felt from head to toe. In messages large and small, the people of the Treaty People Gathering were making their case for change. •

The Umbilicus

Throughout the years of resisting Line 3, and especially during the past year of opposing active construction, I've wondered about what nature thinks of us. The land defenders, the folks chaining ourselves to the machines. The prayer ceremonies, the marches down dirt roads. The scouts walking through forests and wetlands, the drones buzzing through the skies. Nature bears witness to humans fighting other humans. Love fighting greed. The future fighting the past. What does the rest of the web of life think of our struggles?

Before one of many nonviolent actions to protect the Earth inspired by Giniw Collective — our Indigenous women and two-spirit-led effort to live in balance and protect what remains — we met in a place filled with giant oaks whispering the past. As we gathered under the trees, my heart felt their powerful, quietly rustling voices.

They are giants who remember the Dakota and Anishinaabe before, during, and after colonization. Once, they were seedlings who heard the prayers of the humans their ancestors knew, who listened to the tobacco laid by humble hands and grew taller. As they grew, the familiar humans changed: there were new arrivals. New, pale faces with hands that razed entire forests, that pulled sturgeon after sturgeon from the nearby rivers to rot or burn, while Indigenous faces grew gaunt and haunted.

Seedlings-now-trees bore witness to the building of clapboard homes, to the arrival of plows and foreign agricultural practices that ripped apart the earth and erased what was before. Familiar Indigenous faces removed to reservations, to places away from the oaks who knew their voices.

So many relatives cut down, sent elsewhere to build more homes or lavish mansions, to build dams in rivers and mills in the currents. The trees who survived tasted the water change, ingested pesticide runoff and the chemical byproducts from newly built factories upstream. The thinned forests were quieter, the clear-cut forests were silent.

The familiar faces slowly returned, their numbers similarly diminished. Fewer hands remember the tobacco and how to pass on messages. The language of nature is fainter. Lips struggle to shape forgotten words, and the deeper, wordless connectivity pulses through a weakened umbilicus. Time trundles on. The oaks' shadows grow and wane over generations.

From above, the figures darting toward the exposed oil pipeline that cuts through the woods look like water insects dashing toward a branch floating on a stream. Minutes later, the figures are atop the metal snake, inside its dark depths. Others are chained to heavy equipment that has ceased the grating, clanking rhythm that razes the trees, rends the earth, and brings in more steel pipe. Songs drift on the breeze, some older than the humans singing them, stirring memories of the time of seedlings and rich ecosystems. They are singing about the water, about a basic truth of life: we cannot live without water.

New humans arrive, these ones uniformed and armed. Their belts are full of plastic zipties, their hands clutch batons, the expression in their eyes ranges from annoyance to eagerness to uncertainty. The little group of people singing has formed a watchful line, holding their animal-hide drums and braids of sweetgrass up in the air. Drumbeats reverberate heartbeats through the tense air. Those in uniform threaten to use "less lethal" force if the crowd continues to stop the metal snake from sending its poison through.

The singers have formed a tight knot now. A standoff ensues. The screams of cutting tools echo through the watching trees. Cotton hoods are pulled over the heads of those calling themselves water protectors. The rest of the group shouts their support. Some weep, some chant, some stand with defiant, silent jaws. Eventually, the water protectors are cut from their chains, pulled out of the pipeline, thrown into the dirt, and cuffed. They are loaded into waiting vehicles and driven away. The machines they chained themselves to are silent, the pipeline remains above ground; they have stopped a day of work.

The knot of humans still here in the woods begins to sing again. They walk to the nearby river and lay tobacco down in the earth, in the water. Their words trickle through the dirt, through the roots. The weakened umbilicus between humans and nature flickers briefly. An eagle appears, drawn by the message making its way to the above.

So it goes for months, through snow and ice, summer heat, and a historic drought that decimates rivers, as Enbridge simultaneously pumps out the remaining puddles and drills its pipeline under riverbeds. At one point, the company pierces a water aquifer. Millions of gallons spill as the Earth cries out. At another, hundreds of water protectors overtake a major Enbridge pump station, their rallying cries fierce and brave on the already torn-asunder earth.

The machines worked at a frantic pace as more songs rang out, as more water protectors remembered their own humanity. Twenty-four hours a day, seven days a week, the clanking, metallic cacophony ripped through the forest. More eyes watching, more messages sent, more humans trying to stop the machines, to reach the ears and hearts of other humans. The din reached a peak as more and more of the Earth was torn apart and the pipeline was buried inside the new scar — then grew quiet as Line 3 reached completion.

So it goes for months, through snow and ice, summer heat, and a historic drought that decimates rivers, as Enbridge simultaneously pumps out the remaining puddles and drills its pipeline under riverbeds. At one point, the company pierces a water aquifer. Millions of gallons spill as the Earth cries out. At another, hundreds of water protectors overtake a major Enbridge pump station, their rallying cries fierce and brave on the already torn-asunder earth.

A lone water protector kneels at the edge of the Mississippi headwaters. Tears drip into the now-cloudy water, one site of the nearly 30 chemical spills during the Line 3 build. "I'm so sorry, we tried so hard," I whispered. Tobacco floats across the tiny stream's surface. The thick rushes sigh and the water swirls. A chickadee calls. The cicadas buzz. Their voices sound clearer. The umbilicus feels stronger. A new pathway to an old pathway feels nearer.

A generation awakening, remembering that we can live in balance, turning away from extractive comforts and toward community with all living beings. Acts of selflessness pushing back words of ego. We cannot know what the web of life thinks of humanity's struggles: whether nature hopes for us to choose the right path or to finally fall into self-destructive oblivion. We still have agency over our own strand, our own place. Imagining and building a world that doesn't run on endless, extreme extraction is far less difficult than convincing ourselves we can live without water, without soil to grow food, without clean air to breathe. We must choose our path, or our choice will be made for us. •

WATER KNOWS NO BORDERS

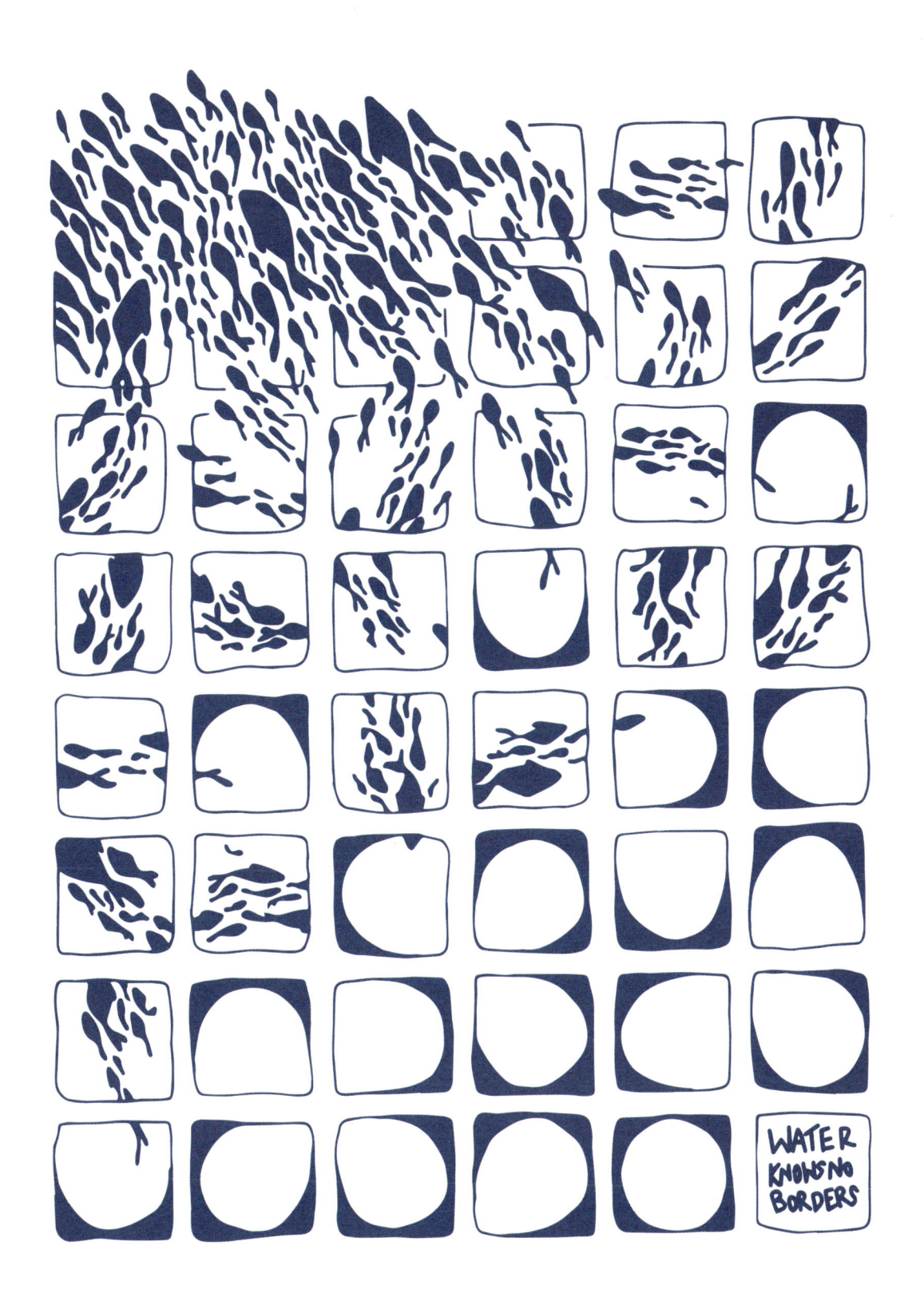

The people who cooked throughout the movement to stop Line 3 sustained people both physically and emotionally. When situations were bleak and morale was low, someone was always around to hand out burritos or pass out the millionth granola bar.

The cook team for the Treaty People Gathering worked to produce small miracles, three times a day. As the event neared 2,000 people in one of the largest heat waves of Minnesota history, the team worked out of a small grain silo. The planning team learned to comply with the cook team's requests as efficiently as possible.

On the evening of the second day of the Gathering, some of us are sitting behind the stage to finalize the schedule for the following day. It's past 9 pm, and everyone has been up since 5 am to make sure everything will run smoothly. We're hot, sweaty, and delirious from sleep deprivation. We get a walkie call from the cook silo, saying they are coming to us with an ingredient list. Assuming this might be some bags of chips that we can pick up at the EasyOne down the road or that this might be for later in the Gathering, we brush it off. We are handed a paper plate with a penciled list on the back, say thank you, and go back to talking.

As the team examines the list, we squint our eyes and read the list more closely: 40 pounds of potatoes, 22 loaves of white bread, etc., etc. In addition, we slowly come to understand that this scratched, paper plate, penciled list… are immediate needs. The cook team won't be able to provide for everyone tomorrow if they do not have these 40 pounds of potatoes by the morning.

We decide that I should go to the Walmart in Detroit Lakes, 40 minutes away and closing in an hour. I grab two friends and a passenger van that I have never driven before. (I do not grab my license, as I left it at home.) The three of us have a list of 12 bulk items we need, ranging from bread to watermelon to romaine lettuce, all written on the back of a paper plate, and 50 minutes until Walmart closes.

Screeching into the Walmart parking lot, we pass a few late night stragglers picking up last minute grocery items and hoping to find the best munchies. Laughing, we divide and conquer with 10 minutes to go before closing. I decide to save watermelons for last, as they will be the bulkiest and heaviest to carry.

Potatoes, check. Carrots, check. Watermelons… nonexistent. Circling the produce area, I start to panic. How on earth could we have driven across rural Minnesota at 11 pm to come up empty handed?! I frantically call another organizer on-site to see what we should do. "Just get pineapple and get OUT of there, you'll be fine."

As a team, the three of us get to the register with two minutes to spare. Our haul has started to gain attention from the other staff and customers, and a circle begins to form around the young person with glitter eyeliner and a huge diet coke who has started to check us out.

Of course, questions start to come. "What is this for? Where are you taking it? Why did you come here at closing time?"

Anxious about how people could track our location and send law enforcement to the Gathering space, I start making things up.

"Oh… this is for a music festival."

"Oh really?! Where?"

"…Southern Wisconsin."

"What? Then why are you in Northern Minnesota?"

"…We are passing through and this seems to make sense!"

Our cashier then tells us, "You all seem so fun, I want to go! What is the name?"

I am sweating at this point. "Oh umm… the festival is actually tomorrow, so it is far too late to get tickets, sorry!"

Somehow the cashier is STILL checking out our items.

"I really think I could come, why won't you talk about it?"

"… I am so sorry, I just think it is closed," I say.

It is at this point I realize I am wearing a t-shirt that says, "Honor the Treaties, Protect the Water, Stop Line 3," a bandana that states, "Stop Line 3" all over it, and a lanyard that says, "Host Team: Treaty People Gathering, Stop Line 3." All subtlety is out the window. We race out of Walmart.

Past midnight, we make it back safe. We unload all the groceries. We laugh and breathe deeply and sleep hard.

The next morning, we receive a message from the cook.

"Where are the watermelons?" •

Editors' Note: The following is a conversation between two neurodivergent folks reflecting on the way their neurodivergence affected their experience in the struggle against Line 3. Both speakers identify as autistic people with ADHD. The transcript has been excerpted and lightly edited for clarity.

"The Slow Life"

A: It's just interesting to reflect on what it is like containing those identities and also existing in spaces where — there's just like, a whole lot of different kinds of people, and a lot of interacting, a lot of socializing.

B: *Really, what first comes to my mind is just how people are more conscious in movement spaces, period. Like, than your average Joe on an everyday basis. I'm going to be treated differently. And not to say that it's always better or worse, or anything at all, but just that, in general, the way that we try at least to see each other in movement spaces, because of the entire goal of what the movement spaces are for, right?*

A: I think that's definitely true, that we're all almost hyper-conscious of who we are in relation to each other, and how we want to be treating each other in the future, what we want the world to be looking like, and that means being really inclusive. And it's pretty unique. This was like, out in the middle of the woods, and really engaging in a lifestyle that was almost utopic, or was this—

B: *Yeah, we were trying to actively make the space better, right? We were trying to make that space, like, what we wanted to see, in every way that we possibly could. So, that's just not the norm for everyday. Most people are not trying to make spaces comfortable for everyone else.*

A: And it was a lot of people's first time kind of living in an intentional community like that. And I'm sure you can speak to this, too, but I found that it was really a welcome change for me. I really struggled in academia and having jobs. I've always seen myself as "not functional" or like, not worthy, or I've really internalized a lot of things because of the way I operate in the world. And that is in a world that is, you know, is capitalist and prioritizes—

B: *Productivity.*

A: —getting ahead, and productivity, and there was a pace and an unlearning of urgency. And I just thought that that was a really wonderful learning moment, for me, at least, as a white person coming into this space, and especially as a neurodivergent person, I think it was like, Oh, our way of life is — or the, the society that I've been brought up in, that is not how it needs to be. And this is a very concrete example of things being different.

B: Yeah. No, I remember in my, in my own little head, sometimes I come up with little titles for things. And I remember I was kind of entitling this adventure or whatever, this activism, this whatever, as "The Slow Life." Because I liked it. And I was, it was slow. You know, it wasn't — you weren't so caught up in the hustle-bustle — excuse my language — bullshit.

A: Bullshit.

B: —of every day. You weren't worried about the stuff that society tells you is real, but is undoubtedly just made up by society. Wherever you aren't so constantly worried about all the social rules, you actually can focus on the things that you feel like really matter. And I feel like, within "The Slow Life," you know — I had enough time to process my own internal state. And, I don't know, I completely learned a new way to live, that had never really been an option to me before. Ever. It was always that I had to push myself harder and harder and be stronger, and always just be striving for something different, and never just being, like, okay with where you're at. And I think especially being neurodivergent, personally — I remember telling people there, that it was the first time I ever really started taking care of myself and felt I was able to take care of myself in the ways that I needed to.

A: That's really interesting.

B: Like in a regular society, I have to not only be the breadwinner for myself, but also be the homemaker, right? Within, oh what is it called, the "nuclear family" or whatever, you're literally doing all of it yourself, and you don't have that community to back you up. I have certain things I can't do for myself. But when I was in that community environment, having three meals a day, that were going to be there—

A: That's huge, yeah.

B: And obviously, when it was my turn to help cook, that's great. But, you know, I find myself on lots of days eating once, because I don't have enough strength within myself to do all of it.

A: Yeah, I have the exact same issue.

B: So, the structure of it was really interesting to me, as a neurodiverse person. So there was a lot of things that I just found were like, wow. Life doesn't have to be so hard.

A: I think that's a really good point that I felt, yeah, a lot more *eager* to take care of myself when I knew I was being looked after by others. And could be looking after my comrades in turn. Whereas yeah, I, day-to-day, just do not have it in me necessarily to know what needs to get done and in what order, or where to prioritize things. And it's like, alright, well, the day-to-day, the way of living, the way we are going through the day, that's been pretty much established. And we're doing it all together, and I have everyone's support, and that's really, really meaningful. •

A part of me is still there, at camp, in the woods of northern Minnesota, fighting a pipeline. A part of me always will be…

But I have left, as many did, on to jobs, cities, school, apartments & friends' couches

Not many were still around, when the temperatures dropped & we stayed inside our hallway of a kitchen to sip tea by a giant woodstove with a leaky door

But those who left were still with us, in funny stories, and nostalgia, legal zooms & signatures of camp names locked away in the walls

They were still there & so am I…

> A part of me is still swimming in Red Lake River, when the mussels were alive, and the water reached higher than our ankles, long before the drill ever came near it
>
> A part of me doing the nightly ritual of slapping mosquitos in my tent, that's rolled away somewhere now, waiting for summer
>
> A part of me is chopping wood & frantically dragging around tarps to cover our piles before a rainstorm
>
> A part of me is in Hubbard County Jail, cell B12, glaring at the Bible, refusing to open it
>
> A part of me is perpetually on that stretch of road between camp and the lake that I've walked more times than I can count
>
> A part of me is reading the shitter graffiti, grateful for a moment of solitude in an overflowing camp
>
> A part of me is asleep by the fire, slouched in a camp chair with one of 11 dogs snoring in my lap

A part of me is still there, even though I left

But all of me is still sad & happy & grateful & fucking angry & confused

All of me knows that it's not over

All those parts of me will call me back sooner or later, to keep fighting •

Author's Note: This poem was scrawled on a pillar in the outhouse at Camp Migizi.

Poop Cube Poetry

here   i
empty
   myself.
i   am a
 vessel
   to be
    filled
again and
   again
i let go
 of what
does not
serve me.
and i am
open again
to love
to hot food
to joy
to be filled.
but   to
 receive
these gifts
i must
release
what i
do not need
my waste
is not waste
but   fertile
 earth •

The American Paddlefish is the only confirmed living species in the paddlefish family. Its recognizable ancestor predates the dinosaurs. But now its existence is threatened by shortsighted greed. STOP LINE 3!

AMERICAN PADDLEFISH
(Polyodon spathula)

STAND UP TO ENBRIDGE. STOP LINE 3.

BLANDING'S TURTLE
(Emydoidea blandingii)

"Line 3 was developed and executed with the most state-of-the-art approach to design, construction and environmental management. We're also very proud of the relationship of trust we've built with communities along the right-of-way in both Canada and the United States."

— AL MONACO, ENBRIDGE CEO + PRESIDENT WHO WAS PAID **$17 MILLION** IN 2020 WHILE VIOLATING INDIGENOUS TREATY RIGHTS AND POISONING MINNESOTAN WATER. **STOP LINE 3!**

STOP LINE 3

I hand-made these postcards and sent them to President Biden.

By the summer of 2020, the Line 3 pipeline was in the final year of a long and drawn-out permitting process. This was a crucial moment, when we needed our state agencies to work for us and the environment, not for Enbridge. In August, the Minnesota Department of Commerce, under Governor Tim Walz, had a chance to renew their appeal of Line 3's "Certificate of Need," declaring, as they had all along, that Enbridge had not proven sufficient need in Minnesota for Line 3 oil.

There had already been numerous protests and rallies outside of the Governor's mansion over the years, but with Walz on the fence about taking action, we felt like we needed to escalate. At this time as well, the Sunrise Movement had been employing a tactic of "wide awake" actions — protests outside of prominent politicians' homes in the middle of the night. Drawing on the historical pre-Civil War abolitionist tactic, young people took to the night. With pots and sticks, musical instruments, and anything else that could make a loud noise, they called on their elected officials to take the climate crisis seriously. "If we can't sleep, neither can you." A powerful anthem, building on the stress and anxiety of being a young person in these times.

Seeing the power and strength of these protests, and given the timing, we knew what we had to do. On August 13, we brought together friends, allies, and volunteers, and gathered outside of the Governor's mansion. I remember feeling anxious, as the night was silent but filled with anticipation. Outside of our crowd of young water protectors, not a soul was around. I always tend to feel anxious when a protest is about to start. I held my breath, as our chant lead held up their megaphone.

"WAKE UP WALZ!!!"

A cacophony of sound: people shouting, musical instruments blaring, a drum beating, pots banging, all crashing together in a wave that split the silence in half. The sound continued for a solid minute, as we fully announced our presence to Governor Walz.

Now that the initial anxiety had been released, I went about my duty of keeping watch, both for cops and for disgruntled or angry neighbors. The protest went on, with chants, songs, speeches, and numerous moments of making as much noise as we collectively could. The power of everyone being there, with beautiful banners, music and noise that was both joyous and angry, in a neighborhood that, usually quiet at night, had been forced to wake up, was something I will never forget.

The cops, when they arrived, told us that we could stay a bit longer, but gave us a time after which we had to stop making as much noise. We didn't intend on the protest being an arrestable action, and wanted to make sure that everyone got home safely. So, after hearing from a few more powerful speakers and making as much noise as possible before our time was up, we began to wind down the action. It had been an incredible night of young people coming together and making noise for our future, for protecting water, for treaty rights, and so much more. Before we left, and after the police had at least gone a few blocks away, we all came together one more time to make as much noise as possible, before going our separate ways.

The next week, after a number of other protests and actions had been held outside of the Governor's mansion and numerous emails and phone calls had been made, the Department of Commerce announced that they were renewing their appeal to the PUC's permit approval. •

Megafauna

There were humans I met at camp, there were so many good humans. But there were also so many animals.

I joked often that I was going to start a camp-wide newsletter just to track the goings-on of the animals; now I wish I'd done it. There were puppies (many born at camp), who grew up into dogs, who experienced dog politics (which dog liked who and wanted who dead, which ones kept grudges, which ones were doms versus subs) and dog romances — including, memorably, a lesbian one, when all the female dogs were in heat so the males were kept on leashes, leaving the girls the freedom to hump one another to their hearts' desire. (Sapphic bitches, like many of us.) There were beavers, mostly active at daybreak, which turned the wetland just outside the gate into a magical, mermaidish lagoon. There were chickens and ducks and guinea fowl, and Camp Cats #1-5, some belonging to a person in particular, and others who were collectively cared for, meowing for entrance into as many folks' tents as they pleased. (Proudly polyamorous, also like many of us.) There were chipmunks that bypassed asking for invitations, opting instead to chew their way into tents. There were insects that did the same thing, including a spider we suspected of laying eggs in my neighbor's laundry, moving us to deconstruct their whole tent and shake out every cranny, each spare sock.

But the animals always came back. And we humans are, of course, animals too, large and foolish but animalian nonetheless, which is perhaps our biggest redeeming factor, through all of our many flaws. We couldn't keep out the animals because to do so would be to keep out ourselves. Every effort to do so would, rightfully, fail. Struggling against the pipeline involved unlearning so many different things for me, and a major one was unlearning the distinction between human and animal life. The directive I was confronted with again and again — and keep re-encountering, like a non-binary Sisyphus and their stone — is this: Accept the utter borderlessness between myself and my fellow animal, both human and non-human. The beavers and the forest dykes alike were teaching us the build skills we need to dismantle this false binary of *us* versus *them*, to take down the fences that keep us apart.

So were the ducks, raised from ducklings in the jail support cabin, who in August learned to fly, uncontainable by boxes or sheds.

So was the intrepid bear who sauntered casually into camp one night, all notions of private property be damned, terrifying me and my friend N. as we worked the overnight security shift.

So was the bald eagle who, while I was driving around one very high-stakes morning at sunrise, took flight from the side of the road and promptly nosedived, and would've hit my windshield if I hadn't managed to swerve onto the road's shoulder at the last second, narrowly avoiding being rear-ended by the truck behind me as the enormous bird regained balance and flew away. (This was nearly impossible not to interpret as a sign.)

Such animals brought stark beauty and wildness to even the ugliest man-made situations. "Look around," a teenaged comrade said to me, approximately a half-hour before they became my co-defendant, in a knee-high field at midnight with all the fireflies of Anishinaabe territory above our heads. "Despite all that's going on right now, it's awfully beautiful out here."

Shortly after that, a field mouse inspected me — or perhaps it was a rat, small and pink and fat — during a time when I was immobilized for several hours and thus even happier than usual to receive visitors. I watched them (I don't know their pronouns) in the mechanical sunbeam cast by the flashlight of a cop, a most unwelcome exception to my visitation policy.

I've thought about that mouse-rat a lot since then. I imagine them telling their friends about me, broadcasting it to the rodent public. They seemed to approve of us, at the time. *Go, go,* it felt like they were whispering, with the twitches of their whiskers and the swishes of their tail.

The winds, in times of both staggering heartbreak and panting joy, always seemed to be saying the same thing. •

Words We Said, Things We Felt

I remember shouting at the workers.
Well, some people shouted.
Some people cussed at them, told them off,
tried to make them feel ashamed.
Some people blasted annoying noises,
tried to piss them off.
People did what they needed to do.
We all carried a lot of emotions.
We all wanted the torture of the Earth to stop.

I didn't really shout, to be honest.
Not at the workers anyway.
I remember talking to them though, and singing.
We had a megaphone.
I sang "Wade in the Water"
and "Sittin' on the Dock of the Bay"
but their machines were so loud!
I always wondered if they could even hear us.
So half the time when I was talking and singing, I figured,
I'm really out here talking to myself.
Talking to my comrades.
Talking loud though!

I told the workers that I was Black.
It was one of the first things I said to them,
after my name, and where I was from.
My name is S., I'm from Minneapolis,
and I'm a Black woman.
That's what I would say.
I wanted them to know.

It was another pretty terrible summer in Minneapolis.
It was a year after the murder of George Floyd
but only months after the murder of Daunte Wright.
People were organizing to eliminate the police department.
One organizer was hit by a car and killed,
in a neighborhood not far from where I lived.

I could be back in Minneapolis marching and organizing —
that's what I told the workers.
We are in the middle of a crisis.
Black life is treated like we are dispensable,
and now everyone knows it,
there's no excuse anymore not to know it.

I could be there and my heart aches to be away.
But I choose to be here.
Why?
This pipeline crosses the Mississippi River.
When it spills and poison flows downstream
all the way from here to Louisiana,
which communities do you think are going to suffer?

The fires were so bad over the summer.
It was the drought that did us in.
The Boundary Waters were burning,
and parts of Canada just over the border.
We weren't too far away from there.
Some days, the air was dense and toxic.
People were wearing their COVID masks
outside around the encampment.
It was really hard for asthmatic people.
There were a few days when I really worried
someone would pass out, or be sick.
Later I found out, at least one person did pass out
and someone else got sick.
I told the workers — *when George Floyd said,*
"I can't breathe" he spoke for all of us.
Why are we still mining for oil?!

Later, while talking to the workers,
I would tell them about Jesus.
I figured, they probably already know about him.
I told them, *Water is sacred in every culture and religion around the world —*
Every language in the world has a word for Water.
I wanted them to understand,
why do we care so much about the Water?
And sometimes I saw them watching me and listening.
I loved those moments when I knew we'd connected.
I think talking about baptism helped with that.

We kept thinking that we'd win the workers over,
that they'd stage a walk-out,
that they'd call in sick en masse,
that they'd slow down work on their end.
I don't know that any of those things happened.
They weren't allowed to talk to us,
so I really don't know.
I *do* know that the pipeline finished being built.
I *do* know that workers need work.
I do know that many of us live lives where we are trapped,

or feel trapped, stuck —
like my friends who wished they could be on the frontline,
but just "couldn't get away" —
maybe these workers couldn't get away either.
Apparently Enbridge hired a bunch of Native workers,
so that they could say, "This project has Native support.
Look at the demographics of our team."

It was disgusting, the lengths they'd go to divide and manipulate us.
The many-headed monster.
You cut off one head and it grows two more.
The Windigo, who is always hungry,
so hungry he devours his own people.
How do you kill such a beast?
There are Anishinaabe stories that aren't for me to tell,
but I'll tell you my own opinion about the many-headed monster.
It goes down in one of three ways —

1. At the heart,
2. From the inside,
3. Through a slow, starved death.

Maybe we didn't stop this pipeline.
Not yet anyway.
But I know we hit the monster in its heart.
And I know one day it's going down. •

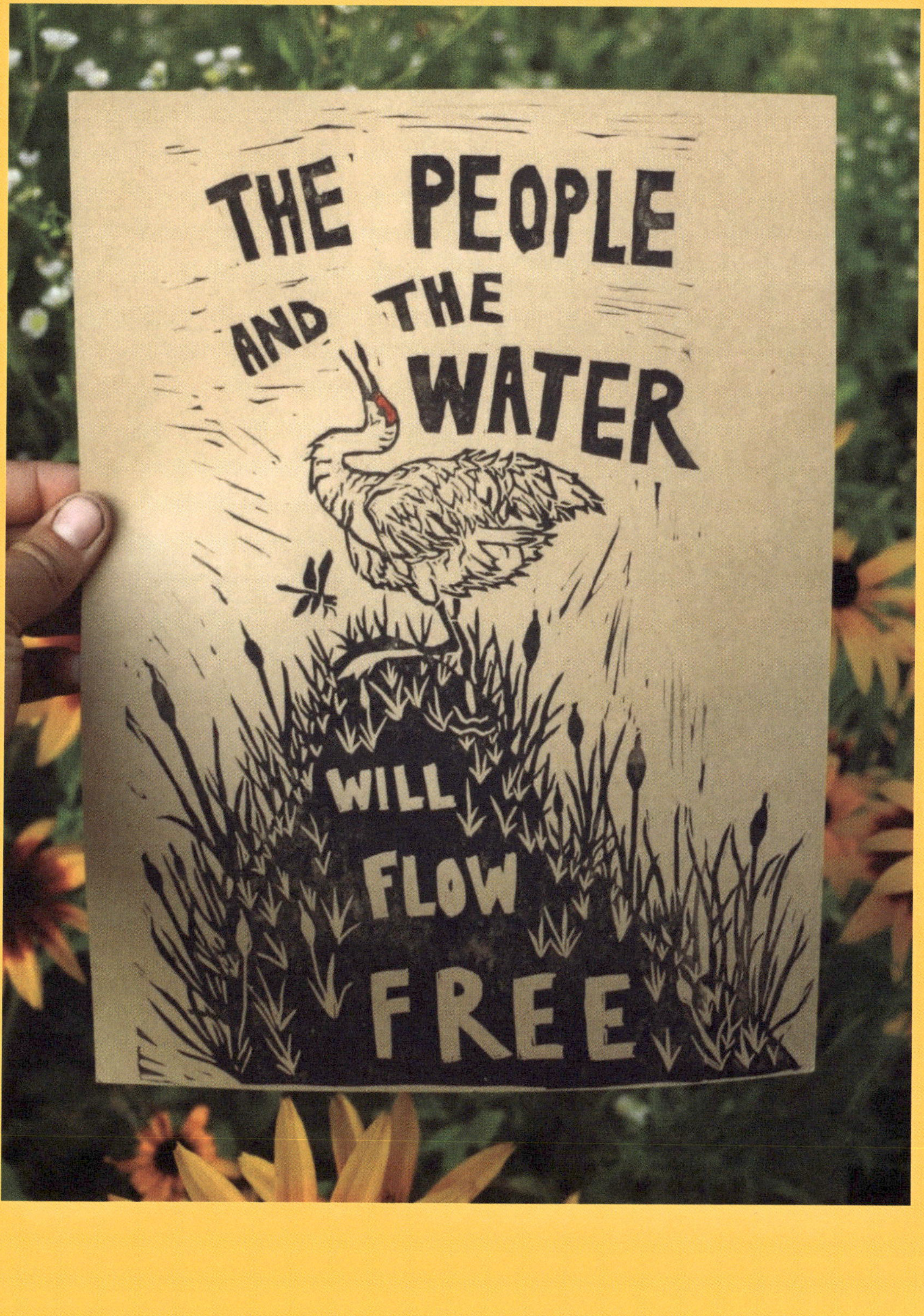
THE PEOPLE
AND THE
WATER
WILL
FLOW
FREE

My entry into the movement to Stop Line 3 began at an evidentiary hearing in St. Paul. My friend and I walked into a massive room downtown that was filled with people, some holding blue squares of fabric, others wearing neon pro-Line 3 t-shirts. I had no idea what to expect. I had read some staggering facts about the climate impact, environmental destruction, and cultural harm that this pipeline posed, but the testimonials I heard that day made it real. When someone's words resonated with the crowd, people's hands shot up, twirling those squares of blue fabric in silent solidarity. After a while, one of the organizers I knew came to me in the aisle and asked if my friend and I would give testimony. Nerves sprung from my gut — what could I add to the record? How could I match the passionate, educated testimonies I'd heard so far? In that moment, I had to identify my stake in the matter. Keep it simple, tell my story. Eventually my name got called from the lottery system, and I anxiously approached the judge. I told her how I was a food educator. How tomorrow morning I was going to cook wild rice with a classroom of second graders and watch them discover this important food. I told her about the 20 wild rice lakes that lie within one mile of the proposed pipeline route and the high probability of small, medium, and catastrophic oil spills. How this pipeline violated the 1855 Treaty that guarantees members of many Indigenous nations in Minnesota the right to harvest wild rice from these lakes. I ended by saying, "Judge, I urge you to deny Line 3 so that I can tell my students tomorrow that Minnesota's lands and waters will survive into their future."

I turned back to my seat and was greeted with a sea of support as blue swatches danced around the room. This community embraced me, and I suddenly felt part of something much bigger than myself. Then I heard the next name get called, my friend was up next! What were the odds? She joined me at the podium and instead of speaking more words into the record, we sang. We sang Mountain Song by Holly Near, a song originally written in resistance to mountain top removal. "You may drive a big machine, but I was born a great big woman. And you can't just take my dreams away. Not with me watching."

Creativity was the stream running through my experience in the stop Line 3 movement. Whether it was an art build or a march carrying Sandy the Loon or a banner drop over a highway bridge or a Musicians Rising for Climate Justice concert — we showed up with art. With our hearts on our sleeves. The world we were building took shape and color in the screen printed t-shirts, the large pledge of resistance, the videography, and the music. This was a movement in stark contrast to the corporate funded efforts behind Line 3 construction, who in one case paid some teenagers to wear pro-Line 3 shirts and sit in some of the limited spots at the Public Utilities Commission hearings.

At the same time as we were resisting a world that chose profits over people and ignored the growing climate crisis, we were also building the foundation for a better one. We practiced at community organizing — listening to each other, gathering around food, calling upon each other's strengths, researching and constantly educating ourselves, getting fed up and frustrated with each other, overstepping, apologizing, then coming back together and starting again.

All the while, using art to express our anger, expose injustice, and celebrate. Once during the Block (Line 3) Party outside of the Public Utilities Commission, where we occupied the block for the weekend leading up to their decision — we held a concert. Four artists took to the stage to fill that corner of downtown St. Paul with their song and their messages of solidarity. During Annie Humphrey's set, it started to pour. At first, we stood with shoulders hunched in resistance to the water dripping down our backs, nowhere to take cover in this concrete covered block. But then, gradually, we let it soak in. Relaxed our shoulders. Lifted our faces. And started dancing. •

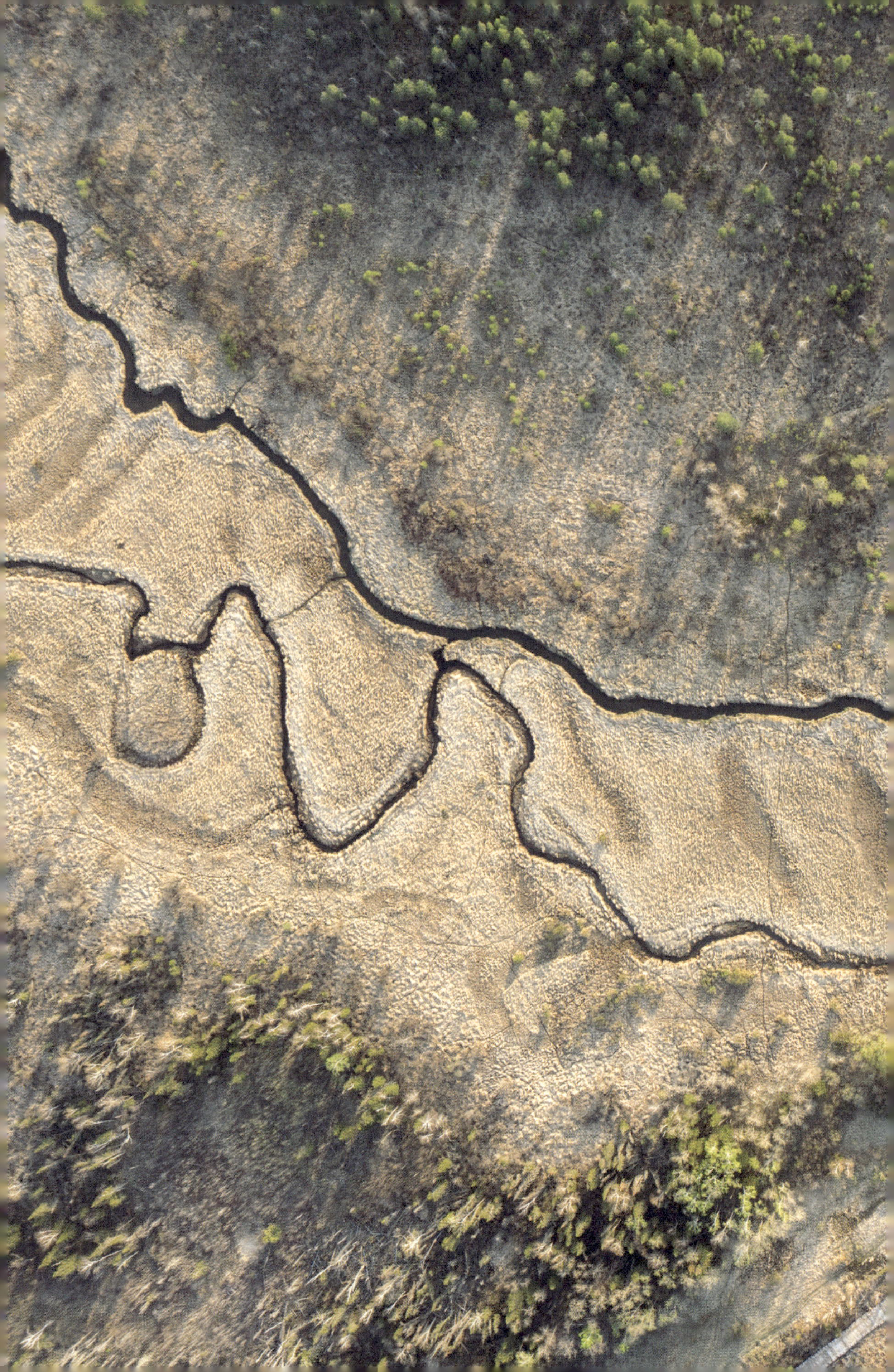

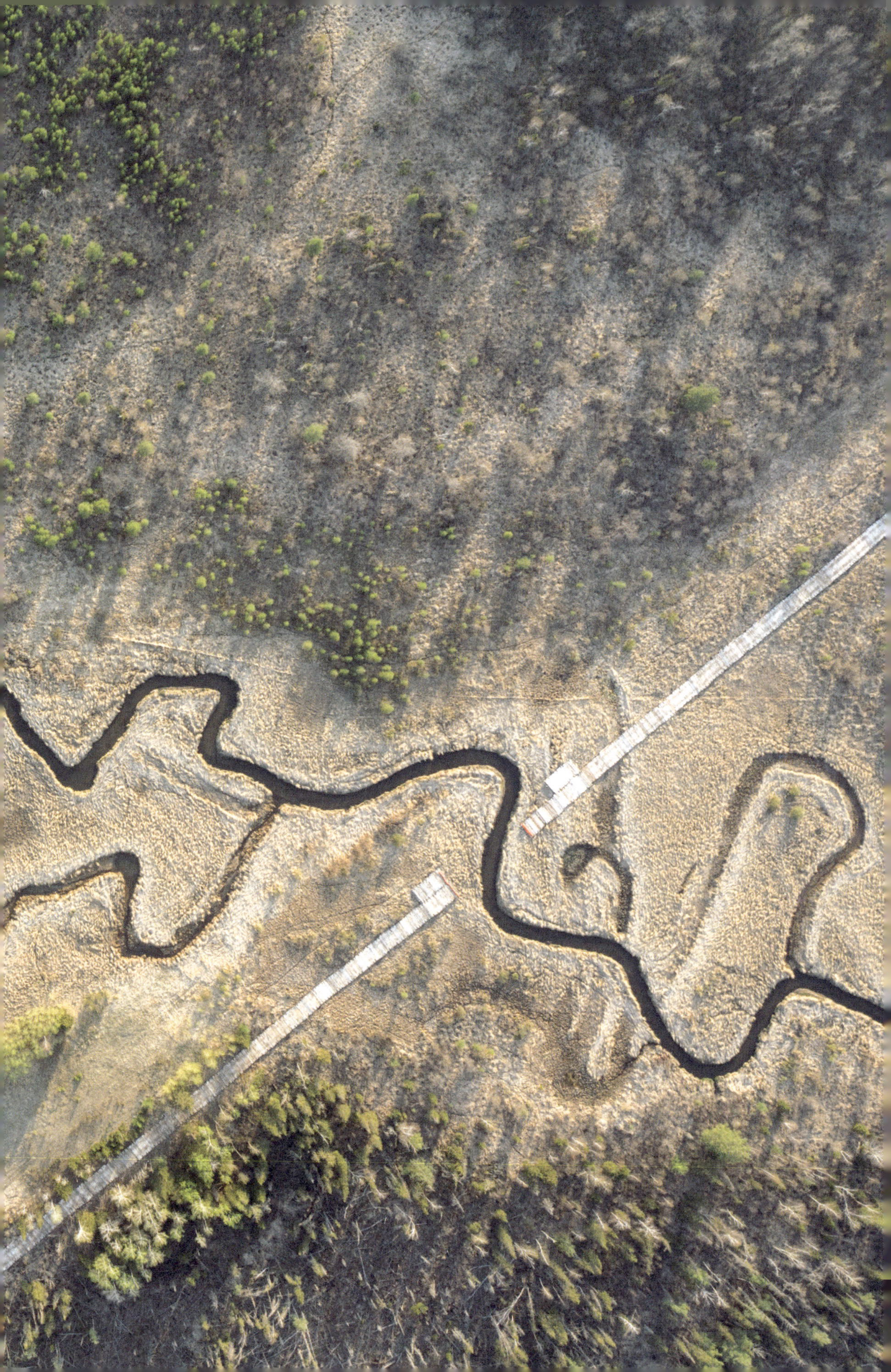

I drove around the circumference of the earth to stop Line 3.

Well, not really. I *did* drive over 24,901 miles, but we didn't stop Line 3.

I'd drive between the cities and the pipeline route.

I'd drive from Duluth out to the river crossings.

I'd drive to jails to pick up our friends, and I'd drive to camp to drop off groceries.

I'd load up my car with art or speakers or a megaphone or zines, and drive to the Governor's Mansion, to the Capitol, to the Governor's Mansion, to the Public Utilities Commission, to the Governor's Mansion, to the Army Corps of Engineers, and back to the Governor's Mansion. Again.

Every five days or so we'd drive to the Duluth Entertainment Convention Center for COVID tests, and then go back every time friends were released from jail.

Once, I took a nine-hour road trip by myself around southern Minnesota delivering Stop Line 3 lawn signs.

Another day, I woke up early, well before the sun, and drove with friends out to Floodwood to meet a group that had driven up from the cities that morning for an action. We collected their jail support forms, handed out sharpies. We described how they would drive, where they could park. We left to drop off the forms and on the drive the sun started to rise. On that cold December morning, all of the tree branches and tall grasses were coated with hoarfrost. The world glittered and sparkled against a pale blue sky. Thin, wispy clouds hung low, suspended in the air only feet above the lakes we passed.

During the Treaty People Gathering, I drove from White Earth to Aitkin County to jail watch, because no one could tell me for sure if anyone was there. When I arrived, there were at least 10 people. They were laying out on picnic blankets, sharing snacks, waiting for friends to be released. I said Hi, made sure they had paper copies of the outtake form, and turned around and headed back; there was lots to do at camp. On the drive, I stopped to cool off in the Crow Wing River. After, as I dried off in the sun, two of my friends pulled into the little parking area. They were on their own driving odyssey, wrapping up tasks some different 150 miles apart, and our paths just happened to intersect.

Sometimes, I drove by myself and sometimes I drove with friends. Sometimes, I drove with strangers and sometimes I drove with people I really don't like that much.

I cried in the car. I laughed in the car. I felt deep, searing regret and terror about things I'd committed to doing while on the road to start them.

Once, I drove by a horse-drawn carriage trotting along on the shoulder of the road.

I struggled to start other people's cars, loaded concrete into a U-Haul, and returned a van to Fargo.

I took calls from the car. I facilitated zoom meetings from the backseat. I called friends on long drives and checked in with my public defender on a short one. Once, we tried to take a meeting from the car, but the rain was so loud on the roof that no one could hear us.

One afternoon, I drove with several thousand dollars of bail money in the glove box and couldn't help checking every so often to make sure it was still there.

I got pulled over for speeding with 50 copies of "A Tilted Guide to Being a Defendant" piled up in the backseats. Then, I got pulled over for speeding in nearly the same spot three months later.

I tailed pipe trucks and Horizontal Directional Drill bits and once, on a particularly weary day, I even followed a truck carrying equipment that ended up having nothing to do with pipeline construction.

I often questioned whether a particular drive made sense. "Wait, why are we taking three cars to the same place?" Or, "What if we get there and they've already left?" Or, "Do we even think this action makes sense?"

I probably don't need to tell you this. You probably spent days and days driving too, worrying about your friends, getting lost, getting tired, feeling hopeful, feeling free. I know that you, too, were willing to try almost anything to stop Line 3, and when they're building a pipeline across 300 miles, in dozens of places all at once, sometimes that means just driving. •

Editors' Note: This story was developed from social media posts. They have been compiled and edited in collaboration with the author.

What does it mean to be a leader? How do I take care of myself, while taking care of my community, and raising children? While I myself am terrified, I worry more for all the people who believe in me, follow me, and are willing to run into battle alongside me. The sound of drumming is constantly in the background, along with soft snores from my friends. I am awake. Others are ready to keep myself and others safe. I say a silent prayer for all our loved ones who have fought. Anger at our elected officials rises, but even more so, so do we. The people are rising, from all walks of life. Every day, I question whether I am doing enough. As a leader, I take it as a personal responsibility to make sure all these people feel loved, uplifted, empowered, and supported. We greet each day again. We are still here.

While others are born into a family, I built a community for myself. The people around me, fighting, are my family. The screams from my community during any arrest haunts me, their cries for help as our beloved medics clean mace out of their eyes, their coughs as the air filled with liquid fire, the look in their eyes as police lift automatics full of less than lethals. I hold no fear of the pipeline itself or even the police and their violence. I fear failing all of the people I love. I often struggle to hold down my breakfast, trying to stay strong for all of them. My stomach churns with the sounds of my community's screams echoing in my head. The bonds we've built in the short time I have known these people, the trust we built being side by side fighting. All of these beautiful, amazing people who have taught me so much. This is me. I stem from the great love that I hold for my community. I stem from the love that is in my DNA.

> *We are a generation of Water Protectors, Land Defenders, and Treaty Enforcers. We are a generation of change, and we are raising generations after us to be the same.*

The rivers need you. They need me. They need us. As a community. I always thought they wouldn't do this, that they wouldn't get this far. The fact of treaties and ancestors and trees and rice and water wouldn't let them do this. The rivers need us. This fight has put me beyond my limits, past my comfort zone. While existing in this fight has come with challenges, women and children have always existed on the Frontline of social change. We are a generation of Water Protectors, Land Defenders, and Treaty Enforcers. We are a generation of change, and we are raising generations after us to be the same. The rivers need you. The rivers and I are grounded in the love for community. For children. We have not stopped. That will never stop. •

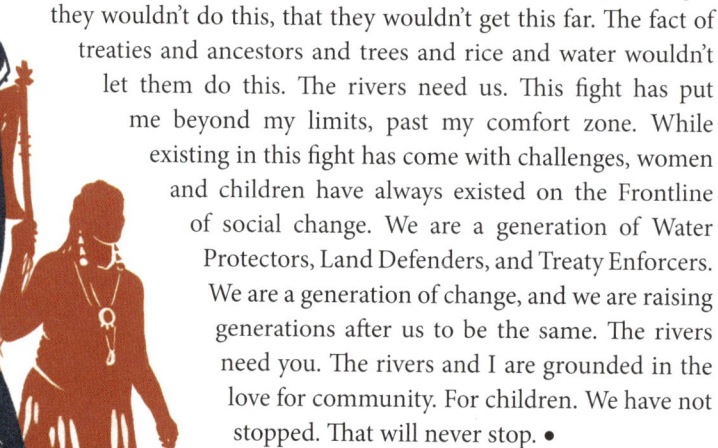

When I got out of jail, I laid down on the ground. I had already been at the end of my rope when they first put me in the cell: low on food, low on sleep, and running on a wave of raw adrenaline that quickly dissolved into listlessness. Jail is designed to break your willpower, and mine was in a position to be easily broken. So it wasn't until I laid down on the ground that I realized I had spent 24 hours without considering the sensation of porous earth under my body, or the wind against my skin. I tend to fixate on things, and I hadn't been fixating on the things that give me life. Comrades from the movement were waiting outside the jail to greet me, and one of them asked me, "Did you hear the storm?" At first I was confused, because I hadn't: the sun was out and the ground below me was dry, just as it had been when I went inside. "It was like nothing I'd ever seen," they went on. "Huge trees blew down. There was lightning in the sky every second." I looked up at the brick wall of the jail, envisioning the rain coursing against it, as if trying to wear it down. "There were so many birds in the sky before the storm. We saw a flock of sandhill cranes on the way back from the action. I heard one group saw an owl. "They continued, naming a whole flood of birds, the mental image of each type of bird unlocking a new emotion in my body. I broke down crying. The world was so large, and we were working for it and with it, and it was still here. •

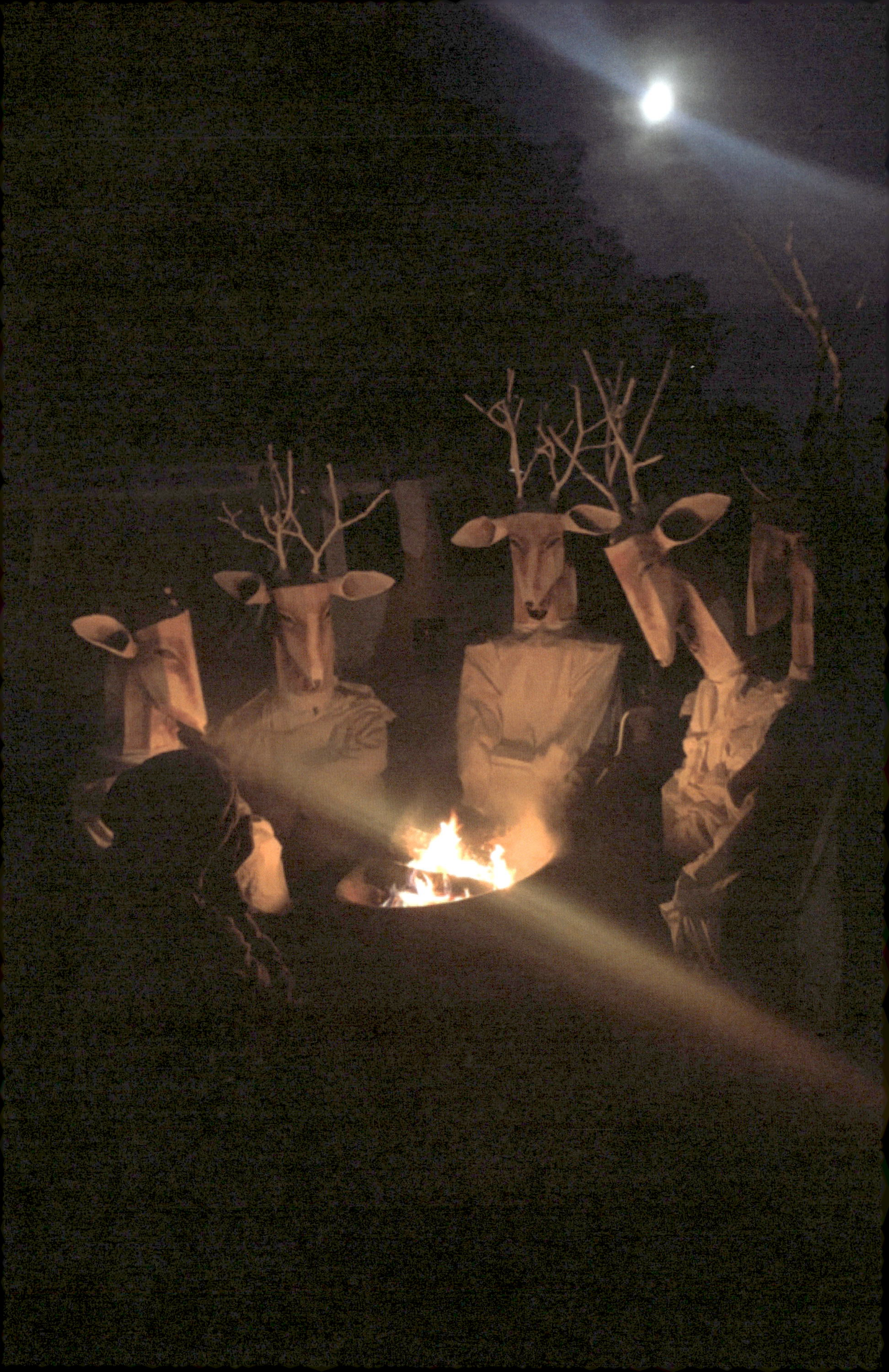

This story takes place at the Welcome Water Protector Center on a beautiful June night. The moon was full and the drilling had been going on under the Mississippi River for days. We had been giving it our all, day and night, for weeks. As we gathered around a roadside fire, suddenly the deer puppets who had made their debut for our winter solstice were coming out of camp one by one. As the deer continued to gather around the fire, I talked them into frolicking down the roadside to where the cops had been staged. At this point, the cops had been staged at the drill site for weeks, 24/7, cops from counties all over the state. We began our pursuit up the road to where the cops were. We were weaving in and out of the ditch and along the shoulder of the road right up to the cop cars, all under the moonlit night. The cops drove off, back and forth a few times on the road as we continued to frolic around the roadside. One last loop from a cop car and our night watch didn't see the cops again all night. It felt so good to laugh and be free in that moment, surrounded with the love for the water and each other.

I was born into a family of Norwegian immigrants. In 1899, my great grandfather was a drover and came from Norway to the Upper Mississippi to build a stable of strong horses to work in the logging camps. I grew up with three brothers in South Minneapolis and celebrated my 50th high school reunion in 2022. Now I live on Dakota Land in Winona County.

I was always an outdoor person; I loved to fish, camp, hike and collect rocks, bugs, and fossils. I went to college at the University of Minnesota and I became a geologist. Now, I think that I know a lot about Minnesota rocks and water, but it was not until last year that I learned from Water Protectors about the culture and true spirit of water.

As a scientist, I'm trained to focus on measurement, repeated observation, and on developing and testing theories to discover truth about water. But I always felt that this really is not enough to actually understand water. I want to know more about the space between hydrology and life, the spaces filled with ecosystems, culture, and emotion. Unfortunately, the heritage of water was rarely on my radar.

I'm almost 70 years old and I'm starting to learn water's spirit from elders and from Water Protectors who were standing up for their heritage in opposition to Line 3. Last year, I was drawn to the spirit of water from the disastrous Line 3 Clearbrook aquifer rupture. I got more than I bargained for when an Anishinaabe elder taught me to see my reflection in still water and to start listening to the songs and prayers radiating from moving water. I learned to hear the silence of still water.

Last September, an Anishinaabe friend from White Earth shared a news release from the MNDNR announcing an enforcement action and restoration order for unconfined flow of an aquifer caused by Enbridge and their contractors. The pipeline trench approaching the Clearbrook terminal was dug too deep and ruptured an artesian aquifer near Clearbrook in the headwaters of the Red River of the North, just a few miles from the Mississippi headwaters. The Clearbrook aquifer was in the middle of ceded Territory, the legendary land where the Water Protectors teach us about Manoomin, the food that grows on the water.

With my hydrology experience, I understood the magnitude of the aquifer rupture right away. Artesian pressure from 30-feet deep that rises nine feet above the ground is a powerful force that is hard to control. Capped by glacial till, the deeper outwash aquifer is recharged miles away at a higher elevation pushing millions of gallons a day through the new excavation.

It was below zero in January 2021 when the worksite turned to quicksand and the water filled the surrounding wetlands and flooded the woods around Clearbrook. The new spring coming from the pipeline trench formed a new stream and was dewatering the aquifer without any attempts by Enbridge or the State to stop the flow.

As a geologist, I could calculate the flow, map the discharge, and calculate the risk to the aquifer and nearby fens, but I didn't understand the human dimension of an aquifer rupture. I knew nothing of Anishinaabe heritage and water culture. As I was writing my assessment to share with the environmental community, I had more questions.

I wanted to know if Clearbrook fens and natural springs were sacred. Was a new spring a threat? Was the water itself sacred? And were the springs around Clearbrook on hallowed ground?

It took the patient wisdom of ages shared by Indigenous movement leaders for me to start to learn the true importance of water. It took the hubris of Enbridge on Line 3 for me to see how persistent colonialism exploits our most precious resources and the people who protect the water. My life is enriched with the knowledge that ancient wisdom still works today. •

Editors' Note: This story was developed from an interview. It has been excerpted and edited in collaboration with the interviewee.

So, there's all this colonization saying that everything's fine, but I don't live in that kind of world. That's ridiculous. I live in a world where we look at trees not just as a product, or this wild rice as a product or this maple syrup as a product. All the plants are food or medicine. That's how we look at them. They're beings, they have a gift for us. And then at the same time, we respect them, too. How would you feel if, you know, someone was like, "How can I use this?" about you? But this is my grandpa. These trees, this water, are my grandpas. So if I looked at my grandpa and just looked at him like he was nothing, he'd feel bad. He'd feel bad for me. There's a way to look at everything. So that's why it's so important for me to keep going, because other people don't see that. They see the money. They've been brought up in a world of greed.

When I was 9 years old, our house burned up and we moved into a teepee, out in the woods. So being on the side of a lake, I got to hear all the water birds, got to catch and see and eat all the fish and deer and rabbits and everything. Turtle soup.

That was the thing, too, when you're a kid, you don't really get to go out. So being in the woods and on the lake, and then watching everybody unload their canoes, and see all the different styles of their knockers that they use to reach out and pull the rice into the boat. And then the different kinds for the different kinds of lakes, because eventually you got to go to different lakes here and there and everywhere. Some years the rice wasn't on this lake because it takes the perfect weather to make that one seed grow, and that's all over the lake. Sometimes some lakes, they just don't produce. The plant doesn't come up. But next year it will be just cool again.

Then there's a little trick to being out there. That's why they don't let us go out when we're young. If the rice is laying a certain way, we go sideways, diagonal through it. We never go against it, break it, because on the head of that rice where all the little seeds are lined up they ripen at different times. So you could go through a trail, and then three days later come back and get the same amount of rice. But if you break that plant, it's not going to come back. You're not going to get that. It might not ripen. He just said no.

I was always on the lake. I know how a boat moves and canoe moves, and then I made my own poles because my great-grandpa, he made bridges, canoes, different kinds of baskets. He grew up and then he was so old. When my dad was growing up, the elders said that he was an old man when they were kids.

So I'm very fortunate to be able to go out and do all these things, to know that I'm doing all these things that my great-grandfather did in the same area. We got wild plants everywhere. We got teepee grounds and different lodges in our yard. They're all for specific reasons. In between all our trails is food, medicine. That's what we have. I get to take my grandchildren and go out in the woods, and they harvest their food, medicine, and the plants.

Here, when they come to Line 3, they're coming from way up there where the tar sands is. Right around Alberta. They're just totally surrounded there. I feel so bad. Like right now there's people still going with that whole oil thing, trying to work for them and stuff like that. Feel bad for them because they're just not awoke yet. People need to see the devastation they've done.

They're trying to still keep it quiet about them hitting the aquifer right by our wild rice lake. And that's what we were there telling them the whole time. They don't care. And what did they do? They hit the aquifer. There's millions of gallons of ice cold water coming out of the ground which wasn't supposed to be up for 1,000 years or whatever. Right? It's changing the temperature right next to one of our wild rice lakes. Hopefully, best case would be that the water is moving a different way. But if it changes the temperature, it's going to take out that whole lake. Because, it's got to be just right for each seed to take off.

So that's really sad. If you went to each lake and studied them, you'd find out that their DNA is different. Everyone is its own being. It's like it's alive. And it's really funny that I have to say it. It's like it's alive. It is! We know that. But society doesn't look at it that way then. We already know that. We understand that. It's like we knew that the water was alive. We've been telling them for years. 20, 30, 40 years ago, the water is alive. Okay, now you're catching on. Some people catch on slow.

My grandfather taught me, and I am teaching my grandchildren, to notice the little animals that live by the clean water, the turtles off to the side over here. That's how you know there's clean water. Then to watch, look at the plants around the spring. That's how you find them. People don't know that. They're like, how do you find them? You got to look at the plants. If there's a plant that loves clean water, there it is coming out of the middle.

So it's easy to do a part, but then to look at not only Line 3, now we're going into Line 5, which is just a continuation of Line 3. Already there's a bunch of grandmas doing treaty walks. I went to go check on them because here I am again. That's all our territory, and then those are our elders. So I figured I'd better get over there. •

WE ARE HERE TO PROTECT THE WATER
STOP LINE 3
PROTECT WATER
WALZ
YOU CAN'T BE CARBON 0 & A PIPELINE HERO
STOP LINE 3
TAR SANDS PIPELINE
PROTECT
CLIMATE • WATER • TREATIES
CUT OFF

WE ARE HERE TO PROTECT THE WATER
PROTECT MISSISSIPPI
WE ARE HERE TO PROTECT THE WATER
STOP LINE 3
YOUR
IS
PROTECT WATER
HONOR TREATIES
STOP LINE 3
STOP
HEAD OF
LINE 3
SNAKE

On This Land Where We Belong

When I learned in 2018 that a tar sands oil pipeline would be built across the Mississippi River just upstream from my hometown, I got into a car with my two young children and drove to northern Minnesota. I needed to see the exact place where they intended to lay pipe, so we followed the Great River Road from Minneapolis toward the spot designated by coordinates on a construction map: the Line 3 Mississippi River crossing. Here, the permits said a Canadian company could drill beneath the water that sustains us, creating what some have called a climate time bomb.

We stood along the roadside, soaking in the sounds, smells, and sights of riverine forests and wetlands. There was a single utility flag in the ditch — a small splash of orange against the lush green of summer, marking the place for destruction.

—

One of the most important things I've learned from my relationships with Indigenous people here in the occupied Dakota and Anishinaabe territories known as Minnesota is the importance of kinship to world-making.

Minnesota is a name derived from the Dakota word for water, *Mni*. Many people believe Minnesota means "the land of sky blue waters," but a more accurate translation is "land where the water reflects the sky." Even our colonial place-names reflect our broken relationships, exposing just how limited our understanding is of what it means to live in place.

To Dakota people, water is not just a resource to be extracted or managed. Water is a relative. To Anishinaabeg, land is not just property that can be bought, sold, or taken from. Earth and all the beings who reside here together are kin.

That kinship is not metaphorical.

I would never say that my mother, my daughter, or my brother are only symbolically connected. We recognize bloodlines, genetic codes, the ways we've nourished and guided each other, and the memories we carry between generations, some of them held deep within our bodies. We are family, capable of loving and caring for one another. Capable of keeping each other alive.

Making kin with place means widening the circle.

—

When I moved back to Palisade in 2020, I moved to an 80-acre parcel of land that had been purchased by Akiing, an Indigenous land trust and community development initiative aimed at restoring an economy rooted in Anishinaabe culture.

I am not Anishinaabe. My people came to this place from northern and eastern Europe, part of a process of colonization that is still underway. We brought with us ideas of property and control that have irrevocably altered the landscape.

Akiing is an Anishinaabe word that means "the land to which the people belong," and last summer, this place became my home and studio. I brought with me questions about what it means to be a non-Native person living and creating from inside an Indigenous Land Back movement.

Akiing sits adjacent to the corridor where the Line 3 oil pipeline is being built across the Mississippi. Two miles away, the pipeline also crosses the Willow River on the very homestead where my grandmother was born 90 years ago.

—

"It's not just a responsibility to protect this place that keeps me standing here," a friend said to me recently. He was reflecting on time he'd recently spent in jail for trespassing on land that had been stolen from his people. "It's still a privilege to be here, resisting further destruction."

> *It's not just a responsibility to protect this place that keeps me standing here. It's still a privilege to be here, resisting further destruction.*

I'll carry his words with me now as a reminder: That kinship, belonging, and taking action out of love are all part of a creative process that's been underway for a very long time. That there is still so much to protect.

That we are the ones who've been called here for that purpose. •

I remember spending all day and night outside of a jail where our friends were held captive by the state. When they were released, there was a beautiful thunderstorm as we drove them home to camp. We spent the entire afternoon running through puddles, slip & slidin' and mud wrestling. It was such extreme heaviness followed by such incredible joy. Living on the frontlines felt like a microcosm of the future, a glimpse into what we all had been fighting for. It was the reason we slept on the jailhouse lawn, the reason we had mud in our underwear, the reason we lived outside, the reason we sang karaoke, the reason we risked everything. We showed ourselves what a world without the State could begin to feel like. •

Editors' Note: This is a compilation of several people's reflections on experiences of gender and queerness in the movement to stop Line 3. Some pieces were submitted in written form and others were excerpted from interviews.

By the time I came to the frontline, I had already worn dresses & makeup once or twice, but it wasn't right. Being there, I saw a kind of womanhood that felt natural within myself for the first time. Maybe others were looking for something similar inside themselves too. Maybe that's also part of why we came. Being Genderqueer is about building a new world within the shell of the old, after all.

—

Why do you think so many genderqueer folks showed up for this movement?

Because I feel like they are also highly oppressed and marginalized, and they understand what physical violence, what bias, what stereotypes — and how those work in social systems — do or have done to their communities and how that's impacted their sense of quality of life, and how to move safely in the world. So it could just be, you know, that at least in the genderqueer folks that I've grown up with since childhood, I think we tend to be more sensitive to our environments for whatever reason. So, we can't ignore harm when it happens. It's such a big, profound experience in our bodies, that either we succumb to it, which for a lot of people has actually looked like self-harm, or, you know, the, the unspoken, which is suicide. Or we become very active and proactive in trying to do something about the situation. And that looks like showing up to a resistance camp.

—

I was questioning when I went out to Red Lake Treaty Camp, and when surrounded by all of the love and support of my queer, trans, 2s siblings I felt a sense of community and home I never had before. I befriended many other trans, non-binary, and 2s individuals and had several enlightening conversations about gender identity and sexuality. I think the added plus of having camp names was exploring the idea of having a chosen name rather than my given one. A lot of my comrades at camp were very respectful of pronouns and gender neutral language as well, which made me feel incredibly safe. I went to camp a questioning cis person and left feeling more safe to accept my genderfluid identity that I've been hiding.

—

To quote a movement lawyer, "Camp names did very little to protect people's identities and a lot for everyone's gender euphoria."

—

I'm not sure if I have a *story* but certain spaces weren't very welcoming to trans folks. Mine and other homies' pronouns weren't used or were hardly used at all. It was usually people older than us, and we kind of gave up explaining pronouns and why we needed folks to use them and ended up just accepting folks' misgendering us. It didn't feel great and made it super difficult to connect with the folks we were camping with. There were never group discussions with organizers about expectations at camp (no racism, homophobia, transphobia here, respect, etc.). It didn't seem important to elders to help start discussions about it either. It kind of felt like we just had to set those needs aside because we came there for a different reason anyways.

—

My name is Mx. S. I am a disabled, non-binary, queer, survivor, descendant of settlers and Turtle Island ancestors. My gender identity has definitely evolved over the time resisting Line 3. I was AFAB (Assigned Female at Birth), and for the entire 30 years I've been in this body, people have questioned and misgendered me.

Witnessing LGBTQ+ community showing up for water, land, four & two legged rights, in such a clear, confident and thoughtful way has taught me invaluable lessons about connection, authenticity, strength, community and responsibility.

Witnessing that I am not alone has given me reassurance, and with that, a bit of confidence, to allow myself to move towards authenticity, as the hetero-normative, cis-white supremacy system in place makes it so difficult to remember that that is the best way to show up.

I feel grateful to witness such movement towards authenticity in our true state of being the environment we are protecting.

—

I brought my dad to Treaty People Gathering. I think that was one of the first spaces that my dad has been in at this point in his life that was so queer in a way that really shook his understandings of things. Specifically, one of my friends who I think was doing jail support at the time, walks up to my dad with like, long hair, facial hair, wearing a skirt, wearing earrings. And this person, you know, introduced themselves with their ridiculous action name. Afterwards, when my dad was trying to talk about people there, he would just switch over to they/them pronouns for most people, because he wasn't sure. When we left (I think) he just understood binaries differently. And why people choose to dress in certain ways and present themselves in certain ways, sometimes to even be intentionally confusing to people. And I thought that was really, really beautiful.

—

The Migizi space was established as a very genderqueer, trans-friendly space early on, and I know that that kind of drew people in, into Indigeneity. That's also a theme, right? That we have been genderqueer for centuries. And, of course, that was illegal. And that was taken away from us, when all of our cultures and traditions and dances were made illegal, and yet, it's a strong, strongly rooted component of being an Indigenous person is that you're not defined by your sexuality. You know, you can be whatever the fuck you want to be. Just show up in community. And show up safely. That's where the impetus is put. So, I think it was a place for people to do that learning, and to experience even, you know, femme-bodied Two-Spirits, in positions of leadership, was profound for people, and also maybe off-putting, and very hard to swallow in terms of like, where they're used to coming into social navigation with and how to be and how to act. It's not very often that we see, you know, femme bodies making calls and taking leadership roles. So, I think that that's part of what was attractive about the Line 3 fight was that every camp was run by matriarchs that had established themselves in this work. And that the space that I was in specifically had established itself as a place where you could come and be safe. Being whatever you are — it didn't matter. We were just happy to have bodies there that would help us fight for Mother Earth.

—

At camp, I had access to a mirror in exactly three places. One of those places was the camera on my phone, which was nearly always dead. The second was mounted on the exterior of a tiny house along the road to the outer parking lot, where I sometimes glanced at myself while passing by and started from my lack of recognizability. The third was the rearview mirror of my car, where I occasionally sat for a half-hour or so on some of those interminable summer afternoons, baptizing myself in the A/C & tweezing my eyebrows. Later in the summer, I stopped tweezing my eyebrows, around the same time that I came to believe in my body what I had long known in my mind: That my appearance, and specifically how closely my appearance hewed to what a "girl" / AFAB was *supposed* to look like, was the least interesting thing about me. And ditto for other people. Genderqueer bodies and faces of comrades became almost indescribably gorgeous to me, both before & after they let lakewater clear away the thick layer of sweat and grit we were all always caked with. I haven't tweezed my eyebrows since. I wear mostly boy clothes now, or as I like to call them, clothes.

—

I remember when the drag show direct action happened, and everybody who I was at camp with was like, *Oh my god*. That came at a point in the summer, early fall, when the construction, all of the drilling was done, and it was really hard to not despair, it was really hard to not find yourself just crumbling under, like, the reality of that. And yet this gorgeous act of resistance and gender fuckery was emerging out of that experience. And it really had me reflect on the way that you know, gender play, gender expansiveness was so present to me in every corner of this movement, in every community, every sub-community that I was even just a visitor in.

—

Witnessing a runway drag show blocking the driveway of a pump station for the pipeline was absolutely revolutionary for me in recognizing the unstoppable power of queer glamor. •

166

This image was taken July 25, 2021, on the Red Lake River next to the Red Lake Treaty Camp. Following the summer's heatwave, we saw a massive die-out of the freshwater mussel population. For several days, shells and mussel flesh floated down the river, and immediately afterward, the water turned murky. These mollusks were responsible for keeping the water of the Red Lake River clean and filtered, and after their mass death, the health of the entire river ecosystem began to decline. This stretch of the Red Lake River is where we held ceremony, swam, played, and fished for dinner. It provided physical and emotional respite from the hot and grueling days of living next to an active Enbridge drillsite. We took water samples and canoed up and down the river to watch for frac-outs as 50 feet away, the HDD drilled the longest river crossing of Line 3. In an act of mourning, we collected and assembled these sun-bleached shells on one of our river rafts. In doing so, we were able to document the clear message this die-out sent: climate change is now.

In December 2020, actions popped off. A tree sit went up, and our friends went cold. A groundswell of emotions, logistics, media, and frantic energy surfaced, and suddenly everyone I knew wanted a piece of it. As a chronically ill member of the resistance community, I couldn't join in on roughing it in the snow like I had in the past. I needed to find new ways to engage.

Being present and connected within my own network felt like a good place to start for me, yet it felt clear that we would need the community to grow exponentially: we needed infrastructure for a mass movement. I witnessed the messy assemblage of group chats, rideshares, and cliques — beautifully decentralized, held together by trust, but with a limited capacity. By February, teams of people who had a wide variety of community connections, virtual presence, and shared fluency in digital organizing came together.

Our goal was to find a way to balance mass movement building with the security culture necessary for direct action. We formed small groups that collaborated on different elements of a broader strategy. My group worked to develop curriculum and launch frontline orientation calls — it felt great to contribute! It was exciting to bring something new into existence, and also nerve wracking to wonder if our new systems would function.

We put up a low gate: attend this training, don't say anything racist or problematic, and you'll be a little more prepared before heading into the territory. I felt like I was living in-between meetings, but that felt engaging and supportive. We worked hard to decide what to include in an hour and a half of zoom time. We invited a filmmaker in our community to produce a piece on decolonization featuring Indigenous leaders, and were graced with an excellent (otherwise unpublished) short film. By March, we were offering one training each week, every other Sunday morning and Tuesday evening. Our small team expanded slowly over the next few months; we brought on more facilitators to manage the schedule so we could participate in other elements of movement building and to accommodate burnout. Digital organizing is, for many of us, both gratifying and deeply alienating.

In September of 2021, the frontlines orientation call facilitators met for the last time to dissolve our training team and reflect on what it was we had done. Deciding when to stop was difficult. It involved naming that there was no longer the same call for masses to the frontlines; the nature of the fight had changed. In that grief-filled moment, we made room for our little community one last time.

The eight of us reflected in turn on our highs and lows and the areas of growth we had experienced over the past seven months. We talked about the impacts our team had on each other and the successes of the movement. We shared stories. I remembered how a sweet and eager person had pulled me to the side at an action once. In the dusty heat, they gushed to me that they knew who I was, that they were up north because the training we hosted was important to them. I was a little flabbergasted — part of me believed we were working in a void, a feeling echoed by my friends. That little bit of connection felt gratifying, and at the same time invoked in me a grief I had a hard time placing. The work we did together was good work, often fun, and also full of sadness.

In our orientation calls and on our team, we had managed to cultivate a tone of inclusion, accessibility, and non-cooperation with the state that I had become proud of. We tried to set the tone for how to show up in radical relationship by — to the best of our abilities despite the infernal limitations of digital communication — embodying those behaviors with the 2,244 individuals who came to our trainings over spring and summer. Sometimes there were five attendees, sometimes 80. Sometimes it felt easy as pie, sometimes the crowd stumped us with an hour or more of questions. So many people tried to seek consultation on sabotage plans in the zoom chat (though we couldn't endorse or talk about that)! So many people expressed gratitude for our work, a thanks I struggled to accept while the good north land was being torn asunder.

Being on the digital end of things felt surreal at times — we talked about it when we checked in on each other. Connecting to a web of struggle and resistance online only to look up from your phone to find yourself alone was hard. To plan and prepare and support systems only to log off and try to be present in an everyday life that doesn't feel particularly opposed to anything was sad. Some days, it doesn't feel like enough. It takes all sorts, a broad cross section of ages and abilities, and some of us can't hold the responsibility and privilege of putting our bodies on the line. The digital intimacies of being constantly in my teammates' DMs and sharing the ephemera of our daily lives certainly nourished me throughout my connection to the struggle. And still: I was grieving for the relationships that were hard to tend from afar, for the connections I had missed, and for the pain being inflicted on the people and the land.

> *Connecting to a web of struggle and resistance online only to look up from your phone to find yourself alone was hard. Some days, it doesn't feel like enough. It takes all sorts, a broad cross section of ages and abilities, and some of us can't hold the responsibility and privilege of putting our bodies on the line.*

I'm so grateful for the organizers who took me under their wings and showed me how we can be in community and apart. They helped me to combat my internalized ableism and to channel my rage into work I could actually manage, like hours online, on calls, furiously communicating and building bridges. My mentors for whom this was not their first rodeo encouraged me to be kind to myself and hold space for an ongoing process of grieving. Communities are born and they dissolve — in their wake, new communities come to life. We have an obligation to honor our losses. The constellations of small groups that came together to love one another and resist the pipeline are now armed with more love, solidarity, and knowledge to continue fighting on the myriad frontlines we face under disaster capitalism. I wish for nothing but love, rage, and space for grief to the resistors of yesterday, today, and tomorrow. •

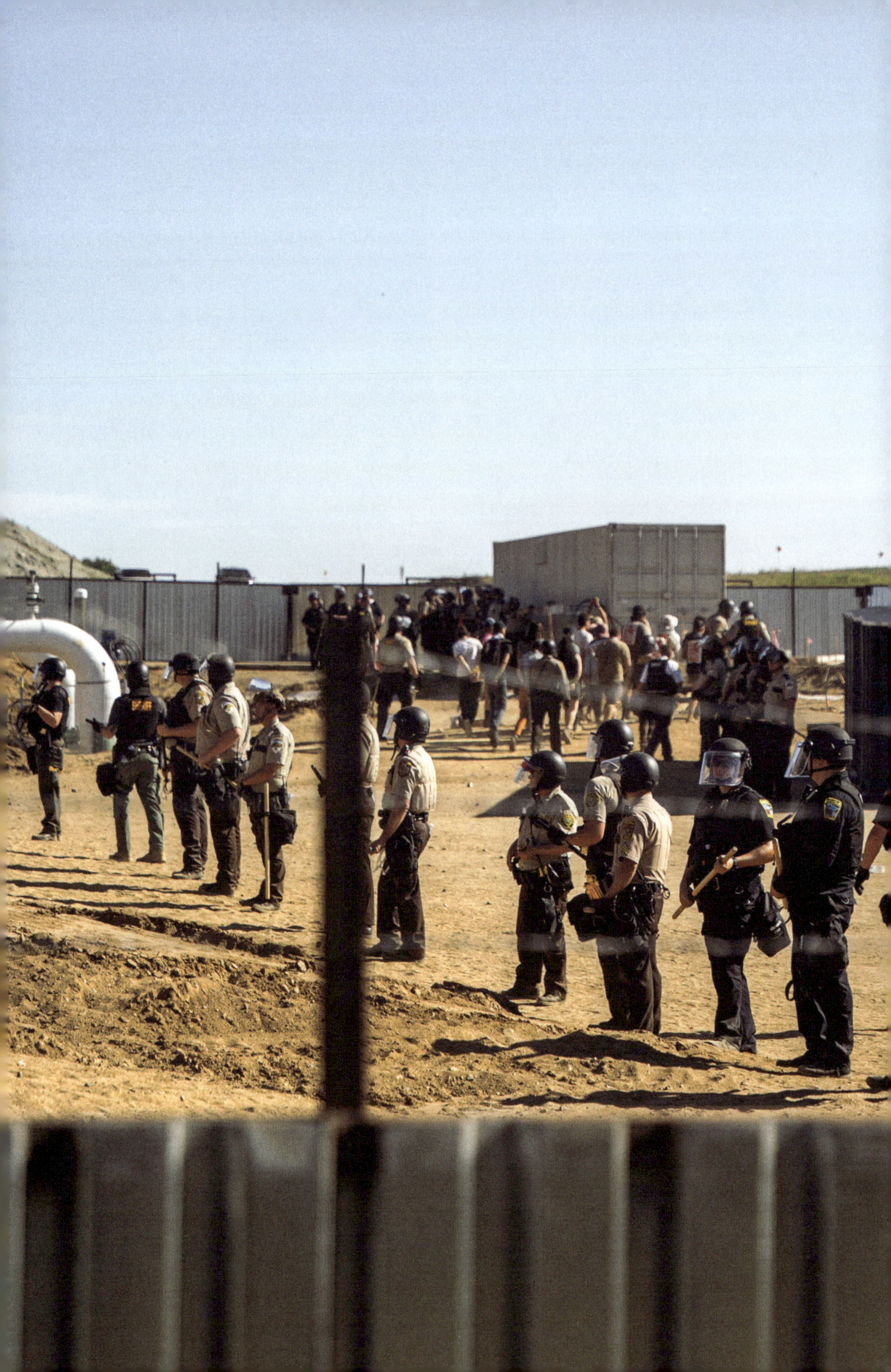

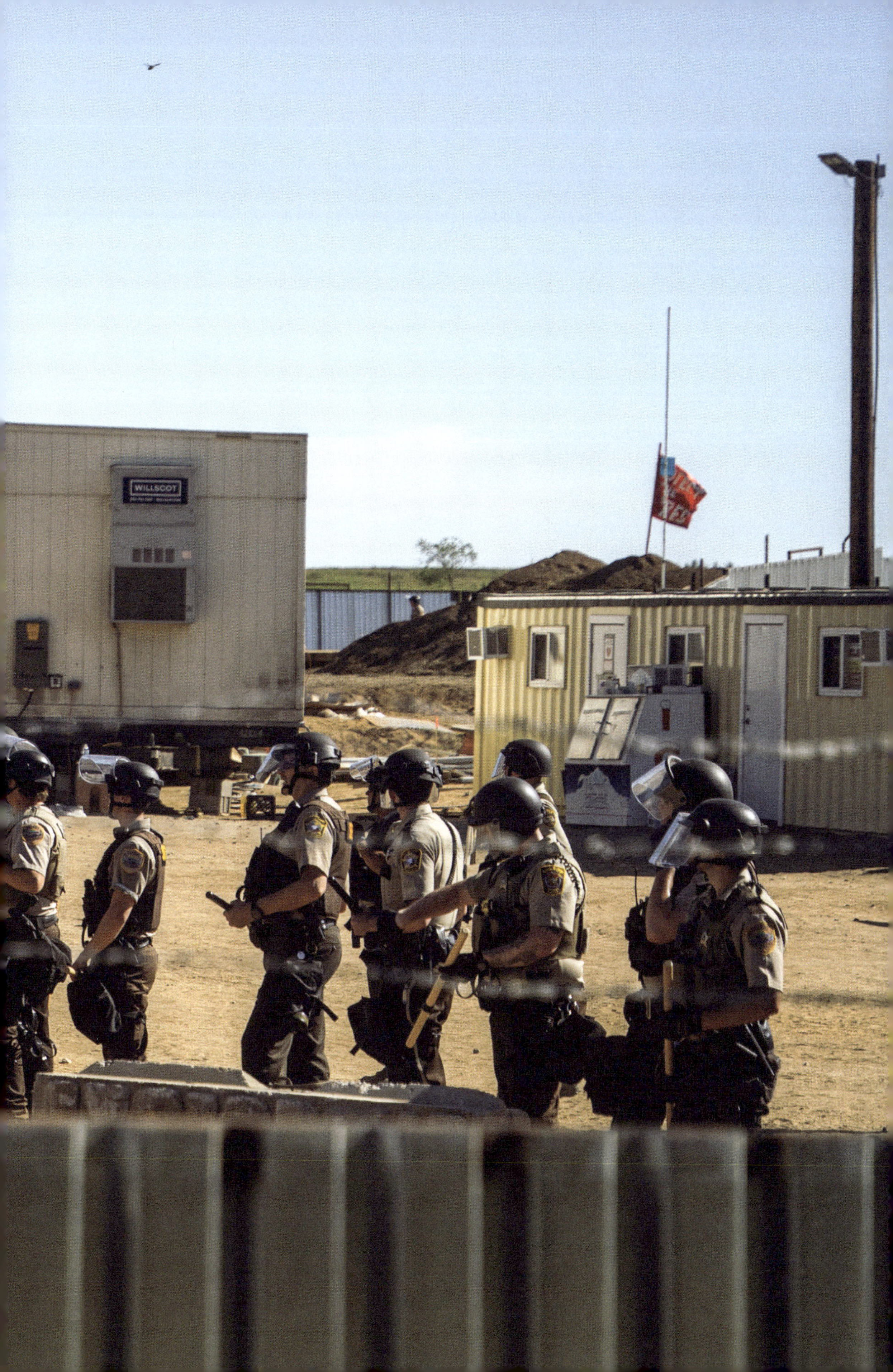
WILLSCOT

My beer was warm, and so was the night. Warm enough that a number of us had elected to hang out on the deck in late April. In front of us, the now indiscernible lake made itself known through its nighttime symphony, and behind us, the house that had been rented for us summited towards the sky with brash caucacity.

Tonight, our group of over a dozen Water Protectors had somehow found ourselves a part of the wealthy lake house community of Park Rapids, Minnesota. We were there with many other titles — puppeteers, artists, scientists, mothers, farmers — to pull off a puppet parade for Earth Day the following day. Some of us had never met, some had spent whole lifetimes kneeling on cold warehouse floors with one another, cutting out cardboard and paper-macheing late into the night. It was that moment in 2021, when the first round of vaccines had become widely available, and there was a nervous giddiness in the air. We were high off of each others' presence, the feeling of being one of many people in a room after a full year of isolation. I remember it as a moment of breaking open, of expanding possibility. We could be together again. We were together again. We had made it.

From the deck, I barely heard the knock on the front door. I did hear the murmurs that rippled throughout our group once the visitor was known: someone had called the cops. My comrades maintained their composure as some of us with more privilege moved forward to talk with them. What did they want? Apparently one of the neighbors had noticed our 18-foot moving van in the front yard and thought that we must be stealing furniture from the Airbnb hosts. My comrade assured them that no, that was a ridiculous story. The simple truth was that we were professional puppeteers and the moving van was full of puppets. The cops scoffed, well then, would we mind opening the back of the van to show them? So, my comrade pulled on their boots, shuffled out to the wet lawn, and rolled up the van door while the cops trained their flashlights on the metal interior. And sure enough, staring back at the police equally as wide-eyed, was an 8-foot-tall bear and wolf, a giant eagle, a black snake, beavers, and birds. A whole menagerie.

Everyone laughed, and the cops left. It was a Trojan horse story, except that our big secret wasn't armed soldiers ready for besiegement. It was just joy. And that joy, that absolute love and zeal for life, will always make us and our movements irrepressible. •

Editors' Note: This story was developed from an interview. It has been excerpted and edited in collaboration with the interviewee.

I did like the fact that we were all very focused on mutual aid, and we also supported many frontlines. Especially at Migizi, we'd go to BLM, to their events, and we were very crossover, and all about helping everyone, anyone BIPOC or LGBTQ+. We'd make time to go out and search for missing relatives, or go to the frontlines in the cities, like for Winston Smith, or we'd hand out food to elders and children around there, you know. That's something that doesn't get talked about much, how much water protectors helped everyone else too. It gave us multiple roles and made it more than just one dimensional. That work gave life to the meaning of what it is to be a protector. •

An 11-Year-Old's Reflections on Camp

This summer, my family drove to Minnesota to help fight Line 3. We went to a camp that had about 100 other people. When we got there, everyone seemed kind of sad. I learned that that was because of the last action where the cops tear gassed and arrested everyone.

After we had been there for a few days, I started to like it more. At first, I didn't like chores like dishes, but I realized that dishes are fun when there are people helping you. Also, you can listen to people tell stories. After that, I started signing up without my mom making me.

One night, there was a talent show. My little brother, our cousins, and I sang Big Rock Candy Mountain. There were mainly songs at the talent show, but there were a couple of other talents. One of them was a jousting contest. One person was on a unicycle and the other was on a kid bike.

One of my favorite things to do was ride my brother's bike down the big hills in camp. That was also a challenge because he has a tiny toddler bike.

One day there was an action. A lot of people went to it, so it was a skeleton crew at camp. The few remaining people were mainly doing security shifts. That day was really quiet. Later, a lot of the people got back, and there was plenty of noise.

There was a lot of weather that we weren't used to, and I was a little shy at first because I hadn't met anyone, but overall, it was a great summer. •

It was a Saturday in December 2020. As I stood outside the room tightening the metal nose clip of my N95 mask before I went in to see my patient hospitalized with COVID-19, I couldn't help but reflect on the past 72 hours.

I reflected on how, the previous Thursday, I'd attended the launch of The Lancet Countdown on Health and Climate Change Policy Brief for the United States. This is a major scientific report that comes out each year as part of a global team's research on how climate change is impacting our health. I was a reviewer on this report and had worked with several health professionals and scientists from across the country over the past year to draft it. And, as with any climate report that comes out these days, we showed how wildfires, extreme heat, and drought are devastating the health of our communities.

I also reflected on how over the past three years, health professionals in Minnesota participated in many steps of the permitting process, citing our strong and consistent opposition to Line 3. We wrote a white paper collecting the evidence on health harms of construction and operation of the pipeline, we showed up at 3:30 am outside the Senate building in St. Paul in 20-degree weather to stand in line to get a chance to testify and share how Line 3 will lock us into decades' worth of emissions impacting the health of generations of Minnesotans to come, gave interviews to media, met with decision makers, and even participated in giving comments to the Minnesota Pollution Control Agency in the middle of the pandemic, while also caring for patients.

I especially recalled how over the past month, I and 200 of my colleagues from across the state who had been on the frontlines of the COVID crisis appealed to Governor Walz to pause construction of Line 3 until the pandemic abated to prevent workers from out of state to travel to construction sites, thus risking their own health and the health of rural and Indigenous communities.

I still couldn't bring myself to believe that on Friday, our state's government had granted permits to start construction of Line 3. Loudly proclaiming that they followed the science, our leaders in power permitted the construction of one of the largest tar sands oil pipelines in the country during the climate crisis, trespassing on Treaty territory, while Minnesota had the highest rates of COVID-19 in the country.

As I felt the final pinch of the metal dig into my skin, I felt numb, empty, and broken. I did not know what my value was to the movement as a scientist and a health professional. If the evidence we brought to the table was not going to be considered in decision making by our leaders, I did not know how or why I should continue my climate advocacy. Was there even a point? Giving in to that despair felt so enticing. If I gave in, I could put down the burden.

I could say, "I tried" and walk away. And best of all, I would never have to go through the pain of finding the courage to go on.

But even as I pushed down on the door handle to my patient's room, I knew that I had to get back to work. I knew that as long as Anishinaabe women and Two-Spirit people led the resistance against Line 3, I would continue to use my privilege as a health professional to elevate the voices of those most impacted. I knew that, when we show up with our broken selves, we can heal, together, with our community. •

I always call them "porta-potties." Some people, inexplicably to me, call them "biffies." A "porta-john," to some. I was tasked with acquiring toilets, whatever you want to call them, for the Treaty People Gathering. An inexpert science, something you never really realize is someone's responsibility. I had mistakenly thought that someone else had it covered, but realized I would need to put it on my own plate if we were going to have toilets at all.

It was three days before the hordes arrived. I received a call at 8 am, while pacing in my bedroom, to inform me that the company I had booked weeks prior couldn't provide toilets to our "protest." It wasn't worth the business to touch it with a 10-foot pole, they told me. I had to hang up and immediately transition into my therapy appointment, which I promptly spent crying about the toilets.

The next day, I drove up, confident that the other company I had hastily found the day before would come through. I had spent the day on the phone with companies, and my supervisor, and the finance team, trying to get toilets paid for. Instead of dealing with the millions of other small tasks that come up before holding a multi-day, several-thousand-person event, I had a one-track toilet mind.

Two hours after I arrived on site, I got the call I should have known was coming. Same story, different company. No toilets on my horizon.

I grabbed two friends and sat them down. Clearly, looking for a rental company in the greater Bemidji area was not going to cut it. We had to think big. I tasked one of them with companies in the Twin Cities, one in the Duluth area. I settled down to focus on Fargo-Moorhead. If they charged a premium to drive them a long distance, I was sanctioned to approve it. The emergency toilet budget was sky-high.

We decided we could no longer try to deceive these companies. No more hiding our agenda. This was a Line 3 related event and we hated the pipeline, and every portable toilet company in Minnesota and North Dakota would know it.

We reconvened with a few promising options (and a lot of duds). We landed on the best deal, K. from M&K Rentals in Grand Forks, across the border in North Dakota and two hours away. I leveled with K., I told him our whole thing with the pipeline. He said all he cared about was that we paid him and didn't destroy his toilets. We were sold.

K. was impeccable. He was prompt. He responded to texts. He brought his son with him. He came back halfway through to clean out the septic tanks and told me I had grossly undercounted how many toilets I would need (poop math, like regular math, was not my strong suit). I had ballparked 12 toilets — he said I needed approximately 10 more. He didn't scold me, though. We profusely thanked him.

A month later, I was texting with someone I met at TPG. They told me that the camp they were currently at had just gotten toilets. I jokingly asked if they were from my guy K. They responded with a beautiful photo of a sunset, foregrounded by potties. The M&K logo was proudly displayed.

It's been nearly a year. I recently got an email from someone looking for toilets for an upcoming event. I sent them K.'s info. I know if they call him, he'll answer. •

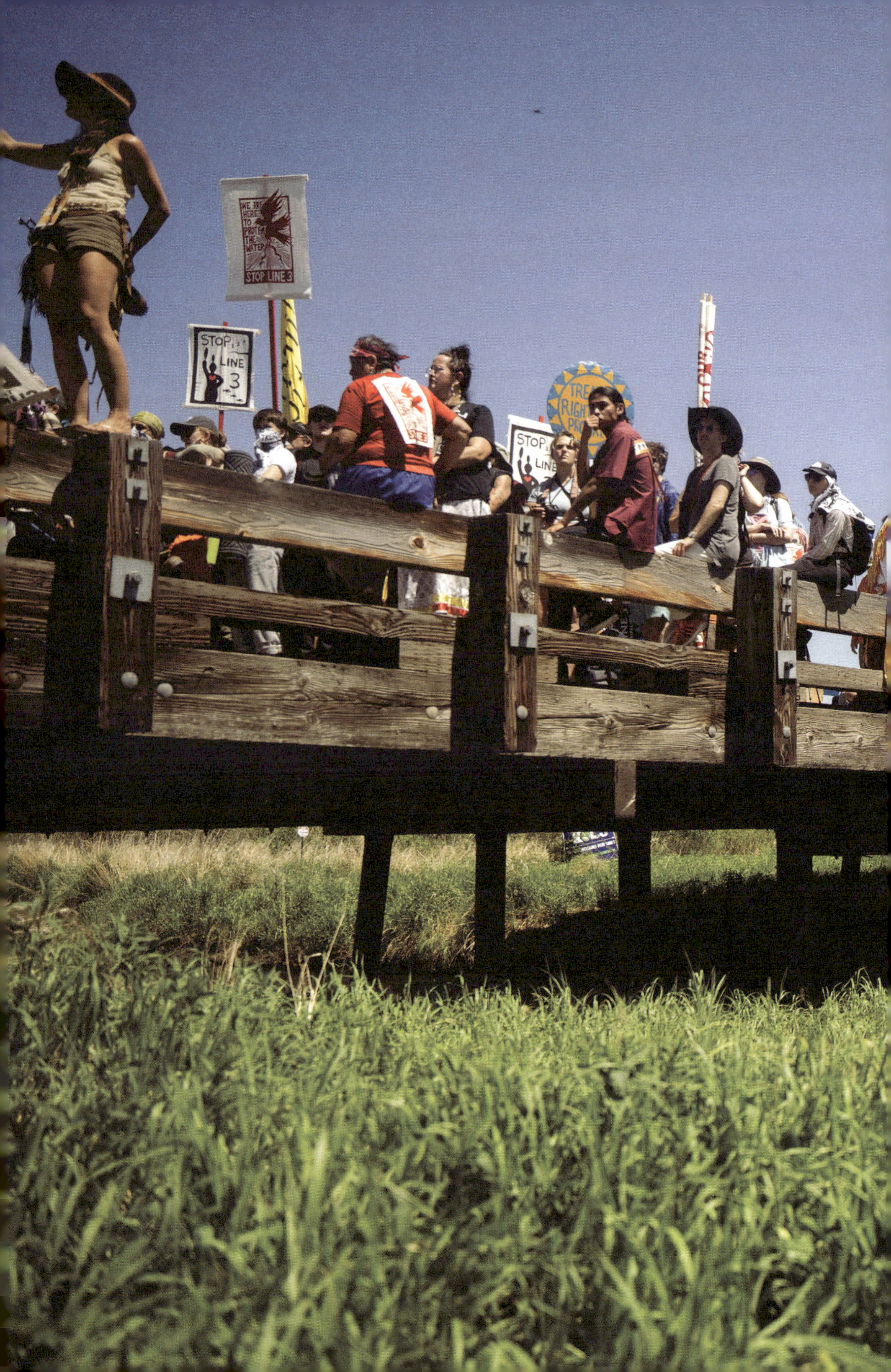
STOP LINE 3
STOP LINE 3

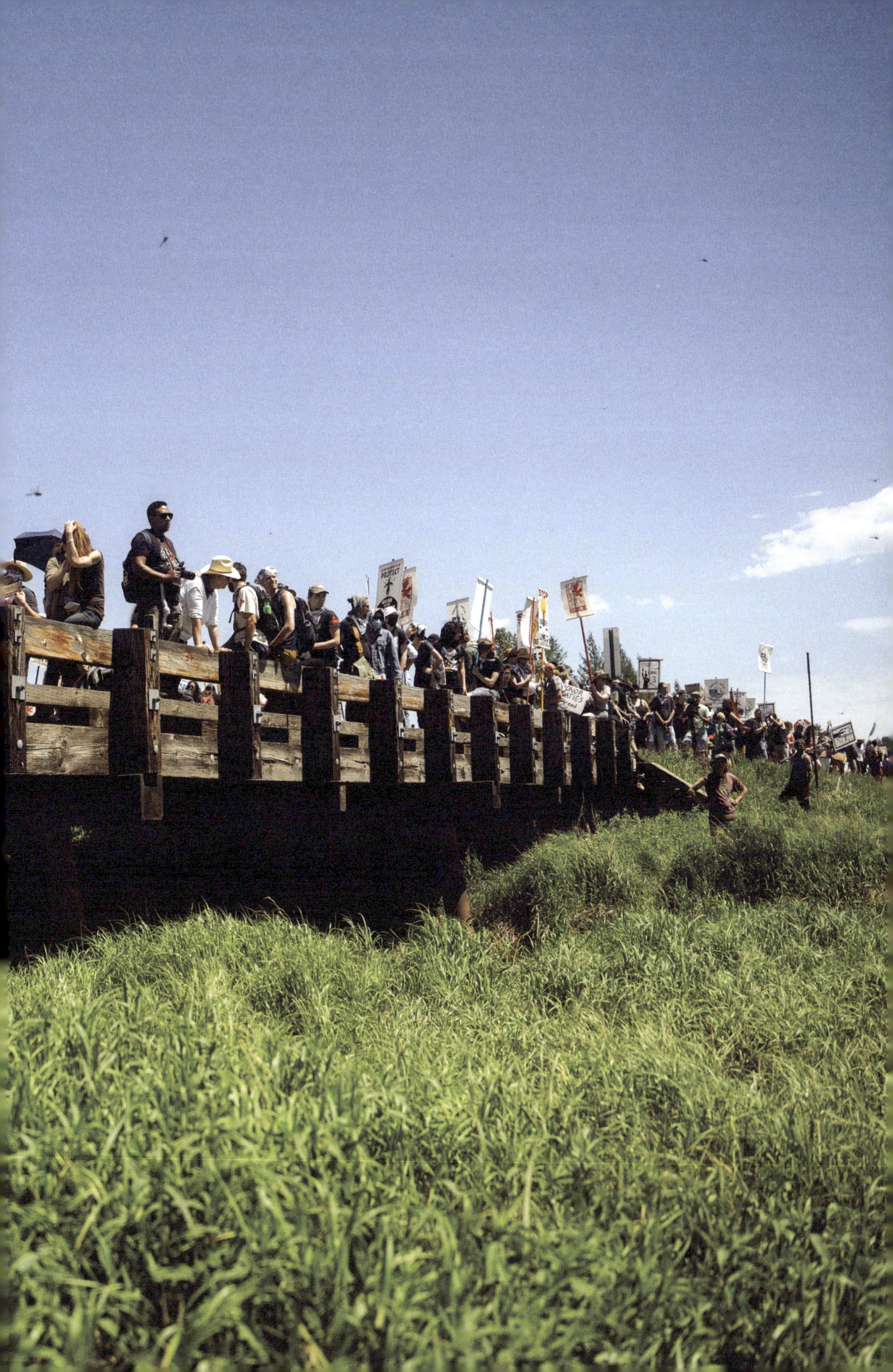

Author's Note: This is a redacted poem, made out of the Statement of Probable Cause paperwork I was given in jail. I wrote it on a ripped-out page from a paperback book, with a contraband pencil that a comrade slid beneath my door while they were on their Hour Out. None of the unredacted words, or the order in which they appeared, were changed in any way, except for the addition of the one bracketed word. All spelling and capitalization inconsistencies below are thus the fault of the police.

Statement of Probable Cause Poem

A Sleeping Dragon responded, aware that Enbridge was Trespassing. He spoke with one protester who had attached themselves to pipe. Left. Observed two protestors who were attached to a backhoe. Shut down the backhoe; halted Enbridge operations. The Sleeping Dragon stated that they were in route to remain free. Brought down the backhoe. The Sleeping Dragon was [not] straight. Used heat to free them. They cost Enbridge over $100,000. •

On December 4, 2020, I wrote in my journal, "Today I had the opportunity to stand at the base of two trees that my comrades are occupying on Enbridge's easement for the Line 3 pipeline. It was a complicated, messy day with a few moments of perfection. The pieces to stop Line 3 aren't quite falling into place yet, but we are *powerful*. We *will* stop Line 3."

The next day, December 5, two of my friends were brutally arrested trying to defend the tree sits. I, like many others, panicked. Some people I'd met a handful of times were living in Duluth for the winter to be closer to the pipeline route. I had planned to move up there after I finished my classes for the semester. But, that day, someone called me and asked, "when are you planning to move up here?" and the answer was so clear: "now. Right now." I packed a bag and drove up in the dark.

By the next night, December 6, I wrote out a thought that I had never let myself entertain over my years resisting Line 3. "We're not even a week into active construction. Everything is so intense and complicated and our tools don't feel adequate. *We might not stop Line 3.*"

My entry from December 8 begins, "Really hard days." And they were. Most mornings, we would leave Duluth early, before sunrise, and drive out to Palisade or Park Rapids to join actions to stop construction. Our friends were getting arrested more days than not, and when they were released from jail, they had to isolate to prevent the potential spread of COVID. The resistance spaces we entered were filled with tension and disagreement about how we should be responding to construction. It was fucking cold, and everyone was sleep deprived and short on trust.

Over the month of December, I prepared to take action to stop construction on many occasions. A day would be spent furtively planning, practicing, gathering supplies. We would try to round everyone up for a meeting, but someone was always missing; out scouting, out at Menards, down by the river. Some days, we'd spend hours drifting back and forth from the fire out to the rest of camp just trying to pull everyone into one place to coordinate. Everyone was trying, really trying, but our humanness and our grief were intractable.

It was emotionally exhausting to prepare for action like this. The whole day before a plan would fall through, my mind whirred with thoughts about what would happen. Would they stop the enormous machines just because we got close to them? Would I be able to fasten my quick links in time? When the cops cut us out would the saws burn us? Cut our skin? How would I handle being alone in a jail cell all night? Why was I so scared when everyone around me seemed so courageous? What did I, in all my privilege, have holding me back?

Later in the month we traveled to a resistance camp to prepare for another action. We spent days in the cold practicing and preparing materials. We fought amongst ourselves about strategy, about roles, about where to do the action, and when. We slept in a trailer with a wood stove that was always insufferably hot early in the night and unbearably cold early in the morning. At some point, some of our friends left, overwhelmed and

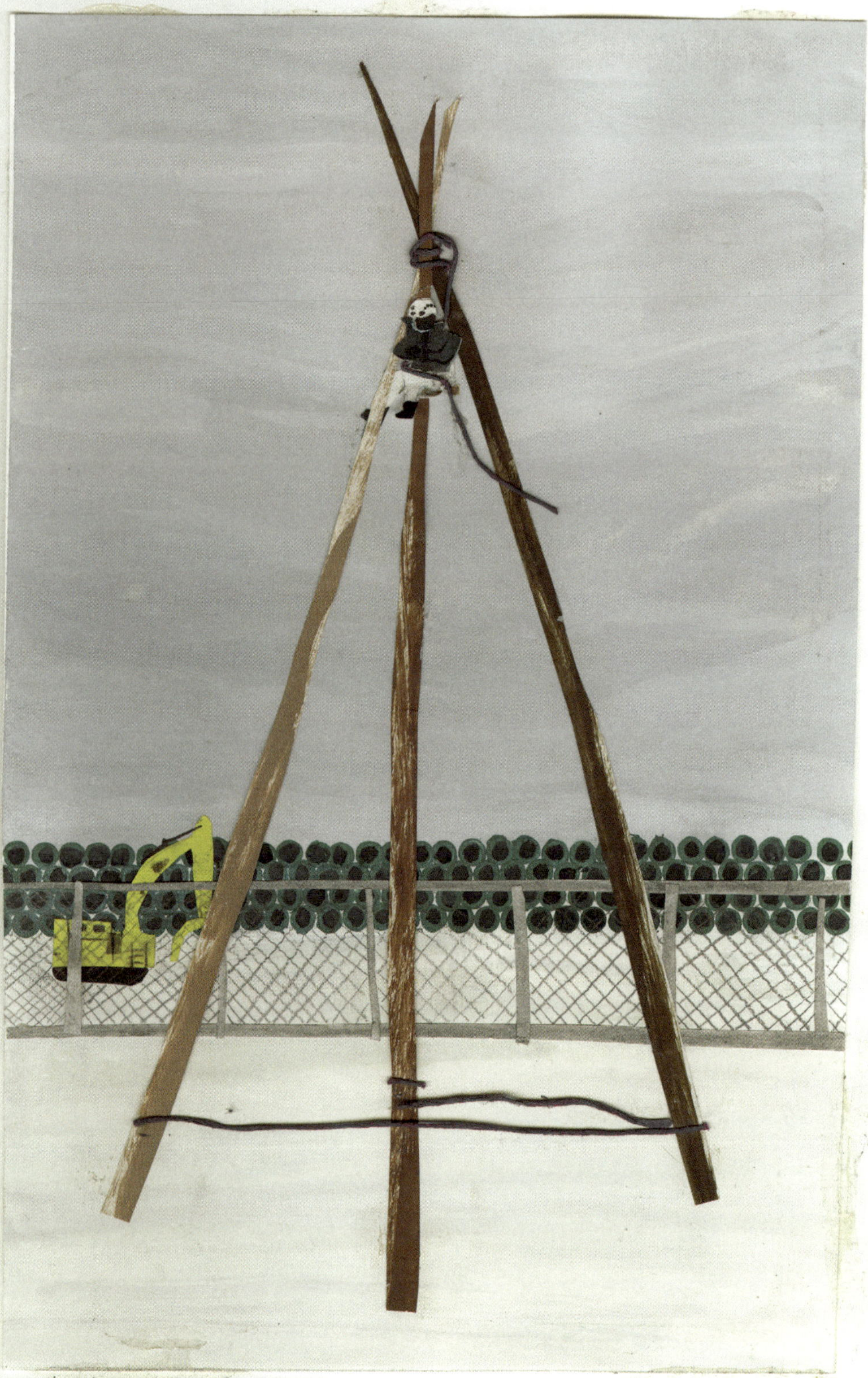

frustrated with leadership, with their peers, with the intensity of our preparations and how dangerous some of it felt. Those of us that stayed kept planning to wrap up our preparations and leave as well. But each day, something would come up that delayed our departure; new information, new people, a new plan. We started to joke that the trailer at camp was a sort of purgatory and that even when we did finally leave and make it home to Duluth, we would wake up the next morning to find ourselves back, in our sleeping bags and frozen sweat, in the trailer again.

We planned to deploy this action three different times over the month. The first time, on December 21, as I mentally prepared for the action I wrote, "Anxious. Fuck. I didn't sleep as well as I would have liked because I woke up panicky at some point. Today will be hard: do your best to be present and grounded anyways. Your people will keep you safe. Tomorrow you will feel so relieved. Maybe not perfect, maybe not satisfied, but at least the unknowns will be known."

And another entry from later the same day: "Rescheduled the action. Re-rescheduled the action. Re-re-rescheduled the action. Not shocking, but the whiplash is definitely tough. Lots of physical and emotional exertion over the past few days. Getting all wound up and focused and then not doing the thing takes a serious toll. I'm less and less convinced that all the shit we're doing is worthwhile."

The next time, we planned to deploy on December 23 until someone mentioned that getting arrested on the Wednesday before Christmas Eve would certainly mean at least four nights in jail. They don't arraign anyone on federal holidays or the weekend. At the time, I was relieved. In the following months, as dozens of our comrades regularly spent that much time in jail or longer, I felt foolish for having been so scared.

In the days leading up to our third attempt, a friend helped me prepare everything I would need for the action. We spent a day packing supplies, and every hour or so they'd go "oh!" and wander off to find another layer of wool, or a pack of hand warmers, or a thermos, anything they could think of to help keep me safe. They graciously stood outside of the bathroom while I squatted in the shower and tested peeing into one of the diapers I was supposed to wear for the action. Ultimately, I decided not to drink any water until it was over. The next day, we drove back to camp and were so busy laughing and telling stories that we missed our turn several times.

The night before we finally planned to deploy, another friend and I tried again and again to start a fire in the woodstove in the wall tent where we were all going to sleep. They had terrible cramps, I was terrified about the action, and we couldn't get the wood to catch. Worse, it was their birthday, and all I could talk about were the plans for tomorrow. They sat with me in the anxiety and the cold, and finally we let ourselves laugh about the fire and give up. One by one, our friends trickled in. Someone started the fire. Soon, we were all nestled in our sleeping bags, packed into the tent, having one final meeting about the next day. Everyone was wound up, goofy. We laughed and laughed. Finally, everyone went to sleep. I laid awake for hours, thinking through every detail of the action again, and again.

And then, finally, it happened. The action was chaotic and confusing and powerful, maybe perfect. I was terrified, I was supported, I was humbled, and I was cold. When I got to jail, I finally collapsed. After weeks of anticipation and disagreement and planning, planning, planning, I wasn't responsible for anything anymore, at least not for a few hours. I drank three cups of tinny water out of a greasy brown plastic mug and fell asleep.

On December 31, as I reflected on the year and what was still to come, I wrote, "This work is complicated and messy and I'm so so grateful. I'm scared too. I'm doubtful. I'm embarrassed and ashamed and apathetic; all of it. But more than anything, I'm grateful for the opportunity to resist this evil project with people I love so much. I'm grateful for all that I'm learning and for every mistake we've made along the way. We won't stop Line 3. We won't even come close. We're not building a perfect movement and we're not doing things right. But we're trying. We're experimenting and learning and growing and striving and I'd rather be here, with these people, trying, than anywhere else in the world." •

We won't stop Line 3. We won't even come close. We're not building a perfect movement and we're not doing things right. But we're trying. We're experimenting and learning and growing and striving and I'd rather be here, with these people, trying, than anywhere else in the world.

I went to my first ever MN350 Pipeline Resistance Team meeting in May 2017. May 4th, to be exact.

I found a parking spot in between the flock of Priuses with "Bernie 2016" stickers on them and walked up to the old brick house on Stevens. I followed the stream of people in the back of the house and walked through the creaky screen door to find a group of people gathered around a large, uneven rectangle of tables made by stacking different tables next to each other. I was a little uneasy being in a new place with people who all knew each other but were unfamiliar to me. In the middle of the table were half a dozen loaves of bread, accompanied by jars of peanut butter and jelly. I was confused by the snack of choice, but I couldn't help but smile each time I saw someone grab a piece of bread and slather on some peanut butter and jelly.

People settled in and an agenda was passed to me. The older man sitting next to me introduced himself and shook my hand. The facilitator got everyone's attention and welcomed everyone to the group. Just as he was about to start the meeting, there was a shuffle behind the side door leading to the rest of the house. Out popped two people about my age, dressed up in homemade costumes. One had on all black with a sign taped to his chest that said "Darth Enbridge," and the other had beautiful hair braided in two small buns on each side of her head. Both were brandishing lightsabers. All eyes in the room were on them as they played out a scene where Darth Enbridge attempted to destroy our water by poisoning it with destructive oil, but Princess Leia jumped in to defend the water. They battled with their lightsabers until Princess Leia hit Darth Enbridge with a fatal blow, causing him to stumble back against the whiteboard with the meeting agenda written on it, before falling to the floor. The meeting room erupted with applause as they bowed. Before taking a seat at the table they both announced in unison, "May the fourth be with you!"

When I think back to that first meeting, my heart swells a little bit. Of course, I knew that defeating the Line 3 pipeline would not be as simple as a white woman with her hair in buns striking a blow, that no individual could do this on their own. I did not know at the time how many hours I would spend in that silly old office. I never would have thought that Darth Enbridge and Princess Leia would become such dear friends in the years that followed. But I did know right away that there was something special about that meeting room with the creaky door and stained carpet. The energy in that space that was so grounded in care and love. And the people that filled the mismatched chairs around the uneven tables were people worth coming back the next Thursday to spend a couple more hours with. •

A Beginner's Guide to Wheatpasting

Supplies:

- 1 cup of flour that a friend liberated from an Aldi dumpster
- 4 cups of water
- A stack of "Defund Line 3" posters sent by a campaign of artists and organizers from around the country

Instructions:

1. Add some cold water to the flour until it becomes pourable. Whisk to remove lumps.

2. Boil the rest of the water and then slowly pour the flour + water mixture in. Be sure to turn the water on low and stir continuously. The first time you do this you will, understandably, keep the heat on for way too long and your flour will burn, smell horrible, and muck up your compost pile when you get rid of it. The second (and third and fourth) times you try will be much better.

3. Remove from heat and let it cool. Store in a large bucket at first and then transfer to a few squirt water bottles. Easy to carry and easier to use (you will learn this helpful tip from a friend).

4. Meet up with friends after dark. Wear black, which is both tactical and also feels a bit goofy. It will get covered in the messy paste by the end of the night.

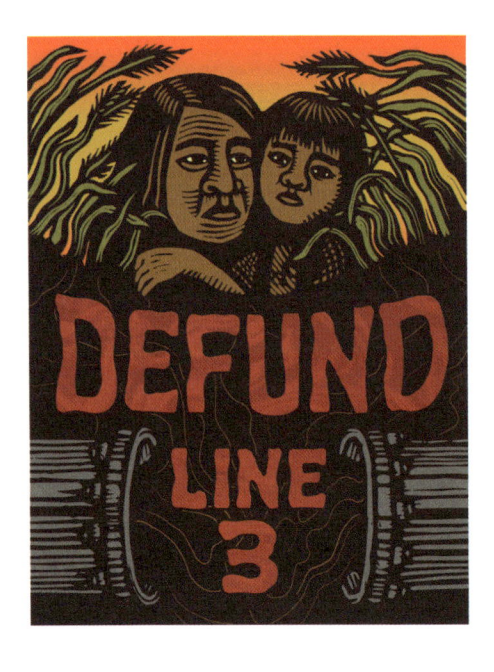

5. Find a target. It should be a fairly smooth surface. Concrete walls and metal electrical boxes are great. Close to (or on) a bank is ideal. You will be a little nervous about the fact that Chase has cameras, but you will run to the window and do it quickly. It may end up slanted but that doesn't really matter.

6. Paint the spot with a layer of paste, stick a poster on, and cover with another layer of paste. It's helpful to have one person with the paste and the other with a poster. You may fumble this a few times but you'll get into a rhythm by the end of the night. The second time you go, you will bring a squeegee to smooth out the posters. This will be the most satisfying part so you and your friends can trade this job back and forth.

7. Try and conceal the buckets and bags when cars drive by. By the end of the night, you will feel both satisfied and hungry for more. You will have walked nearly four miles. You will have put up a few dozen posters.

8. The next day, walk the same route admiring your work in the daylight. "Defund Line 3" will be proudly displayed on bus stops, sidewalks, bridges, and (yes!) bank windows. Over the next week, you will discover more and more posters hidden in plain sight. You will watch photos get shared on the internet and see these posters appear all across the country. You will feel like a part of something big! And it all will have started with some water and flour.

9. You will bring more friends next time, and you will make more paste. •

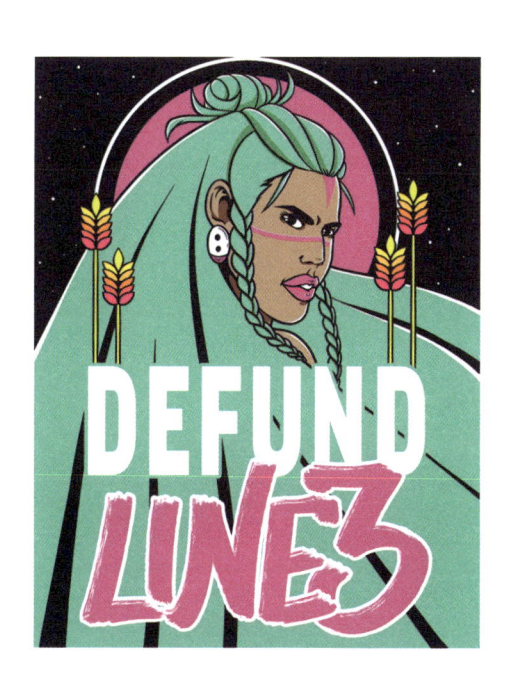

Governor Tim Walz and I were neighbors for 62 hours

Day 1

This story begins at the Treaty Partners to the MN State Capitol event in July 2021, when White Earth's Tribal Council and community members made the four-hour voyage to vocalize another round of dissent against the Line 3 project.

These new statements focused primarily on the 4.5 BILLION gallons of additional Nibi which Minnesota's Department of Natural Resources (DNR) allocated for "Construction Dewatering" midway through the construction of Line 3 without the consent, consultation, or approval of the tribe.

Northern Minnesota was in a "severe drought" according to the USGS and despite the Land of 10,000 Lakes' interconnected watersheds, the DNR determined that displacing 5,000,000,000 gallons of water posed no threat to the ecosystem or manoomin.

Originally we envisioned an outdoor rally on the front steps, but a looming storm had us relocate inside. Capitol Security had stressed that the drums wouldn't be allowed inside if the rally's location changed due to inclement weather.

As members of White Earth's governing body arrived and the ceremonial drums of the Iron Boy Singers made their way into the building, I found myself in direct communication with a frantic Capitol Security staff member repeating the warning that drums inside violated our permit and wouldn't be allowed.

I relayed this to the Chairman who was here to have the voice of the people heard. "The drums are us," he said calmly.

Well, that settles that. Certainly not my place to tell a Sovereign Nation what to do.

I hung up the phone with Capitol Security moments before the thunderous clap of the drum's opening prayer echoed through every marble nook and cranny of the massive symbol of colonial power wherein we stood — Native & non-Natives together — as Treaty Partners, demanding the sixth article of the US Constitution be upheld. I was moved to tears more than once as the rally progressed, but the first droplet fell as that drum made its voice heard, despite Capitol Security's edict.

Sorry, not sorry.

The rally ended, and a small group made the Governor's Residence their next stop. Visiting the Governor seemed appropriate, especially because he no-showed as a "Treaty Partner."

Firing up my '78 Chevrolet Bluebird school bus, I relocated to 1006 Summit Avenue, parked across the street from the small group and nestled myself along the fenced retaining wall in front of the mansion with a "Stop Line 3" yard sign in my lap.

I stayed put after the group left and my colleague J. joined me for a cup of coffee as night fell on the surrounding McMansions. G. arrived and we were graced by several songs which he shared at the front gate.

Day 2

With morning dark roast and yard sign in lap, I watched as parking enforcement chalked the rear streetside tire of the bus.

That was quick — clearly someone didn't want me there. I mean, none of the other vehicles on the street were chalked. What gives?

I wondered if Walz made the call himself having opened his blinds to the 33-foot skoolie with #StopLine3 banners on the side.

Either way, with the chalking of tires the "48-hour to move the abandoned vehicle clock" started ticking.

From inside the bus, I saw Governor Walz depart his mansion via candy blue collector's truck accompanied by his security detail. Each time I'd see him depart like that during my stay, I smiled. Howdy neighbor.

I began writing a letter which I delivered to a security guard who met me at the front gate of the mansion.

The letter was an honest, heartfelt, loving note from a 30-year-old constituent who had voted for the Walz/Flanagan ticket in 2018 because of the Governor-To-Be's vocal opposition to "Any line that goes through Treaty Territory."

Walz did EVERYTHING in his power to approve the project once he gained our votes and took office.

Having left countless messages on his phone over the years voicing opposition to Line 3, there's no way he wouldn't read THIS letter. I mean, if a neighbor of mine walked across the street with a handwritten letter to me, I'd read it. That's being a decent human being, right?

Day 3

I think by this point, most of the neighborhood was getting used to me. Many had seen me or this bus at some point over the years having spent hundreds, if not thousands, of hours talking with ordinary folks about the Line 3 project at parks, festivals, rallies, gas stations.

Passersby stopped to chat, adding to the thousands of signatures on the back of the bus which had been gathered steadily over the years shaping out "Line 3" with a red circle and slash through it on a blue background.

Even now, just a short time after the frontline chapter of the Line 3 fight has concluded, there are signatures on this bus which have outlived their respective owners. Even J., who had joined me that first night as Walz's neighbor, has since passed. On we fight.

Day 4

I had my second letter to Walz written by sunrise. This one simply explained that I'd be leaving, but would await a response directly from him as to why he broke his campaign promises and turned against his constituency, the DFL's platform, and the generations to come.

I delivered letter two to the same security guard shortly before 8am. He expressed hope that other State Patrollers were treating "us" kindly up there in the Northwoods.

Tar Sands Tim never did respond to my letters. •

In June of 2015, thousands of people marched through downtown St. Paul for the Tar Sands Resistance March protesting Enbridge's proposed Sandpiper pipeline and Line 3 expansion project.

Gender Spelling Bee at the St. Louis County Jail

It's booking time. I survived the van ride with a few comrades. I was pretty naked in the cop van. I wore this sexy, maroon slip for the protest, and during the arresting process, it fell off my shoulders and there was nothing I could do about it, my hands zip-tied and all, but accept this violent drama as my current reality. I found this venomous power then in my sexuality as if it were armor, and as I mentally prepared for what was coming, I wore my exposed top surgery scars like jewelry.

I felt like a horse during the first body search that happened in this large, brightly lit, concrete garage area: "Open your mouth. Lift your right leg." I refused to look at the blond cop who patted me down, who misgendered me.

After some moments waiting in plastic lawn chairs, we were escorted into booking and I was still doing my best to grip the back of my dress, with my cuffed hands, to keep my slip from falling down around my ankles. In the booking office, I stood in a line up against the wall with some other boys who I had been arrested with. Presently, a cop, who reminded me of the Trunchbull from the movie Matilda, slithered over to me with a flashlight. She flicked it on, and shone the aggressive LEDs onto my chest, examining my scars like evidence in a crime scene:

"What are these?" she asked me. I stared straight forward.

"Scars," I replied.

"Why do you have them?" she continued.

"I have them because I had a surgery on my chest."

"What kind of surgery?"

"A chest surgery," I said frankly.

"What was the surgery for?"

"The surgery was for my chest," I repeated. And then she escalated to ask "the question":

"What genitals do you have?" At that point, I looked at the Trunchbull cop and around the room that had fallen into this hushed quiet, the gender performance about to begin, a few cops and jailed folks looking over at me. And so, with a bit of forceful drama, I said in my deepest boy voice:

"I've got PUSSY!"

Another cop lady then took me to the back to get some clothes on me. Once behind the curtains, this lady started saying, "I don't mean to be disrespectful, but are you a female?"

"No," I responded, looking right at her and really feeling the force of my trans power in her weak confusion.

"Well, is your sex female?"

"No."

"Were you assigned female at birth?"

"No."

And then she jumped to the "what's in your pants" question, as her colleague had done moments before: "I really don't mean to be disrespectful, but what are your genitals?"

In my head, I laughed. What was with this emphasis on respect?

Sardonically, I looked at her, real straight in the face, and spelled it out for her: "P, U, S, S, Y."

She looked confused and asked me for clarification, but that was all I was giving her and I remained silent. I was honestly a little surprised by myself. I'm normally way shier than this, but this cop had asked me to spell some shit out for her, so I did. And frankly, this was the best joke I've played on a cis person all year. •

Editors' Note: This story was developed from an interview. It has been excerpted and edited in collaboration with the interviewee.

Big Sandy the Loon

Inception: Inspired by a polar bear who used to follow around President Obama, members of the art team realized that no Minnesotan would want to see a loon covered in oil. Upon receiving a request to bring a large-scale puppet to the 2016 Mayday Parade, Sandy the Loon was conceived; born to follow around any Governor who needed a reminder of Line 3's potential impacts.

Specs:

Width: 3 feet
Length: 13 feet
Wingspan: 30 feet

Sandy's head was created before her body and was made rather large — and due to her creators' commitment to precision, her body was made to be proportional to her head. Thus, she has a 30-foot wingspan. Real loons have white on their undersides, and Sandy's white wings were perfect to carry a message to the Governor's 2016 Fishing Opener, where she got her name, on Big Sandy Lake.

Notes on transport: Originally, Sandy would be dismantled each time she went to a new place, as her frame would not fit in any vehicle. She then upgraded to a roof rack with 2x4s and Velcro straps to hold her down. If you keep Sandy's feathers on, you can only drive under 30 mph. If you remove her feathers and carry them in the car with her head and other parts (inside a tote affectionately called the loony bin), you can go as fast as you'd like.

First seen: 05/01/2016 at the MayDay Parade and Festival in Minneapolis. This was her first public outing, and the first time that volunteers learned exactly how unwieldy it is to walk beneath a loon while carrying it.

Never seen: In the news, except for one day when the press was excluded from a hearing in Cross Lake, MN. Disgruntled at their exclusion, a reporter offered Sandy an interview. She was on the cover of the

Brainerd newspaper. Otherwise, she was ignored (perhaps intentionally) by the press, despite the fact that she attended nearly every public hearing on Line 3 across the state. She has also been part of numerous marches: three MayDay Parades, the Park Rapids Parade, the Project Earth Music Festival, Earth Day in Northfield, the Northern Spark Art event, the Gitchi-gami Gathering, and the Treaty People Gathering. She has shown up at the PUC, the Capitol, the Governor's Mansion, and on the frontlines.

Last seen: 06/14/2021, holding space out in the wetlands at Camp Firelight. The evening after the easement was cleared, Sandy was spotted still out in the field. It is unclear if she is being held in the Sheriff's office. Sandy had wanted to do an action for a very long time and took her last stand defending the Mississippi River Headwaters. •

I was a tired elder woman with 56 years of activism behind me — crusty with despair and cynicism. I got wind of people journeying from every direction answering the call to honor their treaty obligation and defend the sacred waters. I was too old to hitchhike and while not at all a camper, I went about securing a tent and sleeping bag. Excitement mounted as we pulled into the campgrounds for the event — the excitement quickly turned into a sense of euphoria! Before me was a kaleidoscope of beautiful human beings busily erecting tents, creating art, joyfully loving on one another. I immediately dropped my cloak of despair and took it all in.

I felt overwhelmingly blessed to be a part of what would surely be a historical moment in time. My 5 am alarm sounded and up I shot — fired up ready to go! The air was markedly different from the day before. It wasn't an anxiety, it was a determination, a necessity, an "it's now or never" gut-wrenching burn. The day was long and extremely hot with no timetable for what where when. Boats and barrels and timbers were strategically placed creating a blockade to inhibit access for Enbridge workers, while many emboldened Water Protectors physically locked down to equipment. We occupied and held down the Two Inlets pump station for 12 hours before the arrests began. During this time, a Homeland Security helicopter flew low to the ground kicking up dirt and rocks, belting us in the face as they issued a warning for us to leave the area. I heard the young Water Protectors saying, "She's badass" to each other. Finally, one of the kids said, "Can we call you Badass Grandma?" I've never felt that loved. I replied that I would be honored. And then we all got arrested.

We leave a big chunk of ourselves at camp when we go back to our home. Leaving this family is heartbreaking, but the tapestry remains and we weave in and out of it as the struggle rages on and we answer the call. I am endeared to every one of you and feel blessed to have the most amazing grandchildren scattered all across Turtle Island! •

Lights of the state in nervous flickers. Frost on barbed wire. Long after the chants fade out,

our shadows remain.

They covered you with a blanket, sparks fly sharp as they cut above your gloved hand.

Lift off

above your head, your arm, your own fear,

and remember the slow sound of water.

Sitting in Aitkin County Jail

we exist outside of time, away from wind in the air and song.

Somehow, the four of us in this single cell still find a way to laugh.

Art made in Aitkin County Jail from the back of a form, scraps torn from a magazine, toothpaste, and ballpoint pen.

Down in the River to Pray

The new lyrics to this classic African American spiritual were written by Indigenous water protectors and allies in the Wadena County Jail after they were arrested for defending the Shell River from Line 3. It has been sung by water protectors across the state in the months since, particularly outside of courthouses in solidarity with those still facing criminal charges for their actions to resist Line 3.

—

Gonna go down in the river to pray
Studying the Anishinaabe way
And who'll protect the wild rice
Creator, show us the way

Oh sisters let's go down
Let's go down, come on down
Oh sisters let's go down
Down in the river to pray

Gonna go down in the river to pray
Studying the Anishinaabe way
And who will kill the black snake now
Great Spirit, show us the way

Oh brothers let's go down
Let's go shut that pipeline down
Come on brothers let's go down
Down in the river to pray

Gonna go down in the river to pray
Studying the Anishinaabe way
And who'll protect the water now
Great Spirit, show us the way

Oh fathers let's go down
Let's go shut that pipeline down

Come on drop the charges now
And come down in the river to pray

We went down in the river to pray
Studying the Anishinaabe way
And we'll protect the wild rice
Great Spirit show us the way

Oh mothers let's go down
Come on shut that black snake down
Come on mothers let's go down
Down in the river to pray

We went down in the river to pray
Studying the Anishinaabe way
And we protect the water now
Great Spirit, show us the way

Oh Enbridge let's go down
Let's go shut your pipeline down
Oh Enbridge let's go down
Down in the river to pray

As we went down in the river to pray
Studying the Anishinaabe way
And we protect our future now
Great Spirit, show us the way •

CAUTION
TREATY
RIGHTS
IN PROGRESS
WE ARE HERE TO PROTECT THE WATER
STOP LINE 3
PROTECT WATER
HONOR TREATIES
STOP LINE 3

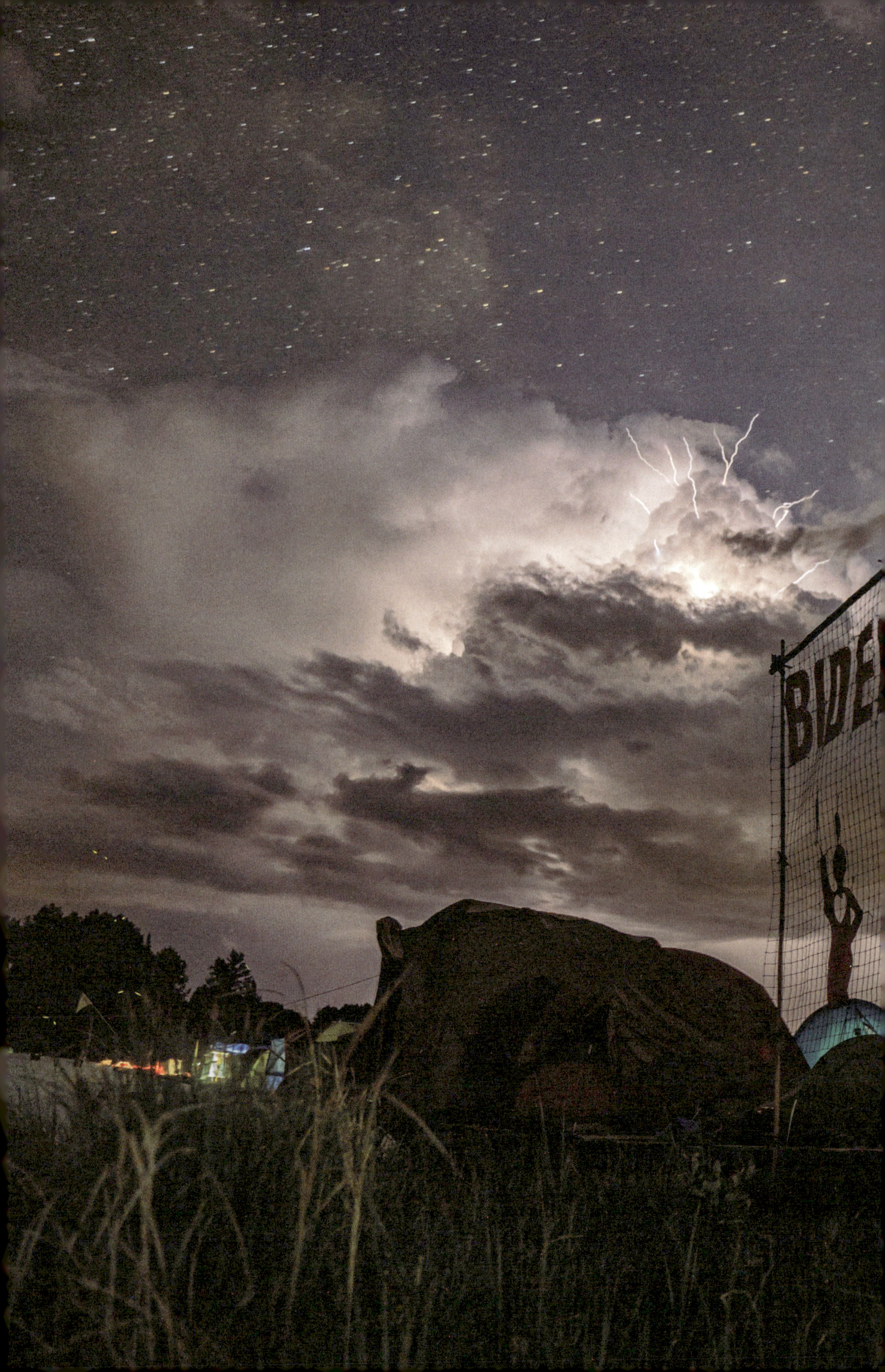

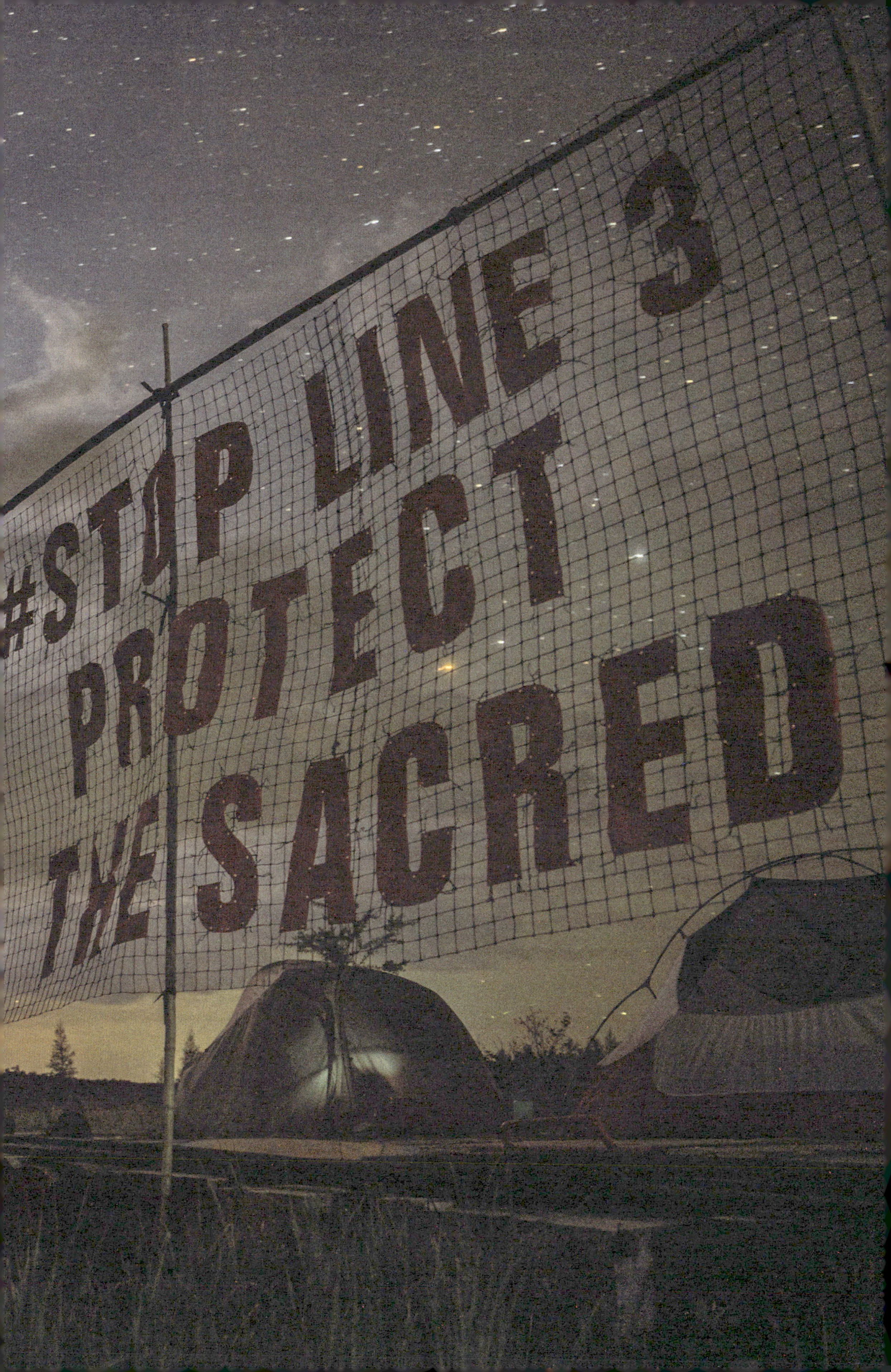
#STOP LINE 3
PROTECT
THE SACRED

restoration

in spite of all that happened we stand on a bridge
in a city bombed-out again by the cold
while another blizzard waits on a bad northerly,
while north of that a strip of bulging ground
waits stripped of trees in its last designation—
declining tract of unwatched churchyard grass where no one goes.
even the anarchists no longer bother—
some fear ghosts; some walked miles
from gas station to bulldozer on wood planks
until they gave up changing and their boots were
lined with splinters and are tired. when we went
between the chocolate shop and park i was thinking
about how i walk. now stopped on this bridge i think
about my awkward lungs so hardly
notice evening drain to the pulp of the sun.
you say ducks cross a shallow pond, i look
down and we watch ducks crowd. i want to speak:

it's been weeks since we talked about the pipeline.
last time it was october—it was almost as if nothing had ever happened
and then there was oil.
we were in another state and nobody called to
ask what one does with defeat.
mostly we passed cigarettes and tried to
flinch a little less at flashing lights because earlier,
in jail, we could think of no reason to speak.
i thought about the humming walls,
ligature without meat, and wanted to know the time.

but world comfort, even world loneliness, returns you.
you would say it repairs. notice it,
outside, comment on the wet concrete
and the underside of lamps and
roots breaking up concrete,
jars of honey, jars of bitter mulch;
it isn't hard when you go outside
to say these hold the earth,

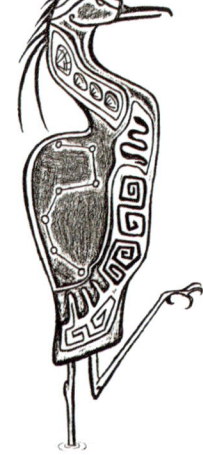

to mean it; you think you're understood.
but though you lost
what you lose in a cell and a gamble
monotony returns.

at first you thought about the earth
over and over,
the same, the same,
the trees the rain and jars on countertops
and crumbs of stone;
you thought about a bone raised like a mountain over the earth,
you called earth a dream in death's head, the body of death our god,
our planet—you tried
like we've all tried.

but we weren't so careful;
in the end you went home.
now add to your notes how bad acre follows acre in the city
and it's even less real than before.
'now now,' someone says,
'leaves all scatter and black water pools; surely
there is love there, surely you can see?' and you smile
and remember to recite the psalms.

even after all the blockades, even after the riots,
the communists, the houseless camps, your own,
even though you've known roads that aren't these roads,
vines can grow over columns,
over a bank. returning to the world returns you
too, it's painful,
it returns you to something that hasn't been alive in years and you give up
on not getting older, forgetting that you've
been a child twice now,
that you've loved twice, you saw a way out

because you're back.
sheepish maybe,
but more likely you don't notice how

cold hours and getaways and what it was your lovers wanted all go.
and the clearest thoughts over bad coffee
come back muddy, and beer on a frozen lake,
ammunition under seats, even snow
in a column of firelight can't last.
you give it back
to the landlord
or traffic on the road, or whatever it was you were fighting.
you can keep wearing boots,
you can buy a gun, but the visions won't come
and you forget the wash of triumph and grief
while black flags wave forgotten over excavators.

someday soon at the end
of another bad night you'll ramble
through the city like you used to
until real anger, that drove hands and legs,
ballet, barricades, flashes
and settles to sleepy self-abuse.
four squad cars could ride away from the curb,
the drivers done kicking someone like you'd pick a hibiscus
and you'd hardly think of it at all because
coming back demands you focus,
to watch the road instead of other headlights,
to enjoy chicken because you refused a steak,
to enjoy changed skies instead of needing a clock,
to be bored. then one day
you give up on peeling an orange,
and soon enough you can make
strange and sudden turns in the street without weeping,
and at last even when slow bones of sunrise scatter over us
we often remember to groan
like some good prayer—
it's mundane again to share. •

Survival Lessons

Up north, the days felt like they were tripping over each other without pausing to think that maybe they should take turns. There was no such thing as one day at a time, because there was not even such a thing as one moment at a time — cramped together in bunk beds or crowded tents where we could hear each other at every second, even (if I may crudely illustrate my point) overhearing the occasional orgasm, we felt constantly surrounded by multitudes of possible experiences in each moment of time. Any given night, someone would be doing dishes while someone would be trying on "jewelry" while someone would be watching the road for cops while someone would be sleeping while someone would be scouting while someone would be undoing themself completely at the unbelievable sight of the stars.

I rolled into the movement pretty late, in February of 2021, when myself and about 25 other privileged college kids set foot "up north" for the first time. I arrived at "scamp," a repurposed summer camp, where I slept in seemingly endless rows of bunk beds and began to familiarize myself with the instantaneous switch between uproarious hope and all-consuming fear that was to become my life, the connection between myself and reality, for what felt like such a long time after.

> *Any given night, someone would be doing dishes while someone would be trying on "jewelry" while someone would be watching the road for cops while someone would be sleeping while someone would be scouting while someone would be undoing themself completely at the unbelievable sight of the stars.*

The switch between joy and terror became righteous comfort for me. As I began to psychologically prepare myself for a red role, whatever that would be, by journaling and reflecting and staring blankly at sparkling snow crystals, I used the intensity of my feeling as a compass for how to act. I followed anything I could find that felt visceral, equating any numbness with complacency, and throwing myself into as much intensity as I could bear.

Summer came, and I began to hear the word "trauma" every so often in conversation. Trauma: shorthand for time travel. The unwelcome gift of experiencing the past, present, and future unravel simultaneously inside of you. Around me, elders and leaders were pointing out and acknowledging the traumatic conditions of what everyone was going through just as I was coming to accept myself as a traumatized individual. A few months before I arrived at scamp, I started experiencing sleep hallucinations. They began when things were going wrong with an ex-partner I had been living with. The first one was about my gaze irreversibly damaging the faces of anyone I looked at, which felt so real I was afraid to make eye contact with anyone for days after I woke up. I had many subsequent ones, some including sleep paralysis, and eventually in May I found my way to therapy and a diagnosis that shocked me, complex post-traumatic stress disorder.

I have told many friends that my word of the summer was "shame." I felt shame about my circumstances. About leaving camp to go to a funeral in July and then taking time off when it felt like nobody else got a break. About being around while feeling too fragile at times to cope with the tasks at hand. I got the feeling that I was taking up resources, space, even food that could have been useful to others. I masked these feelings for a long time, partially because of the fear that expressing them would make people who hadn't thought that much about it realize I was right. But the first time I finally broke down and cried and told a friend, I found out that they felt that way too.

The people who organized and participated in this movement are some of the bravest and most compassionate people I know. I am young, so I was not around for the many bits of history that laid groundwork for this movement (such as resistance to DAPL at Standing Rock). I had never before been part of a group of people so willing to sacrifice to fight the cops and the imperialist government.

But it breaks my heart to think that these same personalities that resulted in bravery and compassion also led to self-hating, self-effacing behaviors. To people's denial of their own biological needs. People who never would have asked anyone else to live in a constant state of vigilance were berating themselves if they were not doing exactly that. These parallel, and often silently fought, battles wore the community down.

I feel protective of the lessons that I learned when I was putting my body on the line. It's hard to articulate them because it's hard to let them get far enough away from the recesses of my chest to even become words. But, in my opinion, the relationship between this movement and trauma is yet to fully be discovered. The movement was comprised of all the people in it, a mosaic of our complex individual stories and what was happening in our lives at the time. Still, there are people I have lost touch with, and I realize that I may have no idea what their life looks like now that our shared experience is behind us. There were many levels at which we were not always fully seeing, not fully knowing each other, that unseeing and unknowing being the cost of our ability to muster up the constant fortitude that our situation required. I tell myself, "We were doing what we needed at the time to survive."

Survival has taught me lessons about how to go forward. That is how I see my PTSD: I can understand my behavior now as a reflection of how I learned to survive previous circumstances. Months out, I still frequently wonder, hope, worry, and reflect about what survival lessons myself and my beloved water protectors will find that we got from the weeks, months, or years we spent together dreaming and resisting under the stars — and whether or not we will shed them when one day we don't need them anymore. •

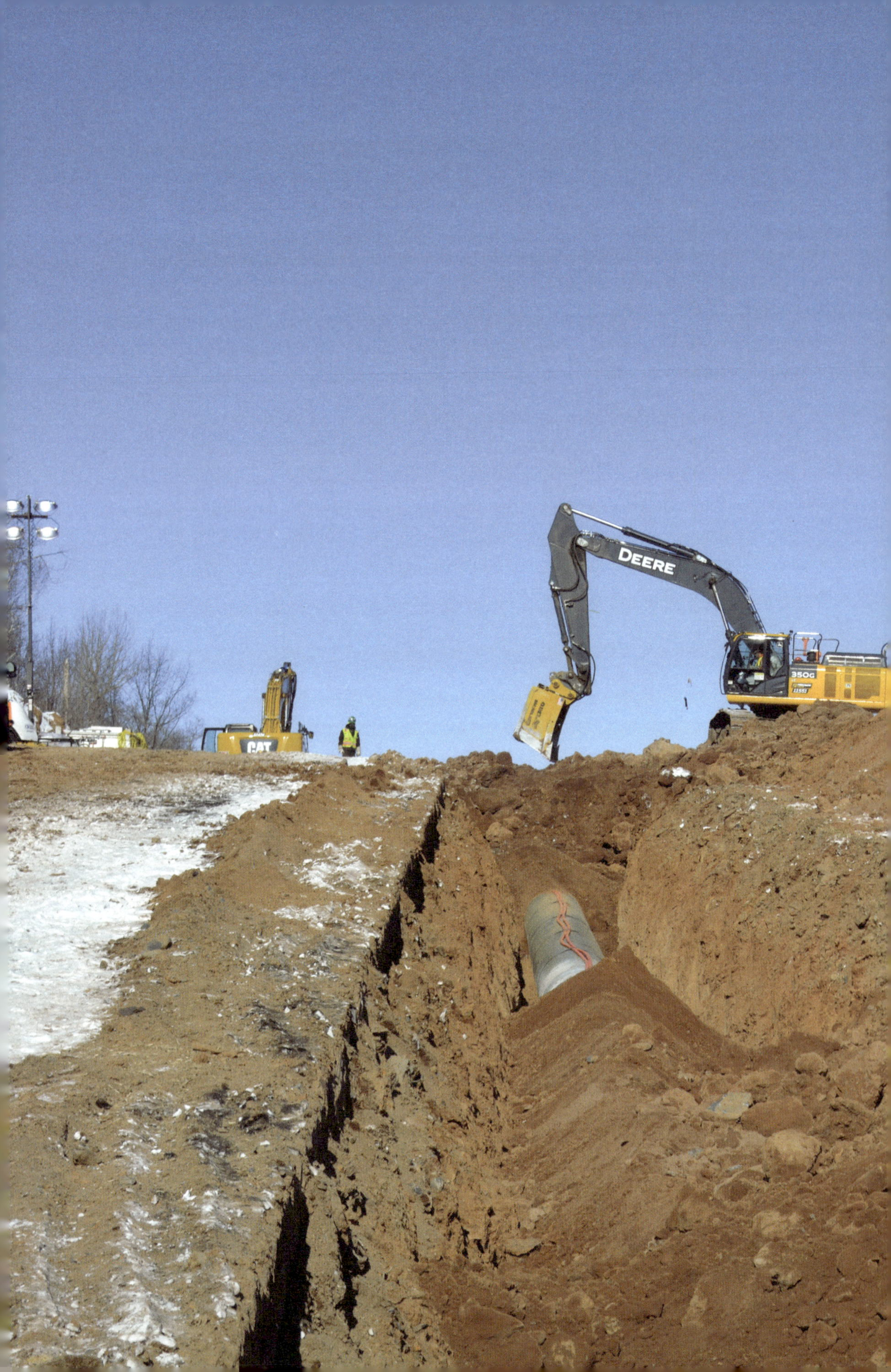
DEERE
350G
CAT

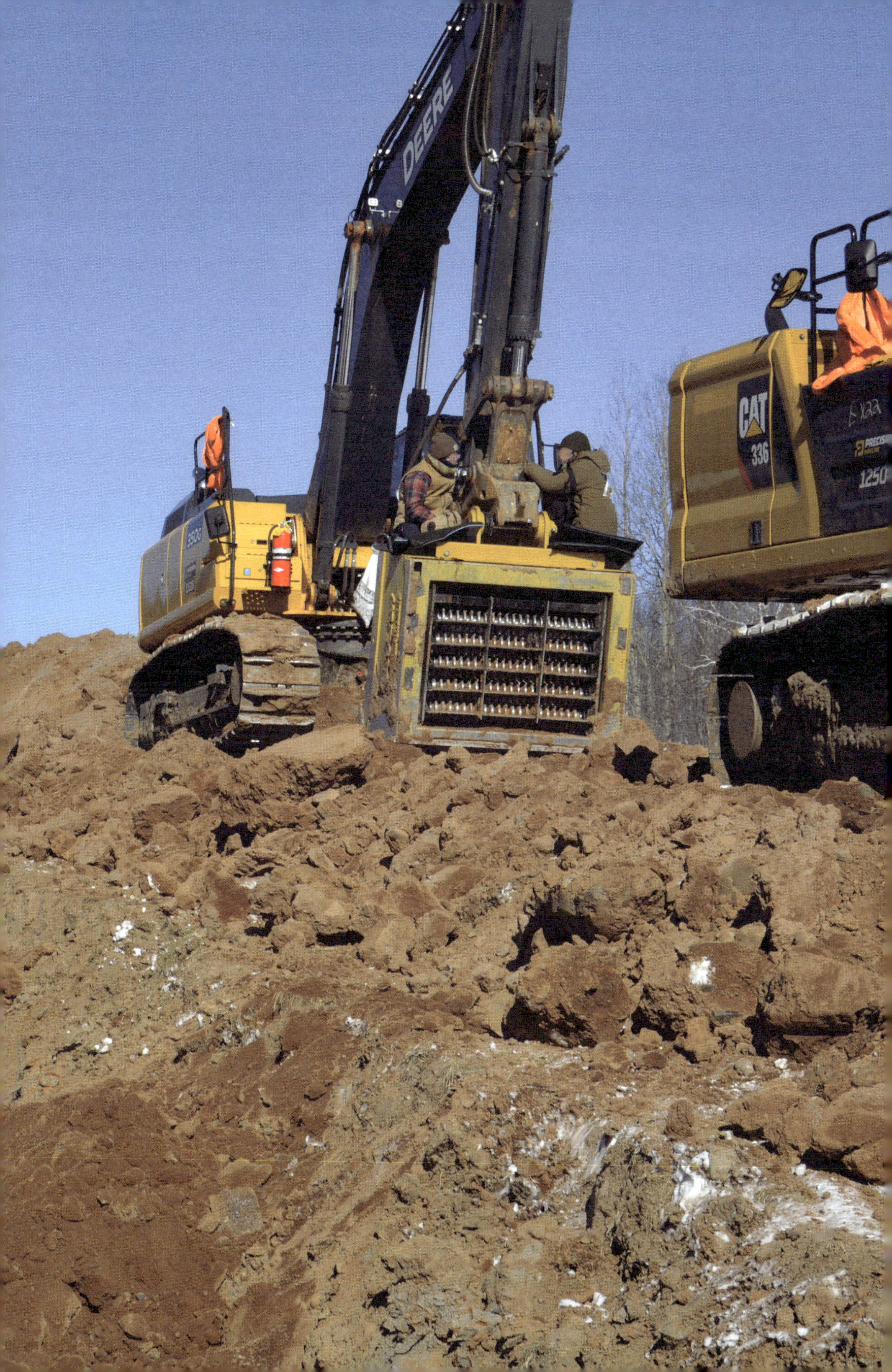
DEERE
CAT
336

Reflections of a Youth Pastor

Churches like to talk a lot about "the body of Christ" or "the communion of saints." Meaning they like to talk about how the members of churches and congregations make up the metaphorical body of Christ that continues to live and serve the mission of the poor and colonized carpenter that was executed by an empire. It's a lot of nice talk, everyone wants to consider themselves a part of the liberatory work that we're *supposed* to do. Yet, having been a member of various churches my entire childhood, and now a youth pastor at a Lutheran congregation, I don't think the communion of saints looks the way that many of my fellow (overwhelmingly white) Lutherans believe it does. The communion of saints is not a bunch of old pious white men with beards, and most importantly, the communion of saints is not within the walls of our churches or within the confines of our institutions.

So, who is the communion of saints? Those who spent their time cooking giant pots of food, laying out sandwich spreads, filling water at resistance camps. At the Treaty People Gathering, the cook team did their own miracle, their own feeding of the roughly 2,500 people at the camp. You are the communion of saints.

The communion of saints includes those who did jail support. Prison or captivity is a common theme in the Bible, as Christ said, "I was in prison, and you visited me." And by God, jail support certainly did this. Those who answered phone calls from people being booked may have felt rushed to gather critical information, but a single phone call with someone scared of what happens next in jail is like a healing balm. They liberated our friends who were held captive by gathering funds and coordinating paying bail, not too dissimilar from the earthquake that freed Paul and Silas from prison. They offered what little they were capable of, companionship and counseling to those recently released, being willing to sit and talk, offer cigarettes, food, and coffee. I imagine that Christ also did the same, sat with those who were suffering or in fear, offered what little he had, and simply sat down and listened. You are the communion of saints.

The communion of saints includes those who put their own freedom on the line for others. Many prophets from my tradition faced persecution for their acts of protest and resistance for the sake of the marginalized and oppressed in their society. And here against Line 3, many of us risked the same. Laying down one's life, or in this case freedom, for the sake of others (both the Earth and the plant and animal life on it, as well as our fellow human, especially our Indigenous siblings) is quite literally the job of the communion of saints if they are to imitate the executed carpenter. You are the communion of saints.

The communion of saints is you, all of you who fought Line 3 together with love and care for your fellow human beings. •

I spent long weekends going north to water protector camps starting in the spring. I got to work with so many amazing people helping build infrastructure for camps. Playing a support role meant that I wasn't on the front lines but I did spend a lot of time listening to all the inspiring folks who came through camp. I tried to distill some of what I learned into this ukulele. I incorporated some foraged materials like mussel shells and wood that beaver nibbled on. When you hold the ukulele, you hold the complex wetland ecosystem and if you are in tune with the system, you can make beautiful music.

On March 5, 2021, hundreds of students from across Minnesota raised awareness about their institutions' participation in the fossil fuel economy. Students at St. Olaf College organized an 18-and-a-half minute "die in," laying in their campus quad — 1 second for every mile of the Line 3 pipeline.

TUMMY SICK ON THE FRONT LINES
4AM. OVEREXERTION
IMPROPERLY STORED BISON CHILI
HEAT + PERIODS
BAD CHOICES AFTER THE VALLINE™

Editors' Note: This story was developed from an interview. It has been excerpted and edited in collaboration with the interviewee.

This has been a battle that has been going on for a long time. I grew up on Leech Lake Reservation. Growing up, when we would drive into Grand Rapids with my grandparents, I would see the billboards saying, "Stop Line 3" or "Protect Water" and things like that. I wouldn't pay any mind to it, I would just think, oh it's another billboard. And I read more about it and saw that it directly impacts my community.

I decided to get in my little car on one of my days off from school, and I drove and got there. It was a solidarity event. There was food, and I remember there was fire, and at that time of year, there was still snow on the ground. I was bundled up.

It was very nerve wracking. Just being around all of these awesome people doing really badass shit. Can I swear? Doing badass shit, water protecting and land defending. I was like, "Wow, this is amazing. How could I have not known about this sooner?"

Coming into the movement — it's gonna sound cringey when I say this — I was a "Native influencer" or whatever on TikTok. I shared different things about my culture, language, the importance of the dreamcatcher to the Anishinaabe. I amassed a bit of a following, and I wanted to use my platform to help spread the word about Line 3. And so I started making content around that. The first few videos I did got a lot of traction. And over the course of the movement, I actually met people who came here from out of state because of my videos. That meant a lot.

I was surprised by the amount of amazing people who are in places you would not expect. I grew up right in Ball Club, which is on the border of the reservation. So, if you drive 10 minutes east on Highway 2, you're in a border town that's majority white. And there is racism. So, when you go out, you're kind of very reserved and quiet and don't interact with people. But coming to find that even members of those communities can fight alongside you, and are willing to throw down to defend the water and protect the earth, is just crazy. It makes me have a little bit more hope in people. And trust. •

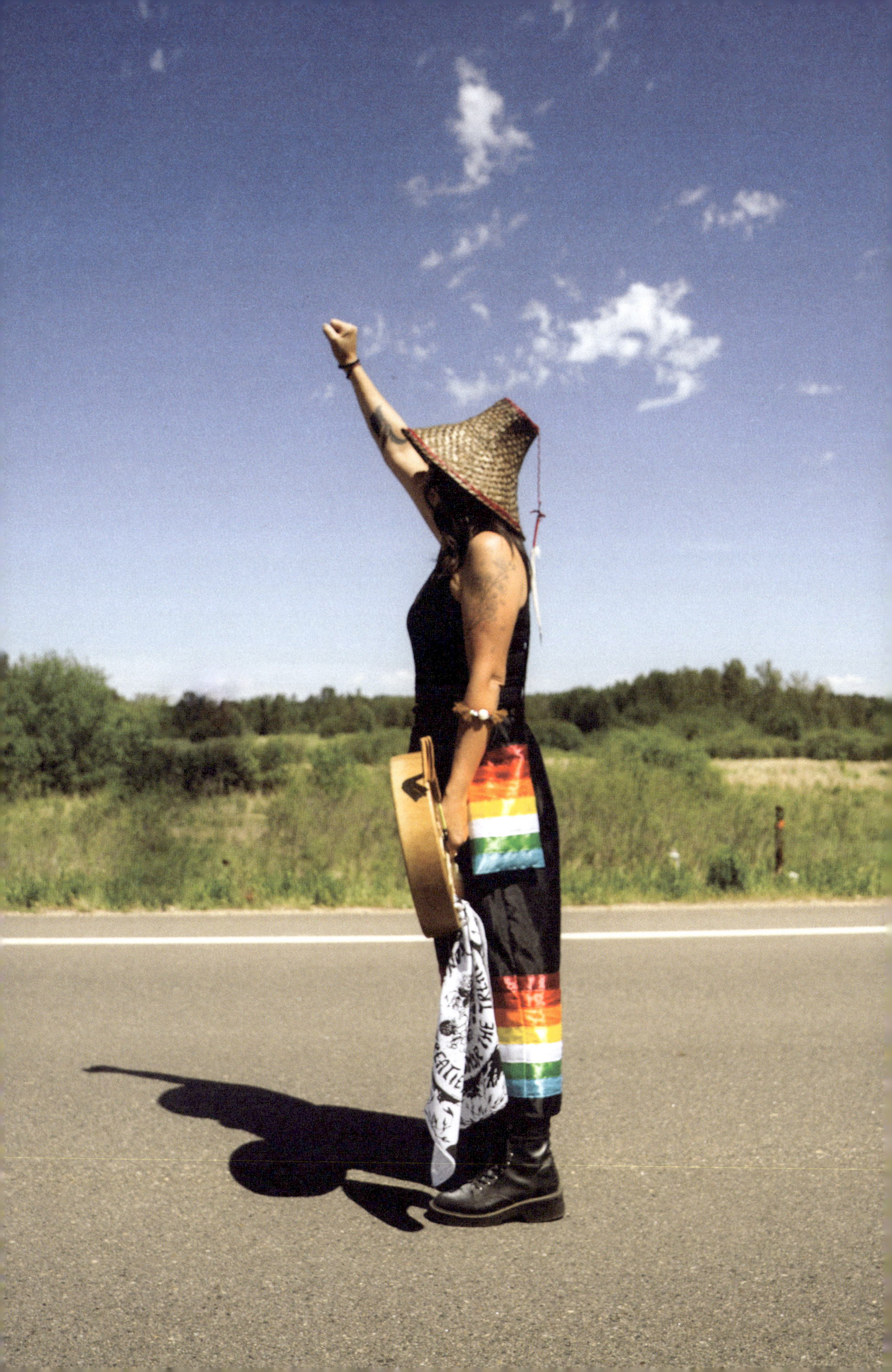

I try not to make a habit out of imposing beauty standards I do not believe in onto any living creature, human or otherwise. But it feels important to document for posterity that the guinea fowl (who ran afoul of the camp I lived in that latter summer of the Line 3 construction process, on acres of woodland in northern so-called Minnesota) were not pleasant to look at. They were, in fact, almost offensively unaesthetic, with Jurassic heads that reminded you gutturally of the genetic link between dinosaurs and birds, and neck wattles that looked like there'd been an oil spill nearby. Which of course there had been. And — they were *loud*! We thought the rooster, a patriarchal asshat who wrought havoc on the camp's hens and puppies alike, was vociferous enough, but the guinea fowl would find their way onto the roof somehow, station themselves there like it was their last stand, and start screaming their neck wattles off, waking up all of the so-called state to hear their complaints.

Somebody told us that they make all that racket not because they're stuck, but because they've lost track of their friends and partners, with whom they bond fiercely. They scream to find their way back to each other. We'd loved them before, in sort of an ironic way. But we loved them a little more after learning that.

One day, when one guinea called out for his partner, he heard no response back. It was too quiet in the woods. For weeks, he looked for her and we did too. Fearing the worst, we made sure he was able to find support with his new chosen family, the chickens. He slept in their coop and eventually stopped calling for his lost partner. We were all devastated. In the midst of a war against the state, any small loss hit harder.

Then, on one beautiful summer day, out of the woods marched his long-lost radiant partner with a *gaggle of baby guinea fowls*. They were parents!

It was the best and most unexpected news we could have possibly imagined for them. Many of us cried, most of us admired their sweet family foraging for hours, and the rest of us took shifts keeping them safe and warm at night.

Isn't this who we all were? Living in community in the woods, screaming out to find each other in the world? •

Even in the early days of pipeline resistance, there were multiple groups working against tar sands pipelines. The groups, via individual members, interacted to some extent but didn't necessarily know or work with each other. Most were working to educate the public about the connection between tar sands and climate change, and they all knew something about the groundbreaking Indigenous resistance. The group I was working with, Occupy Minneapolis, was focused on the last leg of the first Keystone pipeline being completed in Texas at that time.

About the same time, I read a small newspaper article that described a "capacity increase" on the Enbridge Alberta Clipper, or Line 67, pipeline. I brought this information to the next Occupy meeting. It made sense to me to organize resistance to this in-state pipeline, one of several through Minnesota. Line 67 transported tar sands oil, and Enbridge had just filed documents at a place called the Public Utilities Commission (PUC) in order to expand the pipeline's carrying capacity. One person who attended an Occupy meeting was also working with MN350 and invited me to one of their meetings. I liked MN350 right away because they were laser focused on climate change and tar sands pipelines.

The early pipeline group at MN350 had two leaders and met about once a month. They were looking for a specific organizing opportunity in Minnesota. We focused on the Public Utilities Commission meetings on this capacity increase and learning about the ways the public could supposedly influence the decisions of the PUC. The rules of the PUC were new to us and seemed unbelievably illogical. I downloaded the thick "Certificate of Need for a Crude Oil Pipeline Capacity Increase" and read it cover to cover. So began years of reading, learning, and testifying on my part, before a commission that didn't care and ultimately resented us for participating.

One of the first northern Minnesota hearings I attended was on a bitterly cold January night. I shivered from the cold, the stark room, and the oddity of my position: a Minnesotan housewife, who normally brought food for the young Occupiers, testifying in front of a group of older men and before an older male judge. The burly men wanted the pipeline for the income they received from it; they might have been original Enbridge stockholders as well. The fact that two Enbridge contractors had died repairing the old Line 3 one day before another Enbridge hearing on the Line 67 pipeline in this same town made no difference. Afterwards, freezing while refueling at the local gas station, the only farmer who had spoken out against Enbridge recognized us and thanked us for being there. He asked if I had a place to stay that night and was appalled that the five of us were going back to sleep in a tent. He repeatedly offered to pay for a motel room, but we declined and went back to the Indigenous land where Enbridge had four pipelines buried without any payment to the tribe. I remember the sound of cows lowing throughout the night; I expected loons to be calling that far north in Minnesota. I washed a lot of dishes that I found frozen in an ice block of old dishwater. And I kept in touch with the kind farmer who offered to pay for a motel. •

> *The men testifying wanted the pipeline for the income they received from it. The fact that two Enbridge contractors had died repairing the old Line 3 in this same town made no difference.*

It took me weeks after returning from the focal point of the movement fighting Line 3 to remember the joys I experienced. Grief runs deep.

I was really disassociated getting back, feeling like I had left a whole world and entered a completely new one; it felt familiar, but I felt like a new person returning. It took me a while to find where I fit again with the new and exposed parts of myself.

Healing isn't linear (nothing really is), and re-grounding myself was small ups and deep downs, sprinkled in with a fuzzy yellow glowing memory of entering the embracing hug of water the day we got out of jail, here, and the memories of meeting all these new and sparkling people from all over Turtle Island rooted in similar reverence and relationship between all beings, there. Or the spicy crunch of fresh arugula eaten with pickled beets made by a community member and assembled by another community member, all in support of us and each other. The smiling faces, weary faces, furious faces.

I've steadily been able to wrap the grief in with the joy from those moments of the movement in my body. •

I saw it all a little differently

& maybe someday I'll tell you what I mean by this

221

In my diary I referred to it as

"the revolution from an empty room"

(which was only half-true).

A man in a suit parked his car and got out, fiddling with his coat. He had a 25-yard walk to the doors of the Minnesota Pollution Control Agency. I was over on the sidewalk.

I said, "Excuse me, sir, EXCUSE ME!"

I could tell he heard me because his steps stuttered, his eyes flicked over toward me before he studiously made eye contact with the pavement in front of him and speed walked toward the doors.

I went on: "Hi, yes, would you be interested in learning about how Line 3 will put more carbon into the atmosphere than the entire state of Minnesota's carbon emissions?"

He was not interested. Into the doors and gone.

I shouldn't completely generalize. While many of the interactions went as above, we did have some decent conversations too. Some employees seemed genuinely interested in the report, asking us curious questions, or fumbling with their to-go coffees and briefcases to read it as they walked. One even took a small stack of flyers to leave by the water cooler on her floor.

The flyer, actually a four-pager called "A Giant Step Backward," was a summary of a larger report compiled by scientists and environmentalists about Line 3's negative climate and carbon impact in Minnesota. The report primarily used the MPCA's own data to support its conclusion that Line 3 was (and is) a completely unnecessary, destructive, and dangerous project for Minnesota. Yet the MPCA had recently begun the permitting process for Enbridge's 401 water quality permits. The result of our frustration and anger with the MPCA manifested in us handing out their own data in their own parking lot, which we mostly hoped would irk the higher-level decision makers. This was how a lot of our action ideas around that time were born — any opportunity for maximum cheek.

When my two good friends and I (creative action dream team!) first arrived at the MPCA around 7 am, we stood right outside the doors and waylaid employees as they entered the building. This was pretty effective at getting people to take our flyers, but within 10 minutes we were ushered away from the building by bored security guards, who told us firmly that we were only permitted to stand on the sidewalk, on public space, to hand out our flyers. Naturally, the minute they went back inside, we started drifting back to the doors like runners on base, first a few steps, then to the rarely used bike racks, always watching for the moment a guard would come out again and we'd need to skitter back toward the street.

It was a brisk day in March of 2020. In two days, the Governor would declare a peacetime state of emergency and we'd all do a hard pivot toward masking, video meetings, and the brief rise of elbow taps in place of hugs. Subsequently, it was the last in-person activism I did for a long time… but we didn't know any of that yet.

After a while, one friend was having more luck catching people as they drove in, and a few employees would even sit in their cars with the window down, half into the parking lot, and chat with him. These tended to be the ones looking for an argument, but my friend's attentive listening and professorial air were good at defusing the confrontation. Not so much my forte. The other friend and I decided to head to the second parking lot around the back of the building, where we were sure we were not welcome but thought it might take longer for someone to get around to kicking us out. Again (unfortunately), it took only about 10 minutes for a security guard to come escort us away. He told us that one of the MPCA employees had gone specifically to the front desk and tattled on us.

"Oh," we told the security guard guilelessly when he approached. "We didn't know that we couldn't be in this parking lot either. We didn't even realize this was an MPCA parking lot."

"Uh-huh," he said, unimpressed, but we didn't resist him so he didn't care too much. As he escorted us around the building and back to the street, we saw that my friend had been chatting up the second security guard.

"And you know, all this data is from the MPCA's own public record," he was saying.

"Really?" The guard was shocked. "Wow, thanks, man. I'll have to take a look at this!" •

ENBRIDGE
Life Takes Energy
MINNESOTA LIMITED
AN ARTERA COMPANY
• Gustafson and
• EW&C
• Sun Electric

DANGER
OVERHEAD
POWER LINES

After going through the vetting process and being directed to Namewag camp, I was driving cross-country to so-called Minnesota when I received this message: "Hey, you've been approved to come tomorrow. Unfortunately, I won't be here to greet you. Here are the coordinates. They should work with Google maps. Please don't share them with anyone. I would recommend reaching back out to P. and they should be prepared to welcome you." I reached out to P. and…

> hey there! just updating you that i'm a little less than 2 hours away from Namewag — en route and planning to arrive around 4!

Ok cool I'm doing security at the front gate from 4-8 so I'll see you upon arrival

(7 hours later)

Did you make it here?!

> Yes!! I got here around 5!

Oh ok we're supposed to have you check in when you arrive
Are you up by the fire pit?

> ok coming up there now! J. gave me a tour when i arrived

Ok cool not sure I know J.

> what do you look like?
> / where are you?

I'm short with long brown hair and wearing a striped tank
I'm heading up there now

> i'm short, short blond hair in ponytail, purple t-shirt, will be there in just a couple mins

Ok cool see you soon

> sorry where exactly are you?

In the gathering space by the kitchen
Sorry should have clarified

                                                       hmmmm i'm looking for you

I don't see anyone walking around
Are you by the kitchen

                                           i'm by the outside kitchen yes
                                                   by the dishes station

Ah different area

                                         i'm asking people if they know you

Are you at namewag?
Lol I'm by dishes station

                                         i'm at the coordinates M. sent me

I'm so confused

                                                        OMG
                         I'm at welcome water protectors - which was
                            what M. sent me - all day long i've been
                                   thinking i'm at namewag
                                       wow this is a head trip

lol I had a feeling
I thought you were a cop for a second

By the time I finally arrived, the story of the mixed-up coordinates had already spread through camp; the first Namewag comrade I met greeted me at the front gate with, "Welcome to Camp Migizi!" •

THIS IS MY LOVE LETTER TO EACH OF YOU.

- THE RESEARCHERS
- THE FRONTLINERS
- THE JAIL SUPPORT
- THE ORGANIZERS
- THE WATER PROTECTORS
- THE ELDERS
- THE LEGAL TEAM
- THE ARTISTS
- THE BUILDERS
- THE DANCERS
- THE STORY TELLERS
- THE NOURISHERS
- THE COMMUNITY BUILDERS

TOGETHER WE STAND

STOP LINE 3

I LOVE YOU!

TOGETHER WE ARE BUILDING A BETTER WORLD.

I have so much love for each of you.

Those of you who braved the weather and climbed tripods in the freezing cold and scorching heat. Those of you who drove all night and stayed awake to help friends out of jail. The ones who cooked meals for each other and organized food and supply runs across the state. The ones who spent literally hundreds of hours in planning meetings and created resistance gatherings of thousands. Those telling the stories, leading songs and dances, making artwork. Those doing scientific research, leading long legal battles, and everyone, everyone, trying new tactics.

This is what it's all about — building a better world step by step, with everything we have. Using the skills we know, and learning the ones we don't. Unlearning ways of being, and creating new ones. Building vast networks of knowledge, action, aid, and care.

The pipeline is built. Irreparable harm has been done to the land, the climate, and our collective futures — but this isn't an art piece about all the anger and rage and exhaustion I feel — just love for all of you, and a recognition and honoring of this period of time.

I don't feel as if my words get anywhere close, so here is some art, from my hands & heart to yours.

It feels like ages ago when our young family stood in a hotel conference room in northern Minnesota, preparing to comment on a proposed pipeline slated to cut through the county where we lived. We heard that the pipeline would carry tar-sands oil from Alberta, Canada, across northern Minnesota through rivers, lakes, and wetlands to a terminal in Superior, Wisconsin. State agency personnel, County Commissioners, and the consultants in the room were all prepared to rubber stamp the project, as was typical for such things. These folks were sure the project would bring economic prosperity to the region. We stopped at an information booth that showed poorly detailed maps of the route and wondered, where was the water? This project would cut through the headwaters of the Mississippi River. Where were the details?

With a squirmy babe in our arms, we shakily spoke in opposition to the proposed Line 3 "replacement project," its expanded capacity and new route through the headwaters. We felt like lone voices in the room, but we were not. Shortly after us, Indigenous leaders and other Water Protectors came and boldly stated the destruction the project would have on tribal lands, precious natural resources like wild rice, and the harm it would cause Indigenous communities.

Since that first scoping meeting, our family has grown older. We have moved 635 Mississippi River miles to Winona, MN. We see the impact of climate change in our community and our world. I mourned with the great river in October 2021, when Enbridge announced the completion of the Line 3 pipeline and the beginning of the flow of oil. Although the project is completed, the resistance to it isn't. •

I'm a teacher who assigns a lot of Indigenous literature in my classes. I've taught *Last Standing Woman* many times. So, when Anishinaabe leaders called for people to go and put our bodies on the line, I felt like it was literally the least I could do. I had never engaged in this kind of direct action before, never been arrested for civil disobedience. There were many times during our occupation of the pump station when I almost caved into my fear and left. But when those riot police descended on us, and we linked arms and sang for the water, I felt stronger than I ever have. The sun was sinking in an orange blaze, and the dragonflies were everywhere. A young woman beside me pointed and said, "They're a blessing."

I continue to feel blessed by that land, those people, and this movement. Even though the pipeline is running now, and the climate news keeps getting grimmer and grimmer, I feel hope. Every time I meet with my arrestee cohort and our brilliant lawyer, every time I volunteer some data entry for the court-watch team, every time I Zoom into court myself, I know that I am part of something much bigger and more beautiful than I ever knew was possible. •

Something I've learned through organizing against Line 3 is that Nature often shows up as an unexpected participant at our events, protests, rallies, actions. A couple examples that spring to mind are the downpour during the live music at the Block Line 3 Party outside the Public Utilities Commission and an unrelenting blizzard as we demonstrated on the Hennepin Avenue bridge to protect the Mississippi River below us. What might seem at first like an obstacle or adversary, however, can make for a very special moment. Rather than running away, people danced and laughed in the rain while J. continued to sing. While the winter winds drowned out many of the speakers on the bridge, they suddenly quieted while a comrade read a Langston Hughes poem about rivers, giving us all a different kind of chills.

Mother Nature doesn't always show up in an "inclement" manner. Sometimes, she'll come to the party with weather more perfect and unexpected than you'd ever dare to hope for. Such was the case for the Gichi-gami Gathering to Stop Line 3. After nearly six months of difficult and emotional organizing, we turned out about 1,000 people on a late September day in Duluth. My organizing role was around logistics, and I recall being very worried about what the weather might throw at us. Late September on the north shore can produce summer heat, winter winds, and everything in between. And our location, Gichi-ode' Akiing, was a very exposed park right on the lake. I arrived the night before and struggled to find sleep as visions of canopies ripping from their poles, signage taking flight, and sidewalk art washing away invaded my mind.

I awoke early the next morning, got some coffee, and walked along the Lakewalk toward the park. It was a quiet, gorgeous morning. At one point I turned onto the beach toward the shore of Lake Superior. I squatted down on the pebbles, and gently rested the palm of my hand on the surface of the lake as the water lapped at my shoes. A feeling of calm reassurance washed over me. I felt Gichi-gami connecting with me, thanking me for showing up that day, and telling me everything would be okay. It was quite powerful, unlike anything I'd ever experienced. I thanked the water, and carried on toward the day ahead, knowing we were in store for something special.

And how special it was! The weather was perfect, and the turnout surpassed our expectations. The Gathering felt like this string of unforgettable moments, some planned, some a result of spontaneous ideas and creativity. It seemed everyone brought their best selves that day. There really was magic at work. But what I will remember most is the march we took around Canal Park. I found myself marshaling at the front of the procession, and at one point, I stopped to look behind at the colorful, art-packed parade of people that wound impossibly far back — I could not even see the back of the line. And then I looked to my right, toward the lake, and saw the very spot on the beach where I'd stopped that morning. Again, that reassurance came over me. As I panned back towards the marchers, a giant smile on my face, my vision expanded to see not just the people, but the air and sand and rocks and trees and sky and birds and water too, all united in this beautiful moment.

Humans are capable of having such a profound relationship with the natural world. We need not be mere observers of it; we can join with it in common purpose and harmony, if only we can open our eyes and listen with our hearts. This learning is a gift I carry with me from my time in the Stop Line 3 movement. •

My distaste of pipelines started back on August 22, 1979, when a 210,000-gallon pipeline burst just a few miles from my home, known as the Pinewood Spill. To date, about 25% of the oil is still in the ground and the site has been monitored to learn about what happens to the oil after it is spilled.

Many years later, I became the first organizer in the U.S. to fight pipelines, while working for the Indigenous Environmental Network in Bemidji, Minnesota. It was during this time that Enbridge was trying to add Line 67 (Alberta Clipper) and Line 13 (Southern Lights Diluent) to their existing four other pipelines known as their Mainline. The first pipeline was an 18-inch pipeline built in 1948, and the last one was a 34-inch pipeline that was built in 1972. I was working with only a small group of tribal members from the Leech Lake Band of Ojibwe to fight against Lines 67 and 13.

Due to the lack of public support and public knowledge, I realized that it was important to educate and show people the dangers of pipelines. To get people involved, I introduced the idea of leading pipeline tours.

The first tour was on a charter bus that arrived in Bemidji at the Paul and Babe Statues, on the shores of Lake Bemidji. We began the adventure by taking the bus down an abandoned railroad. It was quite the experience for all, including the driver, who loved it!

The people on the tour had no idea of what to expect on this day, or how it would change their lives. Our first stop was at a wetland along the railroad bed. I explained to them that in the early days of pipeline building, due to the lack of equipment, two of the pipelines were placed on wetlands in the winter months and covered with dirt to protect the pipelines from getting hit and damaged. The group was led out into the wetland, where they were able to walk on the exposed pipeline. This was a very powerful thing to experience, as none had ever done such a thing.

The tour then continued to an overlook where the four pipelines cross the Clearwater River, just west of Pinewood. The landscape of this area is stunning, however, a wide-open field is cut into the middle of this landscape with a pine forest on either side of it. This was the path of the pipeline clear cut. It is a steep 75-foot drop from this vista to the swampy river bottom. Group pictures were taken here to show how vast and wide (50 yards) the area is for four existing pipelines. Enbridge was proposing to widen it for the two new pipelines.

This was the first of about 20+ tours. The tours changed over time to include different sites dependent on what pipeline we were fighting.

We went to Cass Lake to view the first two pipelines, Lines 1 and 2 (which actually lay at the bottom of Cass Lake), a pumping station spill (which was never cleaned up and is being monitored), and the site where Lines 67 and 13 were placed.

We visited the Clearbrook tank farm, which holds millions of gallons of oil every day. On several occasions, the Sheriff's Department was called to disperse us, but we were always law abiding and no arrests or tickets were ever issued.

We also started going to the Red Lake Encampment, where Red Lake members started in protest to Enbridge having no easement for their pipelines on the Red Lake ceded lands in Leonard, MN. This encampment was prior to the Standing Rock Encampments. We held the camp for seven months, starting on February 28, 2012. We had to endure several cold nights that measured into the minus 50-degree range. To date, Enbridge still does not have an easement for this land.

Several years later, we added tours of where the proposed Line 3 would first cross the Mississippi River near Itasca State Park and in Bagley, where the Minnesota Pipelines (Koch Pipelines) cross the Clearwater River and U.S. Highway 2.

These tours were important, and they did their job to educate and gain support to fight future pipelines. Throughout the 10+ years of pipeline tours, I would estimate about 200 people have gotten to stand on exposed pipelines, and those people then started the wave by getting their friends and families involved in the fight. There have been politicians, writers, students, actors, and musicians. Many of the people on these tours were vital to the fight as they were executive directors and lead organizers of some of the biggest environmental groups in Minnesota which have resisted Line 3 and defeated the Sandpiper Pipeline. •

Editors' Note: This story was developed from an interview. It has been excerpted and edited in collaboration with the interviewee.

There's No Protecting Without Providing

If community healing isn't a priority, our communities will never be united and our hearts will never be strong enough to keep rising up.

As a rebellious migrant teenager growing up in rural Minnesota, I was sent to a substance abuse treatment facility slash teen prison work camp in the middle of the woods. There, I met another high schooler from a reservation by the biggest lake in the state. We were bunk mates, and even though he loved to fuck with me everytime I was about to fall asleep, he became my closest friend there. He told me about how pretty it was where he lived, so we made plans that I'd go visit him on the rez someday after we got out. A year later, I randomly met another teen from the same rez. I asked if she knew him, and that's when I found out that he passed away a few months after his 18th birthday when he went missing from a party one night.

Years later, I moved to that big lake and got involved in community organizing. We organized around the No Dakota Access Pipeline resistance at Standing Rock, first by raising money, then supply drops, and eventually staying out there for several months. After Standing Rock, I went back to the big lake and helped out with winter clothing drives, weekly free meal distribution, Wells Fargo bank noise demos, and nonviolent direct action trainings to stop Line 3.

After some friends I met in Standing Rock moved to the area, we started a harm reduction collective led by our Native homies from the community. Before starting our collective, I became close friends with a Native organizer from the community. What was new to me was a struggle that they'd been living their entire life. They had seen so many of their family, relatives, and friends lose their lives too soon. My bunkmate from treatment was one of those mutual friends.

We wanted to reduce the number of missing and murdered Indigenous women, teenagers, and relatives in the region. I'd heard about a few cases of femicide and disappearances in the community, and growing up we lived next door to one of the most infamous serial rapists and murderers in Minnesota whose case made international news, but I'll admit that my privilege prevented me from comprehending the scope of the issue.

So, we took to the streets, handing out clean needles and picking up dirty ones. We also made sure our homies struggling with addiction and houselessness had access to narcan, condoms, plan B, any other basic necessity that we could find.

On several occasions, we were asked to assist in conducting family led searches for missing community members. On each occasion, both tribal and city police either failed or refused to respond to families' requests for assistance in searches. In one case, when a family asked the police to initiate a search they said, "Don't worry, she's probably out partying." So, they called on us and all community members one week into her disappearance, and within a few hours one of her own siblings found her deceased. That's when the police decided to respond.

I realized that in this community, tragedies like these were not uncommon. When I was growing up, the only case I recall in my own community was when my neighbor kidnapped, raped, and murdered a young white woman, who had major news and search parties out looking for her from the first day she went missing. That's the kind of attention and outreach I'd thought every missing person received. But as I became more involved in the community, I realized that Native women and youth go missing and get murdered so often, and most people outside the rez don't ever know or hear about it.

When construction on the pipeline began, our focus shifted. Nonviolent direct actions (NVDAs) at construction sites became the focus, and although the pipeline construction industry has one of the highest demands for drug and sex trafficking, we stopped organizing around harm reduction. Lots of people showed up for NVDAs to stop construction, and a lot of the messaging focused on MMIWR, but most actions were not directly targeting mancamps, truckstops, and other hubs for sex and drug trafficking.

Every community of color everywhere has something threatening their land, water, and future generations. And every community would be able to protect and defend itself if its people had everything they needed to survive and thrive.

During Line 3 construction, there were four Enbridge workers arrested with charges related to sex trafficking. But the actual impact was much larger — most instances of sexual assault go unreported and/or unprosecuted. Sex crimes in the oil and trucking industry are systemic. They have and will continue to happen before, during, and after pipeline construction unless effective organizing and action happens. And the only time that the kops ever do something about it is when it makes good publicity, like during the construction of a high-profile oil pipeline like Line 3. The kops will always fail and refuse to respond when it's Black, Indigenous, and people of color disappearing, and they will do anything to cover up their own connections to sex and drug trafficking. Even when the rapists, murderers, and dope dealers get caught, the kourts will never do justice the way community could.

Line 3 wouldn't be in the ground if Enbridge hadn't torn apart Native communities over one reason — providing people's everyday needs. They preyed on tribal members by offering high-paying jobs to provide for their families in the now.

What does it mean to be a water protector and land defender when the communities directly impacted by pipelines aren't the ones protecting and defending their own land and water because they need to provide in the now? We talk about future generations when right now there are children offing each other in the streets and in schools, offing themselves, no food to eat, locked up, strung out, or hungover parents. Every community of color everywhere has something threatening their land, water, and future generations. And every community would be able to protect and defend itself if its people had everything they needed to survive and thrive.

It has been and always will be up to us — families, friends, relatives, allies — to provide for and protect those vulnerable ones by any means. We'll only be free when we can get our own needs met — quality land, homes, food, clothing, education, recreation, healthcare and healing, love, support, meaningful work, accountability, consensus — without expecting kolonial systems to provide them for us. •

Line 3 Villanelle

the river doesn't ask to be earned
though sometimes in dreams she runs dry
deep waters that wandered and never returned

hymns rise from the riverbank dimly discerned
an easeful shadow unfurls the *mooningwane* cry
so easily the river and the bird don't ask to be earned!

remember? how to be both alive and unconcerned?
see how the body became remade beloved in reply
and wandered deep waters wanting nothing in return

remaking relations among dragonfly, fishes, and ferns,
and hum a hosanna as the water runs by
behold! a river who does not ask to be earned

praises both deserving and undeserved as the wildfires burned
sends upwards a thundering of haze to the sky —
searching for waters that wandered and never returned

now brought undone in the current as it churned
offers the barest of prayers sent up between you and I
which still - after all this time - is a river of love who does not ask to be earned
though the deep waters wander and are never returned •

Stealing Baggage

My partner L. and I learned about the movement to Stop Line 3 on TikTok, so we arrived in Minneapolis to join the frontlines without any on the ground contacts there. I'm naturally shy and wasn't sure how to fit into the crowd we encountered in front of the state Capitol. I looked out at the Stop Line 3 signs, orange MMIW T-shirts, tipis and food distribution tents, chain link fencing and cops in brown shirts, and was shocked to see someone familiar. D. and I had only met once or twice at home in Lenapehoking, but running into him here felt like finding an old friend. We chatted a bit before he got up, leaving his bag, to go mingle with the crowd. I seized the excuse to stay on the fringes and confidently told him I'd watch his stuff. D. gave me the kind of look you give a friend who means well but has just said something slightly ignorant.

"Oh, ok," he hesitated. "But you don't have to like, *watch* it."

I immediately felt embarrassed. I hadn't meant to imply that I thought the people here were untrustworthy. Then I felt defensive: of course, the vast majority of them were probably exceptional humans, beyond suspicion or reproach, but taking precautions against theft was just normal, responsible behavior. To think we could just leave our belongings lying in the grass unattended seemed like performative idealism to me. Chagrined, I studiously averted my eyes from D.'s bag.

Three days later, D. went back to Lenapehoking, and I was the one who didn't know where my bag was. I had tossed my backpack to someone when I linked arms with L. in front of the Indigenous water protector locked to the gate of Governor Tim Walz's mansion.

We faced a double line of police in full riot gear; complete with batons, mace, zip ties, and guns. I would soon see these soldiers carry out the outsized response typical of the Northern Lights Task Force, the "security" funded by the Enbridge Corporation. They gave a dispersal order, then chased down, kettled, and arrested those who complied with it. Those of us who stayed to exercise our First Amendment rights were forced to the ground and zip-tied. After a rough arrest that left me bleeding, a strip search, and hours in holding cells so cold that my body finally stopped shivering, all 69 of us ended up in the same place: two nights in the Ramsey County Jail.

For all their weapons, resources, and millions of dollars of funding, the brutality of these police was held up by the same scarcity principle as the pipeline itself. We continue to invest in fossil fuels because we fear that if we don't, we won't have enough. Not enough energy, not enough jobs, not enough money, not enough security. This fear is powerful. It tells us we need to grab what we can, while we can, before someone else does.

Scarcity promotes theft, and pipelines take this thievery to a grand scale. They steal what belongs to all of us: clean water, a planet with livable temperatures, land that produces food and everything else we need. They steal the humanity of the people who build them. Those people, in turn, use intimidation, violence, and imprisonment to try to steal the humanity of those of us who resist.

Two nights of concerted effort to that effect finally concluded with our release into the parking lot across from the jail, into what can only be described as a well-organized, resistance tailgate party. Lasagna, soup, and salad were served out of the back of someone's car. People offered phone chargers, cigarettes, rides, ceremony. In stark contrast to the jail, it was an abundance of community, generosity, joy, and care.

And of course, my backpack was waiting for me. I had no idea who I originally left it with, but there it sat safely in the back of someone's van. My phone was dead so I found L.'s bag and dug for theirs, but came up empty-handed. By this point I knew better than to assume it was gone. I found the van owner and asked if he'd seen a phone.

"Did you check the phone bag?" he helpfully suggested.

My short time in Minneapolis taught me a powerful lesson: there is, in fact, enough. Those who know that feel no urge to steal. Decades of socialization in a capitalist, colonizer country told me that the way to survive was to acquire as many personal resources as possible and then defend those resources from others. This idea was so ingrained in me that I didn't even consciously recognize it — I thought that offering to watch D.'s bag on the Capitol lawn was behaving in a community-oriented way. A few days with this group made it clear that the only people I had to worry about taking my belongings were agents of the state (who did, in fact, take every scrap I had on me, from my wallet to my underwear).

But some things are harder to steal than others. We know the truth of our connection to one another and to the earth, and of the abundance we create when we tend this connection. There is no prison, no task force, no treaty violation that can eradicate that knowledge. While fear of scarcity might give someone the strength to come in riot gear to fight, it is the knowledge of abundance that lets us stand before that aggression with none of our own. "Enough" is not something we can get from the profits of a pipeline. "Enough" is what we started with, what we already had, what we share with each other, and what we stand to lose when we give in to fear and scarcity mindsets. •

500 Comrades

When I wrote these lyrics, I was walking on a frozen lake in minus 20-degree weather. I was at a summer camp that had been rented as a space for young people who were coming up to fight Line 3 for whatever time they could. The group changed all the time and it was hard for me to feel at home. I had come to Minnesota with the intention of passing through, before I became involved in the Line 3 fight. I had participated in a few Line 3 actions starting in the fall of 2019, but I had always traveled to the fight from wherever I was living at the time. I was stuck in a relationship where I felt I was losing myself, I quit a job as a teller at a credit union, and I moved across the country to stay with family, which led to even more emotional tumult.

I ended up packing my bags to go to Minnesota and I felt like I was coming up for air. I felt like I was around people I had known for decades, even though I knew no one. I still don't quite remember what home feels like or what it can mean, but I know that being in struggle with comrades has always been where I feel most at home, no matter where I am.

(to the tune of "500 Miles" by Peter, Paul and Mary)

When I left to fight Line 3
I didn't know I'd be finding me
Now I've got 500 comrades
Who are my home

From the Carolinas to the Golden State
Back up North, day by day
Lord I'm finding, Lord I'm finding
My way back home

I've been at one, I've been at four
Homes up North and there'll be more
Wherever I'm with comrades,
I am home

Well we're fighting the big black snake
And we all know the stakes
Well we're fighting, lord we're fighting
To save our home

For the ones who came before
We will learn and push for more
It's our time to be strong
And take the torch

Stop Line 3, yes we can!
Decolonize and free the land
Yeah we'll make the road by walking
Hand in hand

For our ancestors and our kin
For each other and our children
We'll keep on fighting, keep on fighting
Til we win •

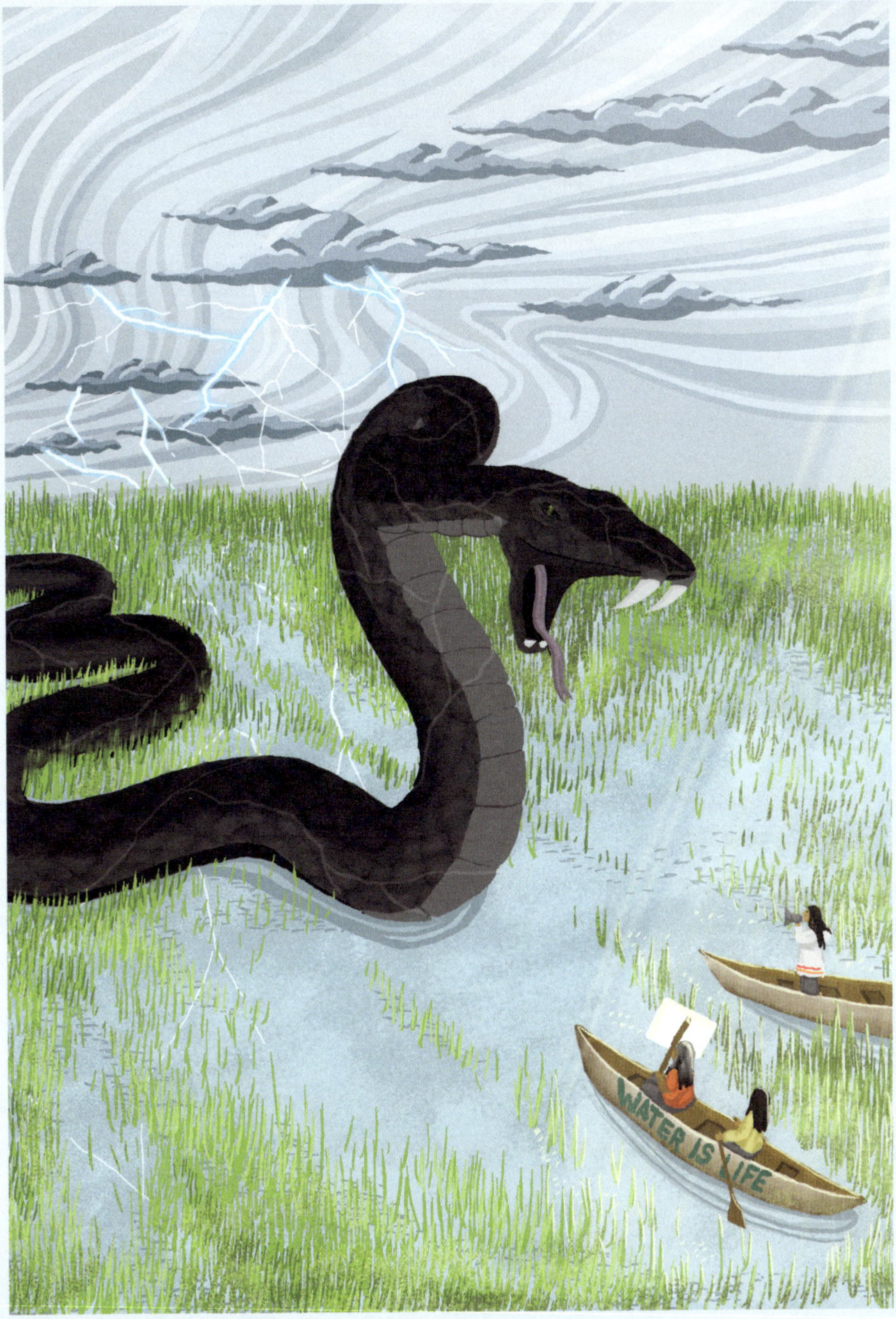
WATER IS LIFE

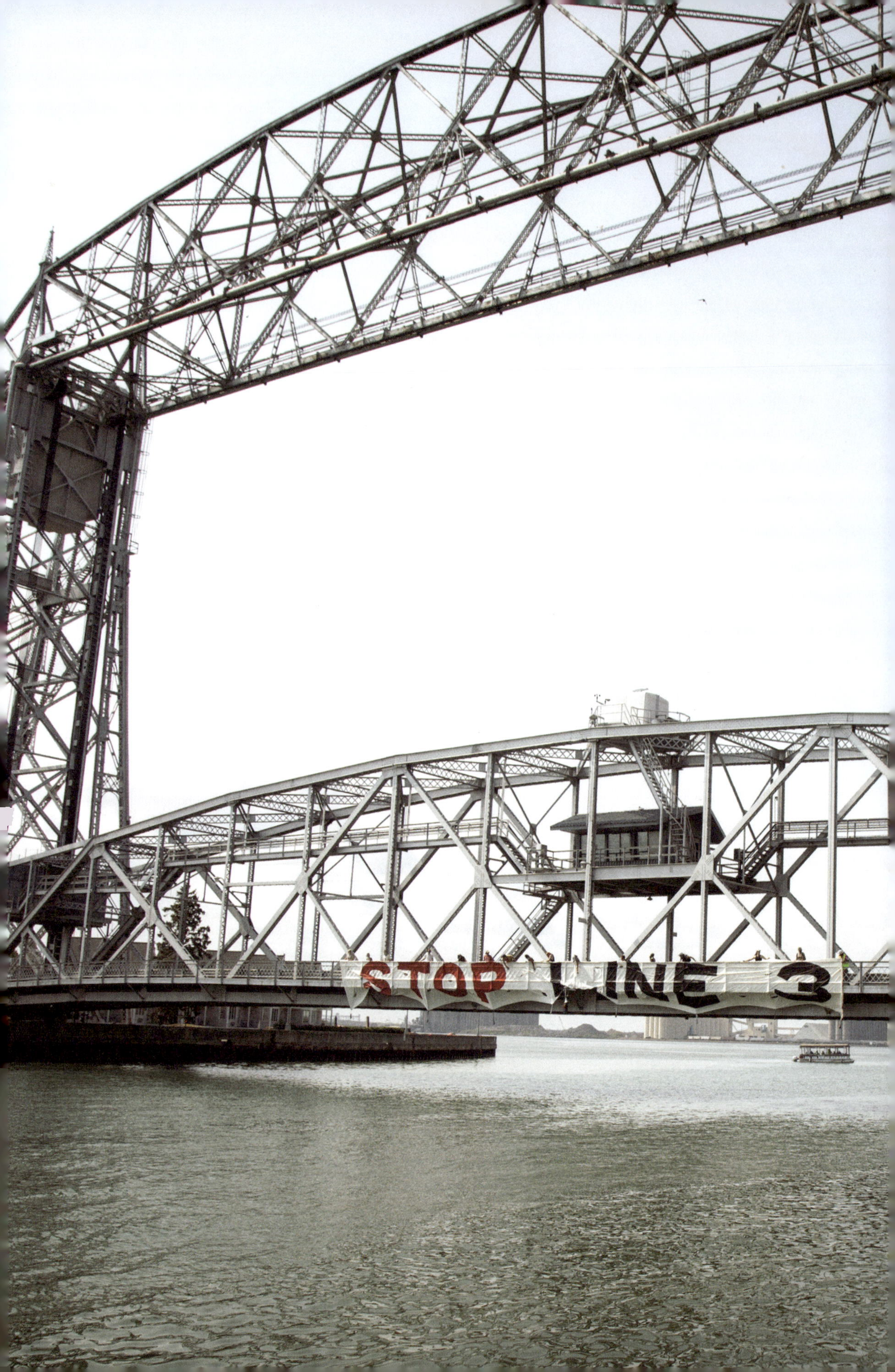
STOP LINE 3

Author's Note: This poem was written as an exercise in personal geography. As someone born and raised on the shores of Lake Superior, the movement to Stop Line 3 for me was shaped by questions of Home. How do places store memory? Can we choose our defining moments or are we destined to erode into essential formations? And most importantly: which stories hold their grip over Time?

Minnesota Point

I lost my favorite day in Duluth

the same day I lost my belief in mermaids.

Because my favorite day in Duluth

Isn't about a Bridge; it's about carpooling.

My favorite day in Duluth, I'd change if I could.

I would choose the hammock by the library or a potato casserole. If I could,

I'd write a poem about pheasant feathers.

But my favorite day in Duluth is a day that could've been played on the Radio.

My favorite day in Duluth is a Goose Statue

and Rose Colored Glasses and VIP passes.

My favorite day in Duluth is a sinking feeling. •

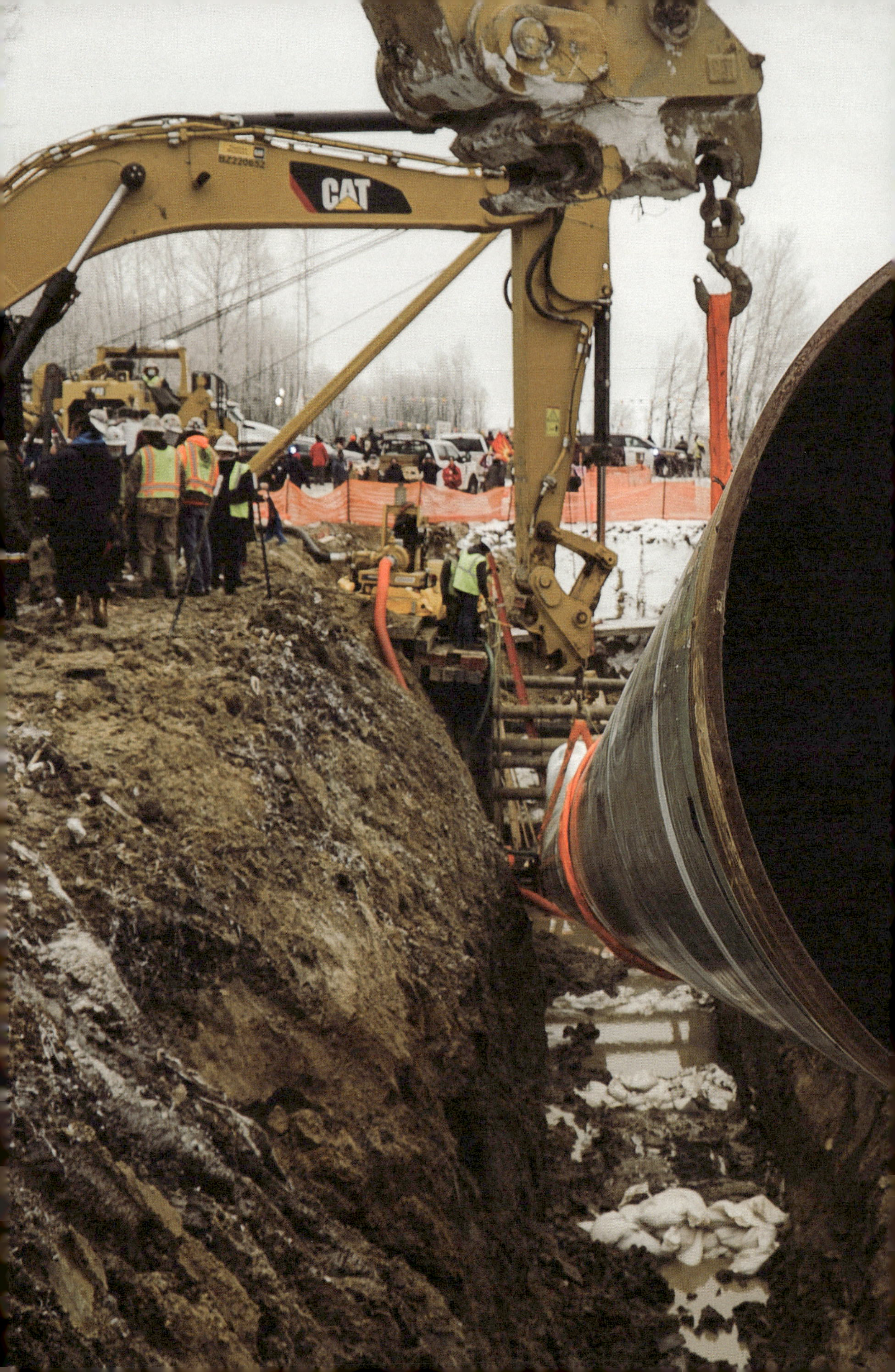
CAT

heart-racing

I had recently moved into a house in Duluth, to be closer to the fight and join some new friends in efforts of direct action against line 3. I was an environmental studies major, and for several years had been searching for some way to play my part in the fight against climate change. When I selected my major, my advisor sarcastically said, "Oh, I see, you want to save the world." I felt patronized and confused. If all the adults at the college understood the weight of climate change, as they claimed to, then how could they continue to live life as usual, without desperately seeking the same answers and action I was? How could anyone who was able, for that matter?

I had finally found a group of peers who were willing to take action against the fossil fuel industry. It felt so righteous and right that I decided to skip Christmas with my family to join them. I lamented not being able to spend time with my sister, who was expecting her second child, but it felt like the proper price to pay for a chance at even a slightly healthier planet. Back then, I had little idea the odds we were fighting against and what the risks we were taking meant.

It was early December 2020, just a few weeks after the MPCA granted the final permits necessary to begin construction. There were two tree sits up in Palisade, on one of the Mississippi drill pad sites. This was one of the spots where they would eventually pull the black snake under a river that provides drinking water to 18 million people. The idea was that if there were two people living in the trees on the path of the pipeline who refused to come down, outfitted with platforms and water and ropes, Enbridge wouldn't be able to cut those trees down and construction would stop, at least long enough to get significant media attention.

The tree sitters had gone up in the middle of the night. Eventually, this same site was outfitted with a double fence, topped with barbed wire, and intensely bright lights that shined all through the night, but when this endeavor first started, there wasn't even a single "no trespassing" sign along this particular chunk of the pipeline easement.

The tree sits were watched around the clock by a rotating team of twenty-somethings missing various amounts of sleep. There were two tents and a fire set up as a satellite camp, within eye shot of the tree sits, on water-protector-owned property.

To our disdain, the morning after they went up, construction began again as if they weren't even there.

All the workday long, we played cat and mouse. We would creep from the tree line on the friendly property, dash across a sparse power line easement, and surround the feller bunchers and excavators that were tearing down the forest. We would stay until the cops were called in from the road to chase us away. Then we would switch clothes and go back. We were able to stop work in 10, 15, 20-minute increments, but it wasn't nearly enough to slow their pace. To make matters worse, the cops were growing increasingly ready to arrest us.

In the afternoon, we watched the machines progress, ever closer to the sitters.

Would they cut down the trees that held our friends? It didn't feel possible, and yet I didn't want to wait and find out.

My good friend, B., decided to take one for the team and chain themselves to the feller buncher to keep it from getting any closer to the tree sitters.

We decided to make double use out of one run and bring some food to the tree sitters while a team helped B. to lock down. We picked someone to livestream, a couple people to stop the machine, and I was one of two designated to carry food for the tree sitters.

"When you reach the bottom of the tree," I was instructed, "yell for them to drop their bucket. Place the pot of macaroni in the bucket and tell them to haul it up. Then get the hell out of there." I nodded and was handed a pot of macaroni and cheese that had been recently made over the fire. Someone dumped a bunch of Oreos on top. Bon appetit.

My heart was pounding. We lined up at the edge of the trees.

I started running when everyone else did. I was wearing winter boots and it was hard to tramp across the field of snow. But I sprinted as fast as I could and I did not let that pot of macaroni fall from my arms.

When I reached the base of one of the tree-sit trees, I shouted for them to drop their bucket. I couldn't see any movement from the platform and so I tried over and over again, "drop your bucket!"

Then I heard someone yell, "RUN!"

Fear flooded my body when I saw four friends sprinting even faster than we had on the initial way across the easement, followed closely by three cops. It was time to go.

When I reached the tree line that indicated the edge of the friendly property, I kept going and headed deeper into the forest, hoping to hide myself from the cops. I was desperately searching my memory of the law for information as to whether or not they could enter the private property, coming up with nothing. I laid on the forest floor for what felt like an hour, still clutching the pot of macaroni as the cheese slowly froze. My heart would not stop pounding.

Eventually, I heard a friend calling us back to the satellite camp, saying the cops were gone. When we regrouped, two of us were missing.

The livestream was one and a half minutes long, blurry white footage and the sound of heavy breathing, followed by a large thump and a yell. Someone who is obviously a cop says, "Here's the deal, we just want you to be safe!" My brave friend, J., that day's designated live streamer, responds, "Then why did you just tackle me?!"

B. and J. did not make it home that night. We didn't see them again until three days later, when they were released from jail.

I'm told they were chastised for singing "Solidarity Forever" in the back of the cop car.

I had never known anyone who had been arrested before, much less participated in the inciting incident myself. I ate an Oreo, soggy with macaroni cheese, trying to process. We had no idea what charges they would get, how serious they would be, what sort of precedent it would set for the rest of us. What were we risking? What were we losing, anyways?

It wasn't until later that I found out that this arrest was the first one since construction had begun.

The sun was going down and construction had stopped for the day. The tree sitters were safe for the time being. It felt wrong, but there was very little we could do other than go and rest. My heart was still racing.

When we arrived back at the little house, I was shocked to find it filled with people. More and more came through the evening, until finally 15 of us were packed into the two-bedroom house for the night. They had all come to support the tree sits after hearing about the day's arrest, and everyone was clamoring to figure out next steps.

I lost any ability to be in the moment. My eyes rested on an envelope sticking out of an advent calendar, our strategic hiding place for $3,000 intended for bail money. We kept it in the event of a day like the one we just had. My mind wandered to what my friends in jail might be experiencing, feeling. I wished I could talk to them.

I snuck into one of the bedrooms and locked the door. I set a timer for 15 minutes and breathed as deeply as I could, giving my best attempt to slow my heart rate. When the timer went off, I opened my eyes and checked my phone to find a text with a picture of a newborn, from my sister.

"She's here! 19 inches, 8 pounds, 4 ounces."

The day had officially become too much to handle.

And yet, days like this suddenly became my new normal. It felt like the whole breadth of human experience was suddenly mine to share in, after months of pandemic-induced virtual reality, and two decades of deadened, destructive business as usual. It suddenly seemed so clear to me that I would either spend my time fighting the machine or becoming it. Absurd happenings replaced the mundane; joy and grief were thrown into sharp relief.

Now, when all was said and done, the blockades that went up week after week did not stop Line 3. But they gave us each other, a huge community built around the drive to fight for Indigenous sovereignty and against the fossil fuel industry. I gave so much of myself to the fight, and it somehow gave even more back. It gave me the special sort of power that can only come from pushing back on the status quo.

I view this liberation-in-resistance as a responsibility. To share and spread, for everything that we can change, for everyone who longs for a stop to the capitalist death machine. •

Author's Note: These are excerpts from correspondence with a company that sells bike locks.

To whom it may concern,

I recently purchased two pure platinum U-locks from your company based on the following review: "We tried everything to break this lock… it can't be done. We tried sawing it apart, using a chisel and heavy-duty hammer, drilling it with a high-powered drill, freezing the joints, and even heavy-duty bolt cutters. Nothing was able to break this lock!"

A comrade and I immediately put the locks to the test. Using the two U-locks to lock our necks to a gate of an Enbridge Energy pump station just felt right. After all, Enbridge, a crappy Canadian Corporation with a shoddy record, is building a pipeline through pristine forests and under pristine water bodies on Indigenous land. This pipeline will transport tar sands oil from Canada to Lake Superior. I couldn't think of a better use for your locks.

We immediately faced two obstacles. First, the gate wouldn't close all the way. Even if it did, your heavy-duty steel U-lock was too big for any of the holes in the gate. We had to resort to using a competitor's chain bike lock to secure the gate and use your U-locks around the bike chain and our necks.

After delaying pipeline work for several hours, a police extraction team arrived. They quickly cut the bike chain with standard bolt cutters — I knew the competitor's bike chain was simply not up to your standards, but we were improvising, and the chain was the weak link in our plan. We went to jail with your prime U-locks still around our necks!

Alas, my euphoria was short-lived. At the jail, the extraction team cut through the shaft with an angle grinder. After 10 minutes, Officer B. cut through one side of the lock. He was very pleased with himself before he realized he was only halfway done and would need to cut through the other side of the steel bar as well. But, within 20 minutes, the lock was in pieces.

I'm reaching out to see if this is covered under your warranty plan. If so, please contact me ASAP as we have much work to do (and we have a couple of bikes too)!

And, finally, I was wondering if you have ever considered sponsorship deals with folks who enjoy your superior products and offer free advertising through blogs and social media. We are not exactly "Influencers," but we will continue to put your locks to the test and share the results with like-minded folks intent on saving our planet! Join us! Be on the right side of history!

Sincerely, J.

N. Woods of Minnesota

(the e-mail response)

Hi,

Thanks for your email!

Amazing story, where did you buy our product?

Was this event published in the local press?

Looking forward to hearing back from you!

Best regards,

T. •

Weeks passed without rain.

To an eye that had not lived with this land for generations, the verdancy of the forest proved deceptive. Insects hummed in the lush undergrowth, full of wild raspberries, sedges, plantain. Pine giants rose above the understory, bursting with birdsong. Even the slap of a beaver's tail could be heard some nights when all was quiet.

Nevertheless, the drought raged onward.

The nearby wetland where ducks once swam reduced to dry foliage. Bears, starving, moved amongst us, scavenging trash. And we had all seen the rivers. Enbridge had just drilled under the Mississippi, a trickle compared to years past, now polluted with drilling chemicals and pillaged by pipeline.

So, you can understand our elation the day the rain came.

Whispered excitement moved throughout the camp, "did you hear it's supposed to rain?" not wanting to jinx it. Clouds billowed in the sky, the smell of damp hung in the atmosphere. Here and there, we felt them, the first drops. And then the sky opened up. Sheets of cool water unfurled upon the land, upon us. Some rushed for raincoats. Others ran for soap. Someone raised their hands in prayer, many others prayed in their own regard, shouts of joy, laughter. Thank you, thank you, thank you, I murmured, hands cupped full of clear, cool, water. As the rainfall continued, small rivers of runoff unwound in the dirt, saturating into mud, forming small ponds of puddles. It was as if inhibition washed away, and into those puddles we jumped. Like children, we raced through the rain, barefoot, shrieking with giggles. Faces, normally gruff, chain smoking, now alight with smiles, some the first I had seen. Someone threw the first mud pie, and soon we were all filthy. We battled, sludge slung without regard, pushing onward until we found ourselves in plain view of the sheriff's car surveilling us. Without hesitation, we continued, belly flopping into puddles, pelting one another with mud. What a sight we must have been.

> *Whispered excitement moved throughout the camp, "did you hear it's supposed to rain?"*

They stole a lot of joy from us, those cops with the rest of the state at their backs. This was an act of resistance, our happiness. And they stole a lot of water from all of us, those alive and those to come, Enbridge did, the state at their back too. This was precious, this rain. Cause to celebrate.

It's raining now, months later, in a different time and a different place. At this time of year, it should be snow. But I can't help but wonder if the water that falls here, now, is the same that rained upon us those many months ago. The water that brought us so much joy, the water that brings us so much life. •

The Mississippi River where Highway 2 crosses it from just outside of Grand Rapids, Minnesota, near the Line 3 corridor. The first was taken in 2021 on my way to Firelight. I stopped because I'd never seen the river so low. The second photo was taken nearly a year after, heading home from my grandmother's house.

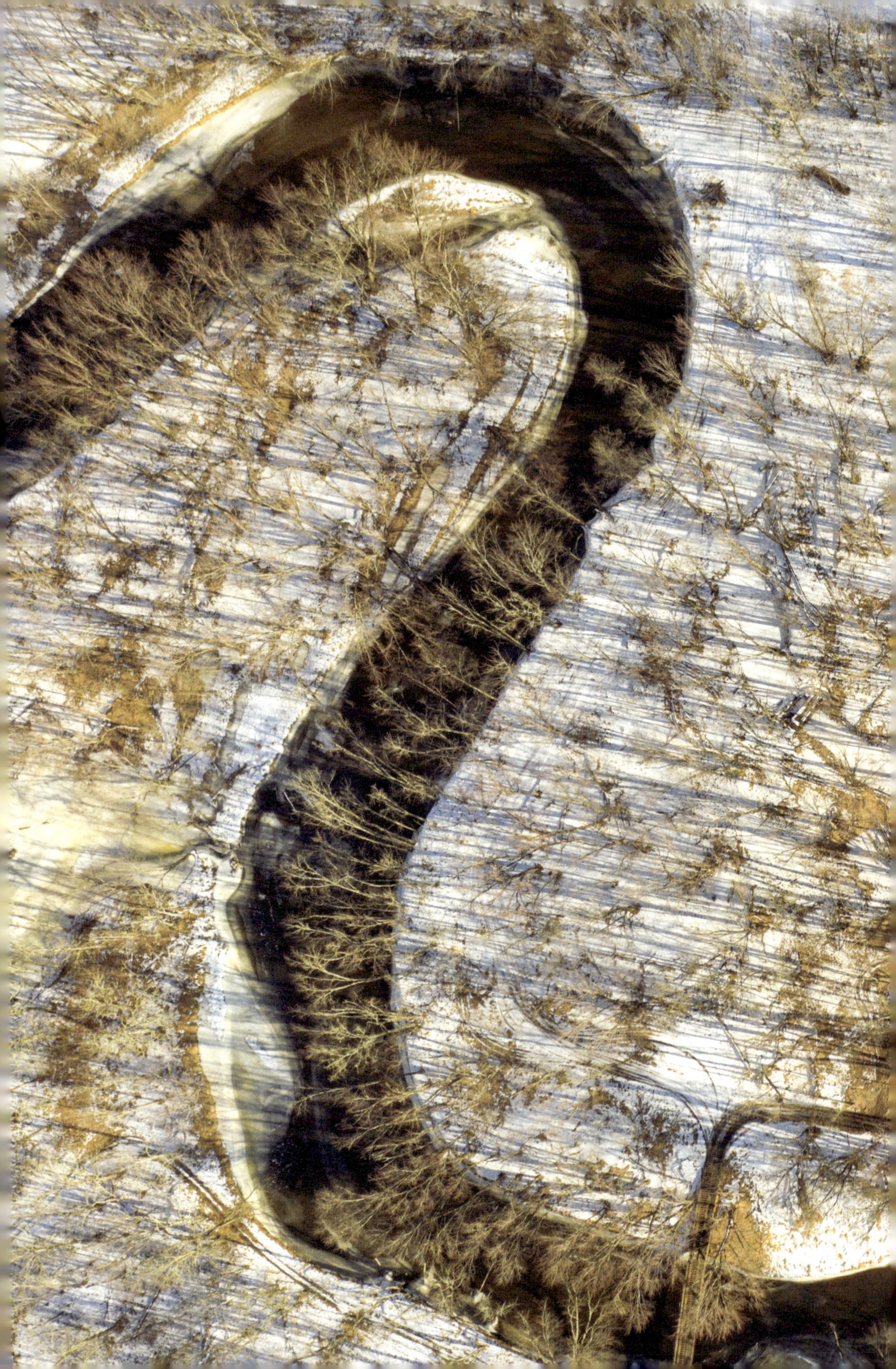

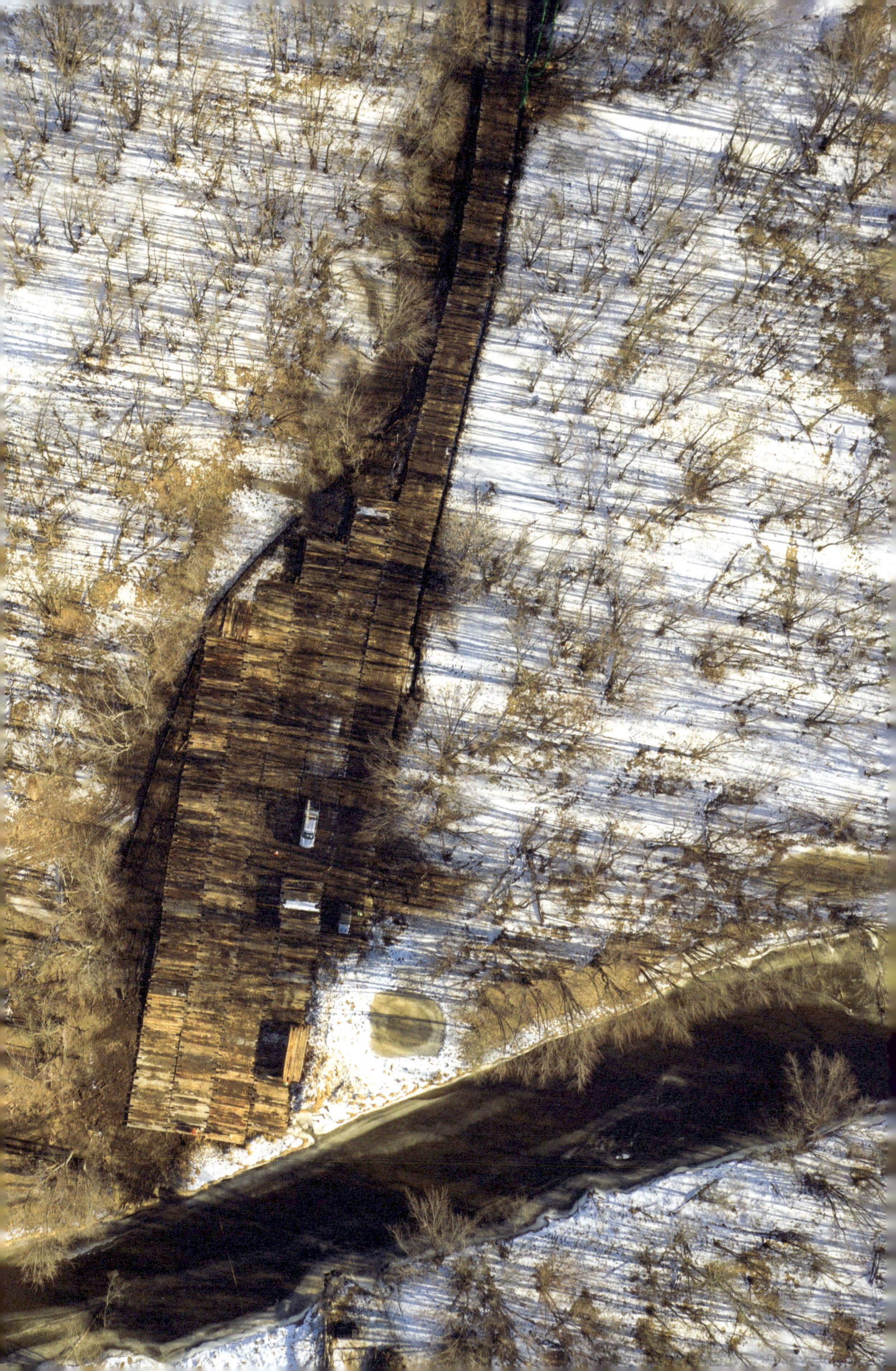

Editors' Note: This story was developed from an interview. It has been excerpted and edited in collaboration with the interviewee.

A Letter to My Future Generations

I'm sitting here looking at a picture of my ancestors and past chiefs, and the chiefs' blood that runs through my veins. I would like to make this a dedication and a letter to my grandchildren and my future generations of family on down the line because I'm thinking about yous! This is what your grandma did back in the day, how she grew up.

Your ancestors, my mom and dad, they brought me to different areas throughout Anishinaabeg territories, from the East Coast to the West Coast, way up in Canada, down to South America. And I was able to see a lot of sites throughout that time, from infancy all the way up until when I left home. During those travels, I was able to appreciate the things that my ancestors had left for me. My grandmas and grandpas and moms and dads, because they fought hard for our home, our environment. The foods that we eat. The waters that we drink. Even the air that we breathe.

So, later on, after seeing everything and being able to appreciate life, I was able to be inducted into the Ojibwe Warrior Society. The Warrior Society came first for me, after having passed the rites to womanhood. After being watched by the elders and relatives and the community I was chosen as one of many to represent the spirit of the Ogichidaakwe, which is my duties and obligations to protect future generations' home environment like we have now. So, that path brought me to the prayer lodge, which is also known as the Midewiwin lodge, or the healing lodge.

The Warrior Society that I was inducted to had to be underground for some time. Back in the day, when the American Indian Religious Freedom Act was enacted, we finally were able to come out and that was in 1972. Prior to that, we were criminalized, put into jails or institutions, called crazy, or just made out to be the villain. We aren't the villains, we were just living our lives.

The prayer lodge and warrior society is where I would like to start at the Line 3 fight. We built a prayer lodge set next to the Mississippi River. Eventually, it's where Enbridge built Line 3, where it crossed the river. When we built the lodge, it was summertime. The clouds were getting gray because it was getting towards ricing season. And it was not just a prayer lodge through the Midewiwin society, it also stood for the healing of the land. Because of the wars, skirmishes, when the settlers started coming in. And the war between the Dakota and the Ojibwe. The memory is still there. So, to heal that memory the prayer lodge was put there and to bring the healing, not just from the past generations but for the future generations and those that live down-water from the Mississippi River. Looking down the Mississippi River where it ends up at, at the Gulf Coast, and leaving here, where the headwaters is, in the Anishinaabe way, we would love to have it leave here pristine.

You know, people from around the world know what it's like to be without fresh water. Overseas, we've got countries having to ration out their days for clean water. Here, people are taking it for granted, with agriculture and the fossil fuel industry and the mining industry. As the Anishinaabe, we need to be able to protect the lands and our waters and our food resources, everything that was written in these so-called Treaties. The usufructuary rights. My inherent rights. But it's getting abrogated time and time again. Even right down to the first agreements. So, this is the hardest life to live, but it's the most rewarding life to live. Because we can appreciate what our homelands can provide for us. You can tap the trees in the springtime to get maple sugar, and in the fall times you can go out into the waters, the wild rice beds, the food that grows on the water, that the creator had guided us here to be able to grow and sustain as Anishinaabe people and to protect it, you know, as a life source. To be able to keep that life source upon us.

That's what we were fighting for. And that's why that lodge was there. To have a space to be able to come to for those who wanted to bring prayers. And believe me, there were people that came from all over the world, who came to enjoy the waters. One thing I was appreciative of was when a delegation of Hawaiians came to pray for the water. They came down to the lodge out there, and as they were finishing up with what they were doing and making their offerings, I started to sing for them. They were so appreciative of it. It was the bond of being able to protect our homelands.

> *As the Anishinaabe, we need to be able to protect the lands and our waters and our food resources, everything that was written in these so-called Treaties. The usufructuary rights. My inherent rights.*

Resisting these pipelines, from Sandpiper to DAPL to Line 3, has been an interesting walk, it's been an interesting way of life as an Anishinaabeg. It's been a hard journey and it's been a hard path. I keep getting told by our ancestors and I know the Creator wanted us to be mindful, prayerful, and to be able to enjoy one another's company. I love that concept, and I love living that. And being able to go back to that joyful, playful, kidlike, adventurous type of mindset, that's where the idea of the prayer lodge came up.

And so, I'll also let my grandchildren, my future generations know this, as Anishinaabe people: We are not small special interest groups. They want to keep dividing us as Anishinaabe people and putting us not only into war camps, also known as reservations, and special interest groups, but these are our homelands that we are fighting for. So, to my future generations and for those who are standing strong today, in the present, *Keep standing strong*. No matter how much they try to criminalize us as water protectors. Because what else can we do? The warrior societies need to step up and keep protecting for the future generations.

With that, I love yous all and there's nothing you can do about it. •

Water protectors install a temporary bridge to cross the wetlands at Camp Firelight.

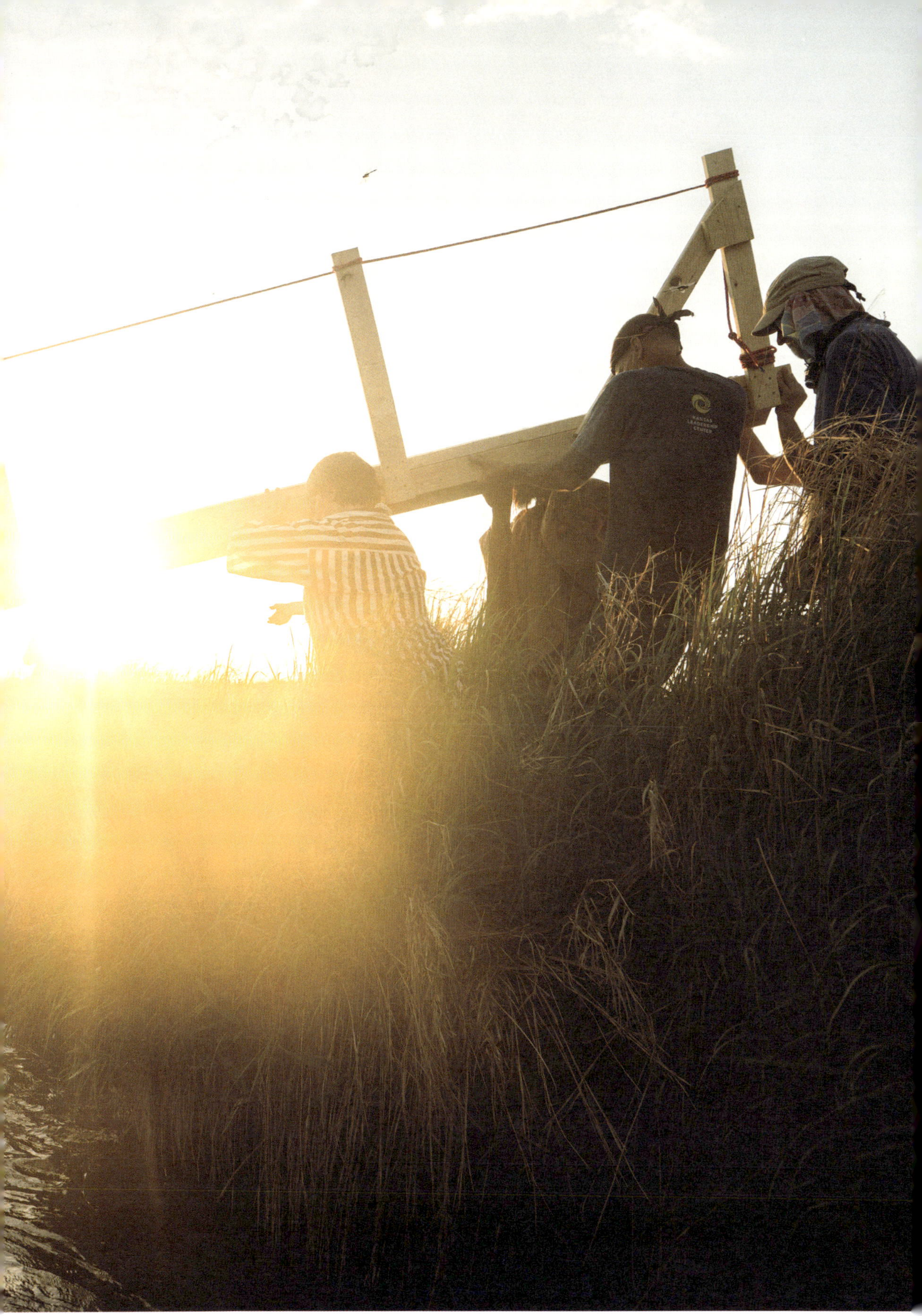

Jail Support

Dear Arrestee,

I need you to know that I gave you everything.

While you were in jail, I called your cat sitter, your partner,
your parents (sometimes they laughed, sometimes they yelled).
I bought cigarettes and hand warmers for when they released you from jail.
I withdrew thousands from my ATM so that you could come home.
I slept with my ringer on so that I didn't miss your calls.

When I had given you all of myself I would cry into the Red Lake River, my friend's shoulder.

I gave you everything and I would do it again.
Because you also gave me everything.
Because you have my heart.

I cannot explain it to the people who weren't there,
but I trust that you understand me.

So remember what we did together.
Remember that you carry my heart
because it is precious and it is heavy

and it is all that I have.

- jail support •

M. picked me up before the sun rose. It was cold, a dusting of snow across the road. We drove together, my roommate, my new friend, and I, to a bridge by the university. I was nervous, but I didn't want this lovely, motherly figure to know that. We got out of the car and breathed deep.

I had just moved here two months prior. It was December 2018. I got involved with pipeline work almost immediately, desperate for something to do after the latest IPCC report. A group wanted to do more low-risk, high visibility actions, meeting twice a week. Mostly older folks, and underemployed me. We called ourselves RAT — the Rapid Action Team. I was thrilled to have something to do, since I didn't know many people in town. I had never done a banner drop before, and frankly, I'm kind of a wuss. I still get nervous doing anything even a little risky. But I was here, ready to fit in, to stop a pipeline.

The three of us swung the banner over the bridge and secured it with zip ties, weighed down by the sandbags sewn in along the bottom. Stop Line 3, it said, a drawing of a bird in the middle. We walked away.

Back in the car, I primed myself to get a picture from the passenger seat as we drove beneath. I only had one shot! I lifted the phone and got the picture, blurry but good enough. I felt a sense of pure and uncomplicated giddiness at what the morning had held. I felt included and involved, a part of something bigger. I didn't know what the next three years would hold, the challenges and tears and endless meetings, how complicated it would become. I simply returned home before 8 am and plopped on the couch, exhilarated with my new life. •

Snow

STOP LINE 3 WE MUST.

I'm wearing everything I own, and it isn't enough. The biggest parka I could find. Toe warmers from the last gas station out of town. Wool socks I poached from my mother. Snow boots I got when I was 14, thinking I'd grow into them, but they stayed a size too big and now I'm shit out of growth spurts and luck. A wave of adrenaline keeps my circulation flowing as we march onto the site, flags waving, eyes looking for blue and red lights.

STOP LINE 3 WE WILL.

Then we settle in, the machines power down, and my toes start to leave my body. I can feel the color drain from each one as they fade out to match this brown and white, torn-earth snowscape.

STOP LINE 3 WE MUST.

I wish they would go numb. Other people always complain that they can't feel their toes. The only thing I can feel now is the sharp ache of frozen feet.

STOP LINE 3 WE WILL.

I've been walking laps on a four-foot course for the past thirty minutes, chanting down to the ice and dirt. We picket line, we jump, we dance, but my feet are too far gone to be revived this way.

STOP LINE 3 WE MUST.

Silently, I wish the pigs would move a little faster, threaten us with something we don't know, do anything really so I can get my feet back into a warm car or prop them up next to the invisible heat of a daytime fire. It is sacrilege to say, but inevitable to think.

STOP LINE 3 WE MUST STOP LINE 3 WE WILL.

Brother, it is too cold for so great a fight.

Even the water takes these days to rest, but we cannot.

STOP LINE 3 WE MUST STOP LINE 3 WE WILL STOP LINE 3 WE MUST STOP LINE 3 WE WILL.

The sun is high, but the day is gray. I've lost track of what we're doing here.

Mud

I am not on solid ground. Things are starting to get a little messy, a little slippery, a little loose. With every step, I risk sliding into the scratchy, leafless underbrush. The mud promises sweeter and softer things to come, but for now it's a hazard zone. My boots feel pounds heavier as they lift fat cakes of prime Minnesota mud with every step. My toes are wet, but at least they're warm. At least they're warm. Warm enough to sit under the steady red pine stands and the spindly aspens, waiting together for our chance to shine.

I watched *Black Snake Killaz* last night and the bottoms of my feet broke a sweat. That was a war documentary, plain and simple. Did I just enlist? Am I ready for what is coming when the strawberry time returns with a crew of excavators and brown-shirted thumbheads out for their sweet red blood? I can't be sure, but my mud-crusted boots keep my place on the frontline.

Dust

These days, these sun-soaked, drought-ridden, bug-bitten days, my feet stink something powerful. The sweaty sandals I've been wearing every summer since I was 17 threaten me with their two weeks' notice every day. I call their bluff and cinch the straps tight whether they like it or not. The sandals are so much an extension of my feet that I have an intricate tan line or dirt line or shit line or god-knows-what line in their image on my arches. It's a shame to be wearing shoes in the summertime, I know, but I refuse to be *that* hippie. Despite the sandals' noble efforts, the good dirt settles in. It takes shelter under my nails, congregates between my toes, holds a morning meeting on my ankle bone. Each night, I pour water from my bottle into my shoes and wiggle my toes around as a pre-sleep ritual. Out here, amidst all that I cannot predict, some things I must insist on, and a clean home is one of them.

Do you think it will ever rain? The dust had an element of charm when it was clinging to my feet, less so when it's in my eyes and nose, turning my boogers brown and adding to the crust in my sunrise eyes. The blueberries in the field are turning brown with thirst. The ground I walk on is turning a shade of light brown that tells me it is just about ready to catch the next gust of wind out of this place. Sometimes I have half a mind to follow it. After all, the big-bad is 65, 75, 85 percent done. I can't keep track of the newest numbers. Still, we finish what we started. We stay until the day oil flows through; many stay even after that. We scratch holes for our toes in the sandy road and we stay.

Concrete

Ten clean toes slowly suffocate in socks and proper shoes, tripping on the smooth pavement.

Not long ago, I could walk up and down the packed dirt of that driveway at midnight with no moon and no headlamp. I knew each divot and muddy spot by feel.

Now, in the flat, gray expanse of the city that stays light through the night, I stumble. In the dark shadow of loss, my feet struggle to find their way, separated from the ground below by layers of
canvas
rubber
polyester
concrete.

Beyond the sting of a real, visible pipeline where there once was just a threat lies the less apparent loss of purpose, of vision, of community that tied my life to its center point for a year.

What now? hangs like so many pounds on my shoulders. What of the land, the birds, the trees, the people? What, selfishly, of me? The rise and fall of collective passion made me somehow unable to pick up where I left off.

Patience, they tell me.

Young feet want to run, though some days it's better to rest.

Inside the shoes with the pretty, clean laces, toes try to wriggle free, to walk barefoot into the world to come. •

Even the river starts small. On a typically gray April day in northern Minnesota, the Mississippi River was at a trickle, slowly regaining its strength in the spring thaw. After even the heaviest rains, the unwitting visitor could mistake this for any other stream. It was hard to believe that I was looking at the same magnificent force that roars through my home base in the Twin Cities. That spring of 2018, I came with a longtime co-organizer to work on a video project and attend coalition meetings. One of our interviewees took us to this riverside spot. After a long day of visiting pump stations, spill sites, and rusted out pipes protruding from the earth, he pointed out which plants he gathers during different seasons and decided his interview would be best here, along the water. It was impossible to forget the environmental carnage we'd seen all day, but short of that, something about that moment between the road and the river reminded us of what we were up here fighting for, not just against. The three of us stood in silence, gazing out at the thin flow of water, the whole scene framed by lanky red pines and the mottled landscape of retreating snow.

Three years later, I return to the same spot, now abuzz with the sheer aliveness of summer along with several thousand people who don't ordinarily live here. They came to carry out a plan that feels so connected to that bleak day so many seasons ago. They call it Firelight. My work is in the years of preparation and backroom battles against the pipeline in its permit stages more than the fiery outbursts of direct action. My role in the action is at a lull, so I walk around to make sure everyone is eating and drinking enough to keep their strength up in the mind-melting heat. My indispensable organizing colleague is here too, and we pause together in the road to marvel at all that went into the creation of this camp over the years. I feel conflicted over our role in it. Of course, we are proud to have stood for something so beautiful and important as the clean water, treaties, and climate for so long, and prouder still of the powerful people we are watching on the easement. And yet, a nagging sense of failure dampens the ecstasy of the moment. It was our mission from the start not to allow construction of Line 3 to begin, let alone finish. This was a scene we hoped we would never have to see. One moment demanded letters to the PUC, house actions, education campaigns, and lawsuits, and this one demands action of a different sort. We do what the moment asks of us. We join the crowd wholeheartedly. •

And yet, a nagging sense of failure dampens the ecstasy of the moment. It was our mission from the start not to allow construction of Line 3 to begin, let alone finish. This was a scene we hoped we would never have to see. One moment demanded letters to the PUC, house actions, education campaigns, and lawsuits, and this one demands action of a different sort.

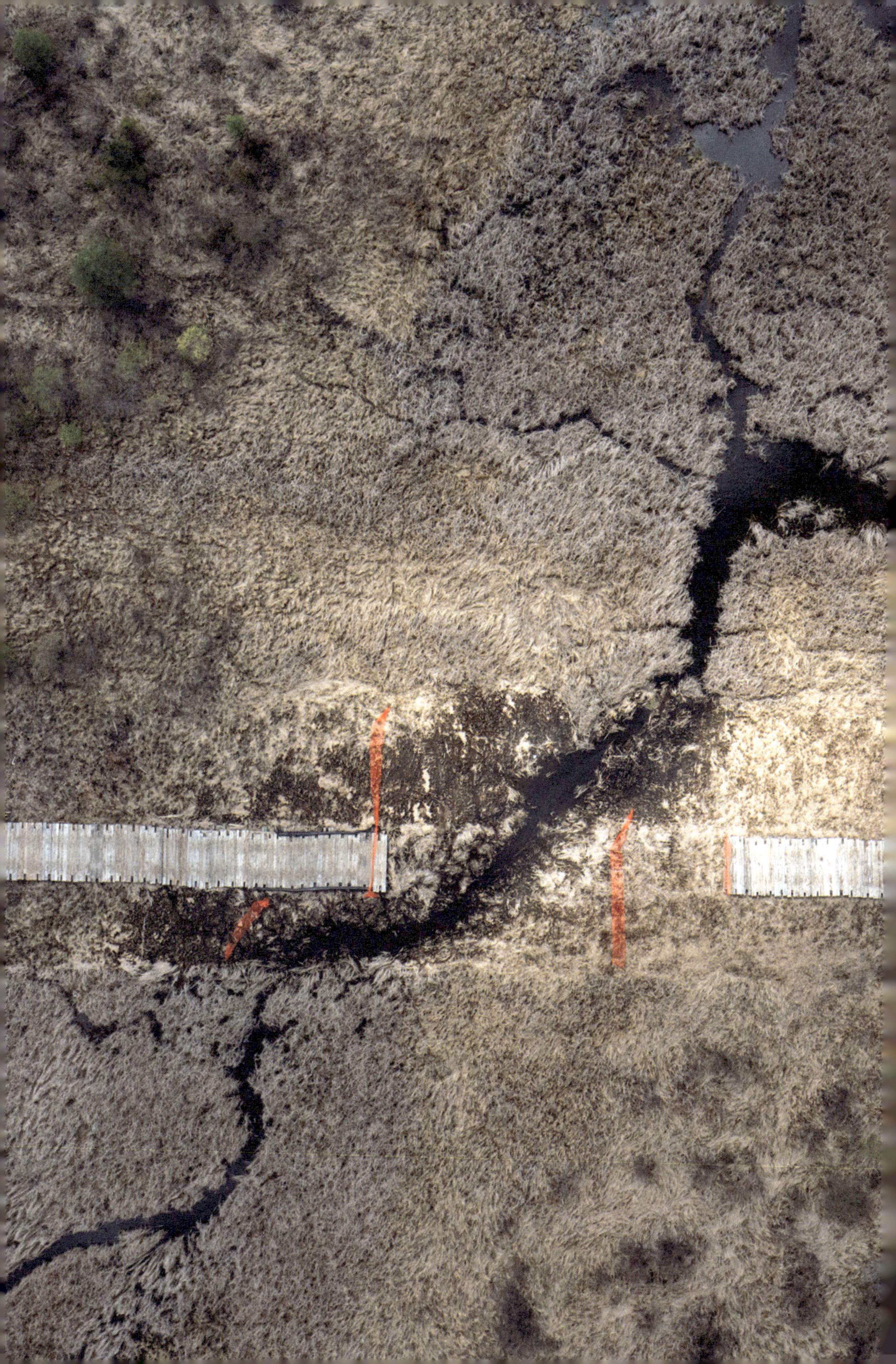

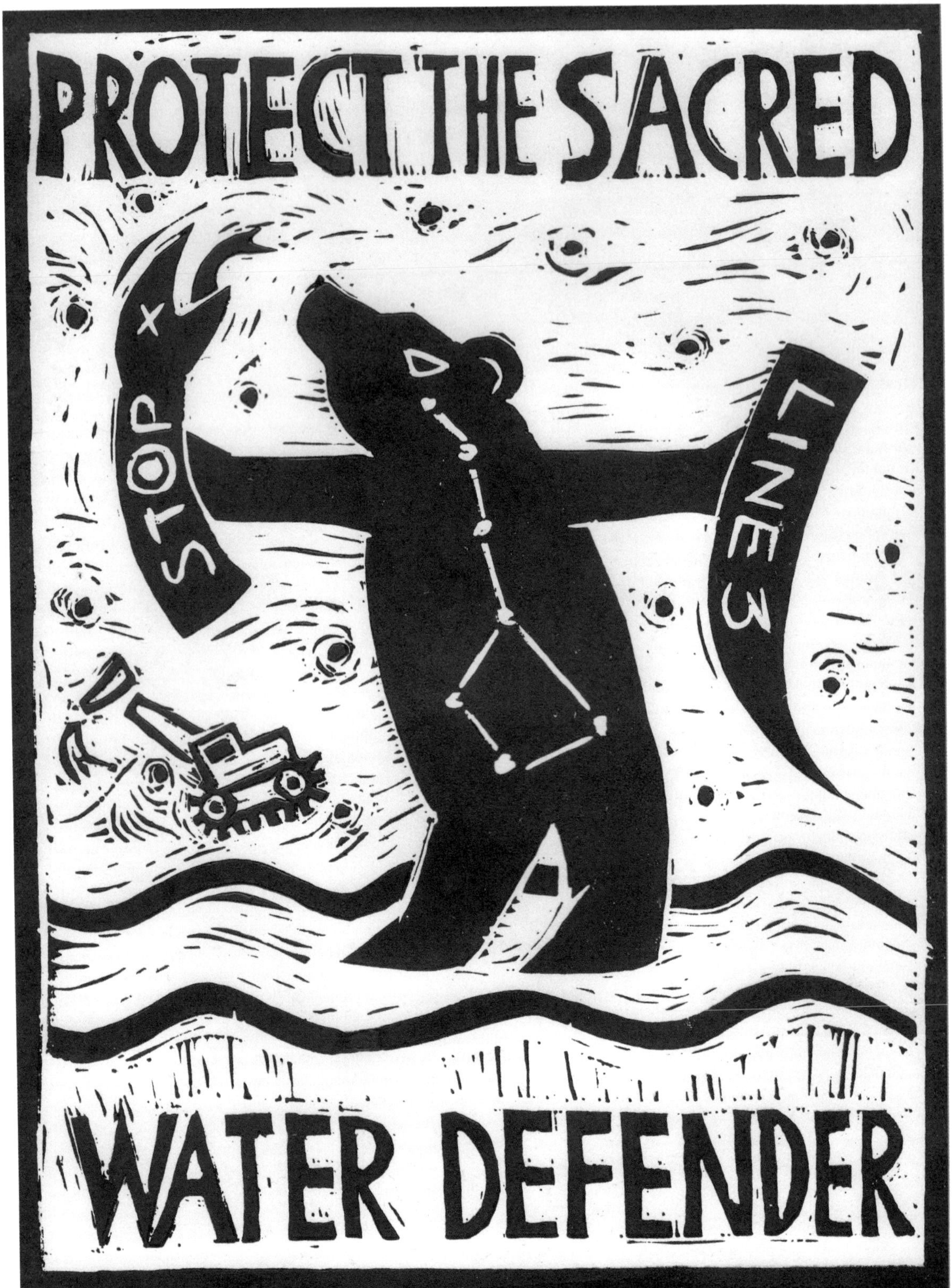
PROTECT THE SACRED
STOP
LINE 3
WATER DEFENDER

Strong Voices

It was a hot summer day at the Red Lake Treaty Camp. By now, construction on the deadly tar sands oil pipeline was approaching the Red Lake River, Miskwaagamiiwi-zaaga'iganiiwi-ziibi. So far, many attempts had been made to try and stop construction, many successfully stopping construction for hours. Most of the brave Water Protectors who were in camp that day were exhausted from resisting the pipeline day and night for days, months, or years. Record high temps, record drought, and forest fires in Canada bringing thick smoke to the area made the fight even harder. Most of the camp was together after the ceremony that morning, check-ins, and a hearty breakfast, contemplating the day.

Watching the unnecessary devastation a corporation was forcing upon the water and land, that will negatively affect so much wildlife and millions of people, lit a fire in many that still cannot be put out. We were all tired but we still needed to do something, at least for the day, to show them we were still fighting and we were never backing down. There was a discussion on the needs of the camp, the needs of Water Protectors, and the need to save the water. Many ideas were brought up and many concerns were brought up. Finally, someone had a brilliant idea. Why don't we start cheering as if someone is stopping construction?

Construction was happening right next to the camp. Many slept in tents within a couple yards of where the pipeline was being forced into the ground. The only thing separating the camp and the construction site was a chain linked fence. Water Protectors had a good vantage point of seeing the site and being able to witness not only the deadly devastation, but also the heroics of humanity when Water Protectors sacrificed their freedom, and possibly their lives, to bring awareness for the need to not shove toxic tar sands oil through precious life-needing water, by trying to stop construction. So, we all gathered on the hill in a spot where we were able to see the whole construction site and we started hollering.

Go Comrade!!!! We love you Comrade!!!

Black Snake Killaz!!!

Water is Life!!!! Stop Line 3!!!!!!!!

WHOOOO GOOO Comrade!!!! We love you comrade!!!!!

And… construction stopped!

Law enforcement and construction workers started searching the whole area. Water Protectors continued cheering the entire time construction was stopped. For nearly an hour, Water Protectors were able to stop construction that day using their voices. A success for the day, uplifting the whole camp and leaving a strong reminder that our voices are stronger than we think.

Speak even if your voice trembles. •

A Letter to The Water Protectors

Late September, 2021

The time is finally here. Enbridge has finished the construction of Line 3. Despite years of activists fighting and obstructing the project, by the time you read these words tar sands oil will flow through it. This reality pains us as it surely does countless others: those who live in the regions the pipeline cuts through, those who have put their bodies on the line to stop it, and those who believe in a world without extractive industry.

We write to you as a handful of friends who have been involved in the campaign to stop Line 3 at various points over the last three to four years. We've also participated in various other social movements and uprisings for many years, including the George Floyd uprising here in Minneapolis, and have become all too familiar with their waves, crests, and crashes. We've seen the traumatizing effects of both state violence as well as the loss of community felt in the aftermath of collective action. We've faced these feelings in the struggle to stop Line 3, we've supported our friends when they've faced them, and we know that right now, upon the pipeline's completion, that you are likely facing them as well. We are writing this so that you know you are not alone in this process.

Climate change is an urgent reality, especially for our current generation. We are consistently bombarded with new information on how fast the arctic is melting, which species are going extinct, or how soon certain regions will be underwater. For most of our lives, we have witnessed if not directly experienced one "natural" catastrophe after another. It only makes sense that when we face the magnitude of the problem, we are gripped by the urgency to take action. We only have so many years, scientists say, before certain changes will become irreversible. The only reasonable thing left to do is to take action, whatever that may be, immediately.

To grapple with the urgent reality of climate change, we've come to understand it as something immanent, not imminent. Climate change already defines our worlds in the present and this realization does hurt us. Yet, rather than see only a dark future looming ahead, this realization frees us to think about how to act against climate change, and likewise against colonial domination, without being constrained to the need for urgency. We focus on immanence because the urgency of imminence feeds into a particular ideology of reaction that ultimately becomes an obstacle in building the change we wish to see. In addressing climate change, the question of *how* we fight is intimately connected with the question of *how we live*, and cannot be separated. This lens of immanence returns the possibility of living to the fight against climate change. When urgency is the priority, life is constantly sidelined in favor of what we are told are the most pragmatic approaches, no matter how much we have to sacrifice to accomplish them. What's a criminal record or a lifetime of trauma in the face of global catastrophe?

But that trauma is real. Going to jail, especially for the first time, is a traumatic experience for many people — even if you get to prepare for it in advance. The loss of agency, the near-total submission to state power is not something to shrug off. Nor can it be shrugged off when it happens to our friends and comrades. It has to be recognized that a lot of what went into the movement against Line 3 was ultimately traumatizing.

To experience this, and to discover that Line 3 was built regardless, only adds to the pain we feel right now. We write to you to say that what you're likely feeling right now is valid. So many people gave up so much for this movement, and their lives have been altered as irreversibly as the planet. We all need the space to come to terms with this, and we hope to offer you this space by naming this experience.

The issue of burnout can't adequately capture the loss and hopelessness of this experience, nor, truly, can our words. We can't offer you a perfect solution or a way out. This is only something we can discover together — by discussing our experiences with those close to us, sharing our feelings, processing them both collectively and on our own. If we can develop networks of affinity groups to carry out direct action, there shouldn't be anything stopping us from developing networks of care and resilience as well. By the sheer fact of organizing and living together for the past months and years, we might be surprised to find out how much of these networks have already been built without realizing it.

It is tempting to ask if it was all worth it — and there's no one who can answer that question except for yourself. We expect many young people for whom this was the first campaign they joined will want to quit activism forever. We won't tell you not to, but we will say that it doesn't have to be this way. The things we can do, collectively, can be beautiful beyond our wildest dreams. We know because we've done it before, and we'll just as surely do it again.

Love to all the water protectors •

Construction Projects

The Line 3 construction project has nothing on the world that we are working together to build. It's nothing more than destruction in disguise. This project has mowed down millions of trees, exposing land to sky it was not meant to see. One risky tar sands pipeline, even in all its hulking 34-inch diameter, its massive 1,097 miles of oily tar sands sludge, is not as big as what we are when we all come together. They've got some nerve to call that a construction project.

What they don't know is we're really out here doing the building work. We wake up every day and dream and work and build the world we want for our grandchildren, the one in which a pipeline proposal would get laughed out of any committee hearing. We are the ones who have descended from those who have done the living and the dying on this land for millennia. Every one of us had that crushing moment somewhere along the line when we looked honestly at the world around us and knew that the pipeline would be completed. For some it was early in the campaign, for others it wasn't real until there was oil flowing through. But we held each other's hands and we saw the thing through because we knew we were there for something bigger. Collectively, we joined together to continue to build, dream, and create something far beyond this lifetime. That is our work as builders, not theirs, and we will continue to construct this world long beyond the time that Line 3 is no more. •

another world is possible

Acknowledgements

These stories and images were collected and edited by:

Haze (Emma) Harrison
Genna Mastellone
Dio Cramer
Griffy LaPlante
Abby Becker (moon)
Ellie Zimmerman
Jessie Foday
Ray Gorlin
Trevon "Rev" Tellor
Melissa Burrell
Mitchell Johnson

We would like to thank all of the artists who contributed spot and cover illustrations in collaboration with our team.

Many thanks to Beth LaPlante for her detailed copy-editing.

Readers can reach our team with questions and feedback at line3anthology@gmail.com.

———

We are grateful to TakeAction Minnesota for their fiscal sponsorship of this project.

Funds to print this collection were granted to our team by The Equation Campaign, Honor the Earth, and the Sierra Club. We are grateful to them all.

———

We would like to extend our deep gratitude to Great-Grandmother Mary Lyons for her thoughtful review of our draft manuscript.

Above all, we would like to thank the hundreds of people who shared their stories, writing, and art with us. We are so grateful to each of you for all you gave to this anthology and to our shared resistance movement.